'Peter Westwood is highly respected world-wide for producing easy to read, common-sense methods which are practical to implement…he presents great advice that is easily applied to classroom practice.'

Dr Bruce Allen Knight, Professor of Education, Central Queensland University, Australia

Commonsense Methods for Children with Special Needs and Disabilities

This fully revised and updated eighth edition of Peter Westwood's book offers practical advice and strategies for meeting the challenge of inclusive teaching. Based on the latest international research from the field, it offers practical advice on both new and well-tried evidence-based approaches and strategies for teaching students with a wide range of difficulties.

As well as covering special educational needs, learning difficulties, and disabilities in detail, chapters also explore topics such as self-management and autonomy, managing behaviour, and social skills. The book offers sound pedagogical practices and strategies for adapting curriculum content, designing teaching materials, differentiating instruction for mixed-ability classes, and implementing inclusive assessment of learning.

Key features of this new edition include:

- Additional information on linking all aspects of teaching to a Response-to-Intervention Model
- A focus on the increasing importance of digital technology in supporting the learning of students with special educational needs and disabilities
- Up-to-date resource lists for each chapter, for those who wish to pursue a particular topic in greater depth

Reflecting cutting-edge international research and teaching practices, this is an invaluable resource for practising and trainee teachers, teaching assistants, and other educational professionals looking to support students with special educational needs and disabilities.

Peter Westwood is currently a freelance education consultant and writer. He is widely published in the field of education and his range of books includes *Inclusive and Adaptive Teaching* and *Learning Disorders*, both published by Routledge.

Commonsense Methods for Children with Special Needs and Disabilities

Eighth edition

Peter Westwood

Routledge
Taylor & Francis Group

LONDON AND NEW YORK

Eighth edition published
by Routledge
2 Park Square, Milton Park, Abingdon, Oxon OX14 4RN

and by Routledge
52 Vanderbilt Avenue, New York, NY 10017

First edition published by Routledge 1987
Seventh edition published by Routledge 2015

Routledge is an imprint of the Taylor & Francis Group, an informa business

© 2021 Peter Westwood

British Library Cataloguing in Publication Data
A catalogue record for this book is available from the British Library

Library of Congress Cataloging-in-Publication Data
Names: Westwood, Peter S., author.
Title: Commonsense methods for children with special needs and disabilities / Peter Westwood.
Description: 8th edition. | Abingdon, Oxon ; New York, NY : Routledge, 2021. | Includes bibliographical references and index.
Identifiers: LCCN 2020026793 (print) | LCCN 2020026794 (ebook) | ISBN 9780367625788 (hardback) | ISBN 9780367625757 (paperback) | ISBN 9781003109778 (ebook)
Subjects: LCSH: Children with disabilities–Education. | Mainstreaming in education. | Special education.
Classification: LCC LC4015 .W44 2021 (print) | LCC LC4015 (ebook) | DDC 371.9–dc23
LC record available at https://lccn.loc.gov/2020026793
LC ebook record available at https://lccn.loc.gov/2020026794

ISBN: 978-0-367-62578-8 (hbk)
ISBN: 978-0-367-62575-7 (pbk)
ISBN: 978-1-003-10977-8 (ebk)

Typeset in Bembo
by Taylor & Francis Books

This edition is dedicated to the many school students and teachers that I have had the good fortune to work with over the past sixty years

Contents

Introduction

This new edition has been significantly revised to keep pace with new developments and current issues in the fields of special and inclusive education. The material within the text represents the most recent research, policies, and practices, as reported in the professional literature. This edition continues to provide practical advice for teachers and tutors, to enable them to apply evidence-based methods when working with students with special educational needs and disabilities. A chapter is also devoted to the needs of gifted and talented students.

Recent guidelines for the *National Curriculum* in the UK and the *Australian Curriculum* now give far more specific attention to how curriculum content, teaching methods, instructional materials, and assessment procedures need to be adapted and differentiated for students with special needs and disabilities. Similarly, in the USA, the *Common Core State Standards* have had implications for teaching and assessing these students.

In all chapters, new approaches to teaching and classroom management have been described, with increased coverage of the contribution of digital technology and e-learning to the field of inclusive education. Links have been made in all sections of the book to the Response-to-Intervention Model, with its three tiers or levels of intervention. Without exception, all chapters are fully supported by the most recent studies, up to and including 2020.

I have continued to take an international perspective on the topics addressed in the book, drawing heavily on research, policies, and practices in Britain, Australia, and the United States. I hope that all readers will find something of value in the material here.

My sincere thanks to Alison Foyle of Routledge for her ongoing support over many years, and to my copyeditor Jacqueline Dias for her careful attention to detail.

Peter Westwood

Chapter 1

Special educational needs, learning difficulties, and disabilities

It is appropriate to begin by delineating the population of students whose management, education, and development are the focus throughout this book. The first chapter provides essential background information on the nature of students' special educational needs, and on the existing policies, guidelines, and models of support. The following four chapters describe various disabilities and impairments and how these may affect learning for some students in today's inclusive classrooms. Attention is then given to the special needs of students who are gifted or talented. The remaining chapters of the book present practical approaches to supporting and teaching these students through early childhood, the school years, and into adulthood.

Who are the students?

In the UK, the *Special Educational Needs and Disabilities Code of Practice: 0 to 25 years* (DfE/DoH, 2015) defines students with special needs in these terms:

> A child of compulsory school age or a young person has a learning difficulty or disability if he or she has a significantly greater difficulty in learning than the majority of others of the same age, or has a disability which prevents or hinders him or her from making use of facilities of a kind generally provided for others of the same age in mainstream schools or mainstream post-16 institutions.
>
> (p. 15)

In the UK, students with special needs are those with intellectual impairment, a physical or sensory disability, health problem, attention deficits, reading and writing problems, or behavioural and social or emotional difficulties. Statistics issued in 2017 indicate that just over 14 per cent of the school population in England had been identified as having special needs (DfE, 2018). Under the policy of inclusive education, most of these students will be placed in mainstream classes and supported with additional resources. It is expected that the curriculum content and teaching methods will be adapted to enable the students with special needs or disabilities to participate, and they will follow the normal curriculum as far as possible (DfE, 2014a) (see Chapter 15). Those students with the most severe and complex needs may still need to be placed in a special school or unit to receive an appropriate educational programme. Advocates for 'full inclusion' in the UK and elsewhere argue that even students with the most complex needs should attend mainstream schools; but in 2020, data from 31 countries across Europe indicate that all countries still use some form of fully segregated settings for some learners (Ramberg & Watkins, 2020). The same is true of other countries outside Europe.

In Australia and New Zealand students are described as having special educational needs if they cannot learn in the same way as other children (AngloInfo, 2019). In Australia, the term disability encompasses children with an intellectual or physical disability, vision impairment, hearing impairment, language disorder, mental health condition, or autism (ACARA, 2014a; 2016a). A policy of inclusion also operates in Australia and the mainstream curriculum often needs to be modified to accommodate the needs of those students for whom additional support for learning is required.

Educators in the USA prefer the term 'exceptional children', rather than 'students with special needs' (CEC, 2019). Exceptional children are described as having differences that occur to such an extent that they require additional services and modification to school practices. In the USA some 14 categories of disability or special need are specified in the *Individuals with Disabilities Education Act* (IDEA) (US Department of Education, 2014). These categories are: autism, developmental delay, intellectual disability, orthopaedic impairment (physical disabilities), specific learning disability, speech or language impairment, traumatic brain injury, hearing impairment, deafness, deaf-blindness, visual impairment (low vision) or blindness, multiple disabilities, emotional disturbance, and health impairment. Under IDEA, individuals with special needs, as identified by appropriate professionals, are entitled to support between the ages of 3 to 21 years. Data from 2015–2016 indicate that some 13 per cent of the US public school population was being served under IDEA (NCES, 2018).

There are other students in every country who fall outside any official classification of 'disabled' or 'exceptional' but who experience learning difficulties, particularly in acquiring functional literacy and numeracy skills. In the past these students have been referred to by many different labels—'slow learners', 'the-hard-to-teach', 'under-achievers', 'children who find school hard' and 'students who struggle.' When these students are also taken into account together with those formally identified as above, it is estimated that in most countries about 20 per cent of school-age children have some form of special need, either long-term or short-term. The actual proportion in any one school varies greatly according to influences such as the socio-economic status of parents, parental standard of education, and level of socio-economic disadvantage in the catchment area served by the school.

In an attempt to simplify identification of the population of students with special needs in various countries, the OECD (2007) created three convenient categories. These categories of special need and exceptionality are addressed in the later chapters of this book where the nature of the support and teaching they require is considered. The categories are useful in that they neatly summarise the diverse group of students with learning problems and special needs found in inclusive classrooms today:

- students with identifiable disabilities and impairments;
- students with specific difficulties in learning, or with behavioural and/or emotional disorders;
- students with difficulties arising from socio-economic, cultural, or linguistic disadvantage (including those learning English as a second or additional language).

Other students not specifically named in most special education policies may also require additional support in schools. These students include those who are intellectually gifted or with a specific talent that needs to be developed. In the USA and Canada, gifted students are regarded as part of the population requiring special provision, but in the UK and Australia they are recognised instead in separate policies and curriculum guidelines, particularly in reference to providing early identification, acceleration, extension, and enrichment.

What are 'special needs'?

The special needs of students with learning difficulties and disabilities tend to be associated with two main areas — those that relate to *cognitive difficulties* affecting learning and those that are termed *psycho-social and emotional problems* affecting a student's personal development and social adjustment. The two sources of learning difficulty are not mutually exclusive and many students have problems in both areas (DfE, 2013c; GOV. UK, 2013; 2015).

Cognitive difficulties

Cognitive difficulties cause major problems in processing information, remembering, reasoning, and responding within a school curriculum. The difficulties can be linked to a variety of factors, including the level of a student's innate intelligence, reasoning ability, verbal skills, perceptual abilities, information processing efficiency, attention and memory (Astle et al., 2019). These factors will be discussed in later chapters in the context of particular disabilities, and also as they relate to learning within particular areas of the school curriculum.

Psycho-social and emotional difficulties

Difficulties in psycho-social and emotional development are related to personal characteristics such as poor self-esteem, lack of confidence, anxiety, poor self-regulation, negative attitude, low aspirations, poor social skills, and limited resilience or hardiness (Schwab, 2019). Many students with special needs display at least some (often several) of these characteristics, which teachers must seek to change for the better. Schools that have the services of a student counsellor are fortunate because that person can also help with the psycho-social needs of all students and can work closely in tandem with teachers (Lindelauf et al., 2018).

Students' special needs must be identified and addressed as early as possible to ensure that their time in preschool and school is profitable and that they maintain good motivation to learn (Lithari, 2019; Rose & Shevlin, 2020). When a student's learning difficulty or disability results in frequent experiences of failure rather than success, then the path ahead can be daunting unless the student receives all necessary support and encouragement.

Learning difficulties

Children with learning difficulties fall into one of two possible subgroups: (i) those with *general* learning difficulties but with no disability or impairment, and (ii) those with a *specific learning disorder* (SpLD). Specific learning disorders may be further identified as either *language-based* or *non-verbal*. Children with general learning difficulties represent much the largest group of those needing support, at an estimated 12 to 16 per cent of the overall school population (Westwood, 2017). Children with a *language-based specific learning disorder* are fewer in number but include those whose learning difficulties may be associated with speech problems, receptive language weakness, and severe reading difficulties (dyslexia) (LDAA, 2019). The smallest group of students are those with a *non-verbal learning disorder* (NLD). Their difficulties are not associated with language but are mainly due to problems in fine motor coordination and spatial awareness.

As indicated in the following sections, the learning characteristics of these subgroups are rather different but they all share a common need for systematic and direct teaching, as described in later chapters. Almost all students with learning difficulties begin to exhibit their problems very early in their school life, so the sooner they receive targeted support the better for their long-term prospects.

General learning difficulties

The term *general learning difficulties* is used throughout this book when discussing students of average or a little below average intelligence who are not in any way intellectually disabled or with sensory impairments. In the past these students have often been labelled 'slower learners' or 'low achievers.' The IQs for this subgroup are typically reported to be between 80 and 100; but in the case of any students from disadvantaged backgrounds or with emotional or behavioural problems, their potential IQ can sometimes be well above 100. Poverty, disadvantage, and absenteeism in particular are known to be major causes of students' general learning difficulties in school.

In some cases, the problems these students encounter are exacerbated by inappropriate or insufficient teaching; but the cause of general learning difficulty usually cannot be attributed to a single factor. Many learning problems arise from a complex interaction among variables such as the learners' cognitive ability, effectiveness of the teaching received, perceived relevance of curriculum content, emotional and financial support from home, absences from school, the student's confidence and motivation, and availability of individual support when necessary. Additional factors also contribute to a failure to learn, such as distractions in the learning environment, the health of the learner, the interpersonal relationship between teacher and learner, and social relationships within the peer group.

Until recently, teaching methods and instructional materials were rarely investigated as possible causes of a learning difficulty; but now it is readily acknowledged that inappropriate teaching and curriculum materials can present major barriers to learning. It has even been suggested that many of these students would not have learning problems at all if schools improved the overall standard of teaching and attended better to the needs of individual learners (Clarke, 2018; GOV.UK, 2014a).

While many cognitive, psycho-social, and environmental problems do exist for children with learning difficulties, these problems should not be viewed as obstacles that are too difficult for teachers to overcome. Rather they should be recognised as clear indications of areas of need that must be targeted through high-quality instruction. The evidence clearly shows that teaching for these students should involve clear presentation of information by the teacher, explicit instruction in skills and learning strategies, active engagement by learners, guided practice with feedback, independent practice, and frequent reviews or revision. Research evidence indicates that students with general learning problems do best in structured programmes of this type (Andres, 2019; Hattie & Yates, 2014; Masters, 2014). It is also clear that digital technology is increasingly proving useful for improving basic academic skills and motivation of students with general learning difficulties as well as those with disabilities (e.g., Cranmer, 2020; Lee, 2019; Mutlu & Akgün, 2019).

Specific learning disability

The Learning Disabilities Association of America (LDAA, 2019) defines a learning disability (or learning disorder) as a condition that interferes with an individual's ability to store, process, or produce information. The Association indicates that this disability can affect an individual's ability to read, write, speak, spell, and compute mathematically. A specific disability in reading is referred to as *dyslexia*, and in mathematics as *dyscalculia* (see Chapter 13). Some individuals also have problems with attention, memory, coordination, social skills, and emotional control. It is reported that various forms of behavioural problem are quite common in students with a learning disability (Horbach et al., 2020).

A learning disorder is experienced by some 3 per cent of students of average or above average intelligence (Lindstrom, 2019). In the USA, the category that has seen greatest increase in number of students over the years is that of learning disorders. These students now represent some 34 per cent of children served under IDEA (NCES, 2018). On the positive side, it is also important to note that in recent years there has been an increase in the number of students with a learning disability who are admitted to tertiary education. Many of these students, if adequately supported, go on to do very well in their studies.

The fifth edition of the *Diagnostic and Statistical Manual of Mental Disorders* (APA, 2013) now refers to a single classification *specific learning disorder* instead of the various subcategories used previously. There was concern that these subtypes became too poorly differentiated and were difficult to use for accurate diagnosis. Rather than relying on the traditional single criterion of a significant discrepancy figure between measure intelligence (IQ) and the student's scores on attainment tests, a learning disorder is now identified through a clinical review of the student's developmental, medical, educational, and family history, test scores, teachers' observations, and the student's previous response to any remedial intervention.

It is often argued that children with specific learning difficulties are not identified early enough in school and are simply considered immature, lazy, or unmotivated. Unless provided with effective teaching, some of these children may go on to develop serious social and emotional problems associated with constant failure in school, and some exhibit major behaviour problems. Early identification and effective intervention remain high priorities in improving the educational opportunities for these children.

An important difference that must be noted between the UK and other countries is in the use of the term *learning disability*. In the 1960s in the USA, Kirk coined the term 'learning disability' to identify students of average or above average intelligence with severe reading or mathematics difficulties. The term was then adopted by almost all countries and became widely understood in schools and in the professions. Unfortunately, the UK now applies this term to what all other countries refer to as *intellectual disability* (impaired cognition). This inconsistency in terminology gives rise to much confusion when reading international research literature. In this book, when the term 'learning disability' or 'learning disorder' is used it refers to a specific difficulty in learning basic skills in students of at least *normal intelligence*. The term *intellectual disability* is used exclusively here to refer to students whose learning problems and special needs are primarily due to significant cognitive impairment.

Language-based learning disability

Language-based difficulties tend to affect acquisition of literacy skills, including phonic decoding, vocabulary, comprehension, writing, and spelling (HASA, 2019). The term most widely used for this disability or disorder is *dyslexia*. Other forms of language-based learning disability that accompany dyslexia include *dysgraphia* (specific problem with writing), *dysorthographia* (problem with spelling) and *dysnomia* (inability to retrieve words, names, or symbols quickly from memory). Students with these problems may also exhibit receptive and expressive communication weaknesses (Snowling et al., 2019; Spanoudis et al., 2019). For these students, teaching objectives must therefore also focus on improving oral language skills as well as reading and writing.

Dyslexic students typically have great difficulty developing awareness of the phonological aspects of spoken language—understanding that words are composed of separate sequences of sounds. This lack of understanding naturally impairs their learning of essential phonic decoding skills and they remain weak at unlocking unfamiliar words. As a result, they fail to develop speed and fluency in reading, and their oral reading performance tends to be very slow and laboured. Much cognitive effort has to be expended on identifying each individual word, leaving very little capacity for focusing on meaning. The student tires easily and avoids reading whenever possible. Lack of practice then exacerbates their problem. As Rose (2009, p.10) commented: 'Not surprisingly, young people with dyslexic difficulties generally do not read unless they have to; they are far less likely to read for pleasure or for information than other learners.'

Theories that have been suggested to account for dyslexia have included those that consider it is due to a subtle neurological condition affecting perception and processing of written language. This view has not, however, resulted in any recommended intervention for use in schools. An alternative proposition is that students with a reading disorder are simply 'non-strategic' learners who use a hit-or-miss approach instead of employing logical steps to unlocking print. This view has gained wide acceptance, and it is now agreed that any literacy intervention for children with a reading disorder must include the teaching and practice of effective decoding strategies and comprehension strategies. Much more is said about intervention methods for literacy in Chapter 10.

One area in which students with learning disorders also require well-targeted assistance is at the time of transition to further study beyond compulsory school years (Hamblet, 2014). Universities and colleges are beginning to realise the need to provide specific support for students who are intellectually capable but have problems with study skills. Such support may include accommodations made in the time allowed for assignments and assessments, note-taking assistance, supply of alternative study materials, and additional guidance in beginning assignments.

Non-verbal learning disability

This category of learning difficulty was suggested as separate from other forms of learning disability in the late 1980s. However, the latest edition of *DSM-5* does not include a category 'non-verbal learning disorder'—because its existence as a unique syndrome remains debatable (APA, 2013). This disability category is included here because it is still important to identify the problems described below and to offer appropriate support for a student, even if the difficulties do not represent a separate syndrome.

To some extent, non-verbal learning disability shares some characteristics with a condition known as *dyspraxia,* although the two conditions are not the same. Non-verbal learning difficulties are associated most obviously with problems in gross and fine motor control, coordination, and spatial awareness (Debenham, 2018). The student may appear to be unusually clumsy and poorly balanced, and does not enjoy physical education and sport. Fine motor skills such as handwriting, setting down columns of figures, or drawing diagrams are particularly problematic. The student may have difficulties applying visual perception effectively in tasks such as interpreting details in a picture or diagram, or attending closely to signs and symbols in arithmetic. The combined coordination and visual perception problems cause particular difficulties with many classroom activities including writing, assembling puzzles and models, or handling equipment. Some children with these problems are now said to have a *developmental coordination disorder* (DCD).

The measured verbal IQ of children with non-verbal learning disability is usually very much higher than their non-verbal score. The child's oral verbal skills are usually within the normal range but he or she may have difficulty understanding non-verbal communication cues used by others (facial expression, stance, gesture). This difficulty can lead to problems when interpreting social situations and interacting with other children and adults. In order to develop appropriate social behaviours these students often need help to interpret social situations more accurately. They are candidates for the social skills interventions described in Chapter 9.

Children with NLD can be helped significantly once their problem is identified, because speaking and listening are their best channels for learning. For example, teachers can use much more verbal mediation (clear verbal explanations) when presenting visual materials, interpreting social situations, and teaching physical skills. More time can be given for students to complete work, and more guidance and feedback can be provided. Often students with NLD will leave classroom tasks and bookwork unfinished. To overcome this tendency, they can be taught self-regulation strategies to enable them to approach classroom tasks systematically and to see them through to completion (see Chapter 7). Any students with very poor handwriting can be helped to develop an easier and more legible style and encouraged to develop keyboard proficiency. More than a usual amount of guidance may be needed to help these students set out their bookwork appropriately.

It should be noted that even a few gifted students have non-verbal learning disabilities. If they are not remedied, the difficulties tend to prevent the individual from reaching his or her potential. This issue is discussed in Chapter 6.

Disabilities and impairments

Some students have special educational needs because they have a disability. Their disabilities may include: *intellectual disability* (previously referred to in some countries as 'mental retardation' or 'mental handicap'), *hearing impairment, vision impairment, physical disability, autism, language disorder,* and *specific learning disability* or *learning disorder* (as discussed above). Associated with any of these disabilities one may also find some degree of *emotional disturbance, behaviour problems, social relationship failures,* and *communication difficulties.*

Physical handicaps, vision impairment, and hearing impairment are all regarded as fairly low incidence disabilities—together accounting for no more than 2 to 3 per cent of the school population. Significant emotional and behavioural difficulties are reported in approximately 9 per cent, with double that number of children judged to be at risk for developing such problems (Turnbull et al., 2019). The number of children with social, emotional, and behavioural problems has increased very significantly in recent years.

Intellectual disability is discussed fully in Chapter 2, covering all degrees of cognitive impairment from mild to profound. Intellectual disability is sometimes also referred to as a *developmental delay* or *intellectual developmental disorder*, as in the *Diagnostic and Statistical Manual of Mental Disorders* (APA, 2013). The prevalence of intellectual disability among children has remained fairly stable over the past decades at 2 to 3 per cent. Some children with intellectual disability may have additional sensory, physical or communication impairments, and are described as having *complex multiple disabilities*. These students usually require intensive support throughout their school life and beyond. Chapter 3 provides information about autism spectrum disorders that may or may not be accompanied by intellectual disability. Autism is sometimes classified as a *pervasive developmental disorder* (PDD). In the USA, students with autism now represent 9 per cent of all students served under the *Individuals with Disabilities Education Act* (NCES, 2018). The prevalence rate is similar in other developed countries.

Hearing impairment includes students who are deaf and others with varying degrees of hearing loss. Vision impaired students are those who are blind or with low vision (partial sight). The characteristics and special needs of these students with sensory impairments are described fully in Chapter 5. A very few individuals may have both hearing loss and blindness.

Physical disabilities are described in Chapter 4. The most common conditions include cerebral palsy, spina bifida, traumatic brain injury, epilepsy, and chronic health problems such as asthma, cystic fibrosis, Type 1 diabetes, and allergic reactions. Many of these students have normal cognitive ability to learn but may have problems attending school regularly and accessing resources and therapy. In the case of students with a significant physical disability, there are often mobility problems causing difficulties accessing school buildings and in participating in some off-campus activities.

Provision of education and support

In most developed countries the term 'special needs' has legal significance, denoting a mandated responsibility for schools to identify any such students who are entitled to additional support and extra resources. The term special educational needs (SEN) had been in use in the UK since its introduction in the *Warnock Report* (DES, 1978) and was rapidly adopted in many countries. In 2001 the term used in the UK became 'special educational needs and disabilities' (SEND); and that is also the term used in the 2014 policy of that name in England. The National Health Service in the UK explains that a child or young person is in this category if they have a learning difficulty and/or a disability that means they need special health and education support (NHS, 2020).

It is usually necessary for these students to be assessed first by relevant professionals in order to be classified as having special educational needs and then the nature of these needs must be clearly specified for teachers and parents. Schools are then expected to make reasonable provision so that these students are afforded the amount and type of support necessary to have the same opportunities to learn and develop as all other students. It is anticipated that these opportunities will be available through such inclusive classroom measures as the use of evidence-based instruction, modified curriculum when necessary, and differentiation in teaching approach. In recent years, support has also been provided through assistive technology, flexible grouping of students, additional tutoring, peer assistance, and (where available) the use of classroom assistants. These issues are discussed later in Chapters 14 and 15.

It is now mandated in the UK that any child or young person to age 25 who is assessed as having significant special educational needs must be provided with an Education, Health and Care Plan (EHCP) (DfE/DoH, 2015). The EHCP specifies in detail the health and social care support that is to be provided for an individual, and sets out relevant goals for education. The plan indicates clearly any arrangements that need to be made for accessing additional services in the community. The aims of the EHCP are not only to increase accountability for designing and implementing effective support programmes, but also to keep parents fully informed and involved in the support process. The EHCP helps coordinate any supplementary services efficiently (e.g. medical, therapeutic, counselling). All young people with a learning difficulty assessment who continue into further education or training will also receive an EHCP (DfE, 2016). Data obtained in 2017 indicate that approximately 3 per cent of the school population in England has an EHCP (DfE, 2018).

The requirements for supporting and teaching were made operational in the UK in the revised *Special Educational Needs and Disabilities Code of Practice: 0 to 25 years* (DfE/DoH, 2015). The *Code* places responsibility for oversight of teaching and support for SEND students in school with the Special Educational Needs Coordinator (SENCo). The responsibilities set out in the *Code* are regarded by most SENCos as having strengthened and clarified their role (Curran, 2019). Nevertheless, the principle that students with special needs should be educated in the mainstream as far as possible continues to present many challenges for SENCos and mainstream teachers alike (Hellawell, 2019; Smith & Broomhead, 2019).

In the USA, students with special needs usually gain their support through implementation of the *Individuals with Disabilities Education Improvement Act* (IDEA) (US Department of Education, 2004). This Act had its origins in the *Education for All Handicapped Children Act (Public Law 94–142)* and was amended again in December 2015 through Public Law 114–95 (*Every Student Succeeds Act*; ESSA). ESSA served to replace and update the *No Child Left Behind Act* of 2002. Under the requirements of IDEA, children with special educational needs are provided with an *individual education plan* (IEP) that specifies in detail the modifications and accommodations that are require in the curriculum and teaching method, and indicates any additional services that must be accessed. It is stated in IDEA that:

> Disability is a natural part of the human experience and in no way diminishes the right of individuals to participate in or contribute to society. Improving educational results for children with disabilities is an essential element of our national policy of ensuring equality of opportunity, full participation, independent living, and economic self-sufficiency for individuals with disabilities (US Department of Education, 2004).

The use of an IEP is also common in Australian schools, although it may be called by a different name in some states. The value of an IEP is that it ensures all personnel involved in teaching and managing the child (including parents and care-givers) are clear about the objectives of the programme and the adaptations to curriculum and teaching that may be needed. The active involvement of parents in the education of a child with special needs is now regarded everywhere as essential for obtaining optimum outcomes (Urtubey, 2020). Input from the students themselves, where this is feasible, is also regarded as desirable when planning an IEP that will best meet their needs (Merrick, 2020).

Response to intervention model

One of the more recent school-based approaches to meeting students' special needs is known as *Response to Intervention* (RTI) (Barth et al., 2013; Bouck & Cosby, 2019). Under this model, all children beginning formal schooling receive daily instruction in basic literacy and numeracy using systematic evidence-based teaching. This is termed Tier 1 or First Wave Teaching. During this period of teaching, any children who are not making adequate progress are immediately given additional regular tutoring in small groups at Tier 2. Only those children who fail to respond within a reasonable period of time to this additional support are then considered to have a significant learning difficulty or disability and are referred on to Tier 3 for in-depth assessment and intensive one-to-one tuition (Ludlow, 2014).

The advantages of the RTI model include:

- a child does not have to accumulate many months of failure before being identified and receiving support;
- effective evidence-based teaching methods are used within each tier;
- a child's response rate indicates the level, intensity, and duration of the tutoring required.

There is an urgent need for all teachers to receive more detailed professional training to ensure that they possess the knowledge and skills necessary for teaching children at Tier 2 and Tier 3 (Al Otaiba et al., 2019; Nagro et al., 2019b). At the present time, there is a tendency in teacher education courses to deal only with student-centred classroom teaching methods (Tier 1), not with interventions that can assist students who struggle with learning (Vollmer et al., 2019). It should not be left only to specialist remedial teachers to acquire these skills.

The following four chapters deal in more detail with disabilities and the effect they can have on learning and development. Later chapters present effective methods of teaching and assessment that can be used at the various tiers in the response-to-intervention model.

Online resources

- Special educational needs and disabilities code of practice: 0 to 25 years [UK]. Available on line at: https://assets.publishing.service.gov.uk/government/uploads/system/uploads/attachment_data/file/398815/SEND_Code_of_Practice_January_2015.pdf.
- A detailed description of the students served and the services available in USA under IDEA can be located on 'What is special education?' at: www.thoughtco.com/what-is-special-education-3110961.

- In Australia, the Australian Curriculum Assessment and Reporting Authority has provided information on Students with Disabilities on line at: www.australiancurriculum.edu.au/resources/student-diversity/students-with-disability/.
- A description of learning disorders from the Diagnostic and Statistical Manual of Mental Disorders (5th ed.) can be found at: https://psychcentral.com/disorders/specific-learning-disorder/.
- The Learning Disabilities Association of America has provided a useful summary of types of learning disability at: https://ldaamerica.org/types-of-learning-disabilities/.

Print resources

Ashman, A. (Ed.) (2018). *Education for inclusion and diversity* (6th ed.). Sydney, NSW: Pearson Australia.

Hallahan, D., Kauffman, J., & Pullen, P. (2018). *Exceptional learners* (14th ed.). Upper Saddle River, NJ: Pearson.

Levenson, N. (2020). *Six shifts to improve special education and other interventions.* Cambridge, MA: Harvard Education Publishing.

Obiakor, F., Banks, T., Graves, J., & Rotatori, A.F. (2019). *Educating young children with and without exceptionalities: Contemporary perspectives in special education.* Charlotte, NC: Information Age Publishing.

Van Rensburg, H., & O'Neill, S. (2020). *Inclusive theory and practice in special education.* Hershey, PA: IGI Global.

Chapter 2

Students with intellectual disability

The current view of educators is that all children with intellectual disability can learn if provided with methods and materials oriented to their individual needs and abilities, and if given all necessary support. In this regard, Peterson and Hittie (2010, p.86) remarked: 'When we use good teaching strategies, students with intellectual disabilities learn much more than anyone thought possible.' It is vital that we do not sell these students short by expecting too little from them.

The most obvious characteristic of students with intellectual disability is that they tend to experience significant difficulty learning and remembering almost everything that other students can learn with relative ease. In some cases, there may also be problems with maintaining attention, social interaction and emotional control. It is often reported that mainstream teachers lack confidence when required to implement programmes and differentiate instruction for these students. For this reason, all teachers need to have some knowledge of the effects of intellectual disability on children's capacity to learn and on their behaviour.

Intellectual disability

Intellectual disability was previously referred to for many generations as mental handicap or mental retardation, and the term intellectual disability was not officially introduced until the fifth edition of the *Diagnostic and Statistical Manual of Mental Disorders* (DSM-5) (APA, 2013). It is generally accepted that individuals with intellectual disability comprise some 2 per cent of the general population. Diagnosis is based on an evaluation of the individual's developmental history and the actual repertoire of knowledge, skills, and behaviours that person has acquired (Reynolds et al., 2014). The degree of difficulty each person encounters in learning is directly related to their level of cognitive impairment— mild, moderate, severe, or profound. Students with mild intellectual disability form the majority of this group (87 per cent). They are only a little slower than average students in learning new information and skills, so can usually be educated in mainstream schools if provided with additional support. However, children with more severe impairments may be low-functioning in most areas, and require almost complete and continuous care and management—described as having 'high support needs.' Their education is still provided mainly in special schools or centres, although a few mainstream schools have made efforts to accommodate them.

Intellectual disability impairs cognition in several key areas—language, reasoning, memory, reading, writing, and number skills (APA, 2013). However, children with this disability may have problems not only with schoolwork, but also in developing self-management and acquiring everyday living skills. Functioning is affected in the domains of interpersonal communication, social judgment, and the ability to make and retain friends (Schwab, 2019). Many individuals with moderate to severe intellectual disability may also have physical or sensory impairments. Some students may also have attention deficit-hyperactivity disorder (ADHD) (Arias et al., 2019) a condition discussed fully in Chapter 8.

In general terms, children with a significant degree of intellectual disability usually appear much less mature than their age peers. Their behaviour, reasoning, and self-control are more closely related to their rate of mental development rather than to their chronological age. They have the greatest difficulties interpreting information and solving simple everyday problems (Vise, 2019). From a practical viewpoint, intellectual disability presents itself as an inability to think as quickly, reason as deeply, remember as easily, or adapt as rapidly to new situations, when compared with so-called normal children.

Priorities in teaching students with intellectual disability

In the USA, Britain, and Australia, almost all students with mild disabilities will attend mainstream schools and are helped to access the mainstream curriculum. Where necessary, adjustments and adaptations are made to classroom programmes and teaching methods to accommodate their learning needs (ACARA, 2013; Ain, 2018). Only those with severe disabilities and high support needs will receive their education in a special school or centre.

Mild intellectual disability

When students with mild intellectual disability are included in mainstream classrooms, the intention is undoubtedly that they will follow the normal curriculum as far as possible (ACARA, 2013; Westwood, 2018a). This arrangement is preferable to providing an alternative programme because it includes the students more effectively in the total classroom experience. However, these students may need to produce work at a slower pace, and possibly use different learning materials (e.g., simpler text with more illustrations; structured notes; easier worksheets; different ways of producing written work) (Jimenez et al., 2014; Vise, 2019). Students with mild intellectual disability will also need more frequent direct guidance, emotional support, and encouragement from the teacher, classroom assistant, and peers.

Any necessary adaptations to methods or materials are usually specified in the student's IEP or similar document, along with personalised goals for learning. Chapter 15 describes a number of strategies for adapting teaching methods and curricula.

Moderate to severe disability

In the case of students with moderate to severe intellectual disability additional adaptations are required. This degree of disability often results in significant limitations of development in the following areas, and these must represent priorities for intervention and teaching:

- language and communication
- self-care and daily living skills

- social development
- self-regulation and self-direction
- basic academic skills (literacy and numeracy)
- transition to employment or sheltered work
- independent functioning in the community.

The great dilemma facing those who wish to educate children with moderate to severe disabilities in the mainstream is how to meet their basic needs for training in self-care and everyday living skills within an environment where a standard academic curriculum prevails. Some experts have queried whether the potential benefits of normalisation in the mainstream can outweigh all the problems involved in supporting these children in a curriculum that is not necessarily very relevant to them. Some years ago, Dymond and Orelove (2001, p.111) warned that: 'Functional skills, which were once widely accepted as the basis for curriculum development, have received limited attention as the field has moved to a more inclusive service delivery model.' In recent years little has changed, and the same observation could be made today. There is growing concern in some quarters that 'full inclusion' is unrealistic for the most disabled students, and may even result in some learners receiving an education that is not appropriate to meet their needs (Goodall, 2018; Imray & Hinchcliffe, 2012; National Autistic Society, 2016).

For some students with moderate to severe intellectual disability, a special education setting still offers the best environment to meet their needs. The purpose of having special schools and special classes was – and still is – to create an environment in which objectives for learning, curriculum content, resources, and methods of instruction can be geared appropriately to the students' needs and abilities. A priority in designing such a curriculum is to use content and teaching approaches that will improve the quality of life for intellectually disabled student as they grow toward adulthood.

Learning characteristics of students with intellectual disability

It is generally accepted that children with intellectual disability pass through the same stages in cognitive development as all other children, but at a much slower rate. In most aspects of conceptual development, school-age children with mild to moderate intellectual disability tend to be functioning at what Piaget (1963) referred to as the 'concrete operational level'–they understand and remember best the things that they can directly experience. Teaching for them must always be *reality-based* and must involve 'learning by doing'. Students with severe to profound disability may be at an even earlier cognitive stage, tied closely to sensory awareness. Programmes for these students are described later.

Attention

Individuals with intellectual disability appear often to have problems maintaining attention or attending to the relevant aspects of a learning situation. For example, when a teacher is showing the student how to form the numeral 5 with a pencil, or how to use scissors to cut paper, the student is attracted to the ring on the teacher's finger rather than the task itself. This tendency to focus on irrelevant detail or to be distracted easily from a learning task, is a major problem for a child with intellectual disability when integrated into mainstream programmes without close supervision. Without adequate control of attention, any student will fail to learn or remember what the teacher is trying to teach. Attention and memory can both be improved when a learning task is relevant and interesting, involves action on the part of the student, and is paired with positive and encouraging feedback.

Memory

Many students with intellectual disability also have difficulty storing information in long-term memory. This problem is linked, in part, with failure to attend closely to the learning task, as discussed above; but it is also due to the students' lack of effective strategies for facilitating memorisation. To minimise this memory problem, students with intellectual disability require much greater amounts of repetition and practice to ensure that important information and skills are eventually stored and can be recalled when needed. Many opportunities must be provided for guided and independent practice, revision and overlearning in every area of the curriculum. It takes longer than expected for these students to reach the desired state of automaticity, in even the most basic skills.

Generalisation and transfer of learning

For any learner, the final and most difficult stage of acquiring new learning is that of *generalisation*. A stage must be reached when a student can automatically apply new learning in other situations not directly linked with the context in which it was first taught. It is typical of most students with intellectual disability that they do not transfer what they learn (Turnbull et al., 2019). They may learn a particular skill or strategy in one context (the classroom) but fail to transfer it to a different situation (workshop). It is recommended that teachers consider ways of facilitating generalisation and transfer when planning lessons for students with special needs—for example, by re-teaching the same skills or strategies in different contexts, gradually increasing the range of contexts where practice is carried out, challenging students to decide whether a skill or strategy could be used in a new situation, and reinforcing any evidence of students' spontaneous generalisation of previous learning.

Language delay

A characteristic of many children with moderate and severe intellectual disability is the very slow rate at which they acquire speech and language. Some have a definite speech disorder that makes it extremely difficult for them to communicate; and the frustration of failing to communicate can give rise to emotional reactions and the onset of challenging behaviour (Gerow et al., 2018). A few individuals with severe and multiple disabilities never develop speech, so for them alternative methods of communication may need to be developed, such as sign language or picture communication systems (Inclusive Technology, 2014).

Language ability is important for cognitive and social development for the following reasons:

- language enables an individual to make his or her needs, opinions, and ideas known to others;

- language is important for cognitive development; without language one lacks much of the raw material with which to think and reason;
- concepts are more effectively stored in memory if they have a representation in words as well as in sensations and perceptions;
- language is the main medium through which school learning is mediated;
- positive social interactions with other persons are heavily dependent upon effective language and communication skills;
- inner language (self-talk) is important for regulating one's behaviour and responses.

Early intervention programs in the preschool years place heavy emphasis on developing children's communication skills. These interventions should also be family focused as much as possible. It has been shown that parents can be trained to engage more proactively in stimulating the development of children with language delay (Colmar, 2014).

The development of communication skills is given very high priority in special school curricula, and will be no less important for intellectually disabled students included in mainstream settings. Two obvious benefits of placing a child with intellectual disability in a mainstream class are immersion in a naturally enriched language environment, and the increased need for the student to communicate with others.

Language is best acquired naturally, through using it to express needs, obtain information and interact socially. Where possible, naturally occurring opportunities within the school day are used to teach and reinforce new vocabulary and language patterns. This *milieu approach* is found to be more productive in terms of generalisation and transfer of learning to everyday use than are the more clinical approaches to teaching language in isolation. However, teachers do not always find it easy to integrate specific language development objectives for an individual student into their content-based mainstream class lessons.

Many students with intellectual disability require the services of a speech therapist (Terband et al., 2018), but while this proves to be helpful for some individuals, others make very slow improvement. This is because the individual receiving help may not understand the need for it, and may therefore have no motivation to practise and use what is taught. There is also the usual problem of lack of generalisation – what is taught in a clinical therapy setting does not necessarily transfer to the person's everyday speech.

Social development

For many individuals with intellectual disability the development of social competence and skills presents many ongoing difficulties. The presence or absence of social skills in these students tends to be related to the extent to which they have had an opportunity to socialise in environments other than the home. Within the family, the social interactions between the child and others are likely to be mainly positive, but the same assumption cannot be made for contacts within the community and at school or work. Although community attitudes towards people with disabilities have become more positive and accepting, there is still likelihood that some children with intellectual disability will experience difficulty gaining acceptance and making friends – particularly if they display some challenging behaviours.

Some students with intellectual disability are rejected and marginalised by their peers more often on the basis of their irritating behaviour than because they are disabled.

For example, the presence of inappropriate aggression and temper tantrums makes it difficult for some of these children to be socially accepted. Intervention is needed to eliminate negative behaviours and replace them with pro-social behaviours (see Chapter 8). If the student with a disability is to make friends and be accepted in the peer group, social skills training may be needed (Hallahan et al., 2019).

Strategies for developing social skills are described in Chapter 9; but helping students with intellectual disability form lasting friendships with other children in the mainstream is actually quite difficult. Often students in the peer group who start out with good intentions to socialise with a disabled peer quickly lose interest and fade away. In post-school years, socialisation remains difficult for many individuals with intellectual disability and often they require regular and ongoing support from a social worker.

While stressing the need to increase social interaction with others, students with intellectual disability (male and female) also need to be taught *protective behaviours* to reduce the possibility that they become victims of financial or other forms of exploitation. The lack of social judgment of some teenagers and young adults with intellectual disability causes them to be rather naïve and trusting. There is also a risk of sexual abuse from peers or adults because they may not really comprehend right from wrong in matters of physical contact (Wissink et al., 2018). For their own protection they need to be taught the danger of going anywhere with a stranger, accepting rides in a car, or taking gifts for favours. They need to know that some forms of touching are wrong, and they also need to know that they can tell some trusted adult if they feel they are at risk from some other person. These matters must be dealt with openly in schools and also reinforced by parents. Sex education is an important priority for these children.

Self-regulation and self-determination

In recent years, much emphasis has been placed on using cognitive methods to increase self-regulation and self-monitoring in students with intellectual disability (see Chapter 7). While this approach is proving useful for students with mild disabilities, it is very difficult indeed to employ cognitive training with low-functioning students, for reasons that will be discussed later in connection with autism.

Self-determination is an attribute currently attracting attention in the education of individuals with intellectual disability (Friedman et al., 2019). It is recognised now that too much of the life of a person with moderate or severe disability is typically determined by others. In recent years, educators and caregivers have been encouraged to find many more ways of ensuring that persons with disabilities have many opportunities to exercise choice and make decisions. To facilitate this process, goals must be included in the IEP and in the curriculum for increasing the individual's independence and self-management. Parents, paraprofessionals, and carers may need to be reminded to allow children with disabilities in their care to *do more for themselves*.

Physical fitness

It is reported widely that students with intellectual disability often fail to take regular exercise and have a tendency to become overweight and unfit (Hassan et al., 2019; Pierce & Maher, 2020). This is a negative influence that can affect their wellbeing. As far as possible, schools must endeavor to include these students fully in PE and games activities, and should also encourage out-of-school participation in sports. The issue of childhood obesity is considered in more detail in Chapter 4.

Teaching approaches for students with intellectual disability

Taking into account the stage of cognitive development of most students with mild to moderate intellectual disability, the priority for teaching is to make the curriculum *reality-based* and *relevant*. For example, reading skills should be developed and practised using real books, information on the computer screen, recipes, brochures, and comic books—as well as through the medium of graded readers, games and flashcards. For students at the concrete operational stage in cognition, the principle of learning by doing certainly applies. If they are to learn important number skills for example, they should learn them not only from computer games, instructional materials, and practice sheets, but also from real situations such as shopping trips, stocktaking, measuring, estimating, counting, grouping, recording data, and comparing quantities. A mathematics programme for students with mild intellectual disability should link the regular practising of functional number skills directly to real-life situations, so that basic mathematical thinking is encouraged rather than rote learning. Where first-hand experience of quantitative situations is not immediately available, using videos of such situations (e.g., measuring, weighing, giving change) can be beneficial for improving students' mathematical understanding. Videos therefore offer an innovative solution for bringing more of the school curriculum to life for these students (Al-Salahat, 2016; Blik et al., 2017).

In addition to reality-based learning, children with moderate intellectual disability need the curriculum content to be broken down into simple steps, and to be taught with high-quality explicit instruction to ensure high success rates (Reynolds et al., 2019). Explicit instruction is among the most extensively researched teaching methods and has consistently proved more effective than unguided learning for most purposes. Lessons that employ explicit instruction present information and skills clearly, teach students effective ways of learning, and obtain many successful responses from students during the time available. There is heavy emphasis on practice and reinforcement with feedback from the teacher. Frequent prompting by the teacher or instructor during learning plays an important role in helping students process information, respond correctly, and acquire new skills. It has been found that this type of teacher-led instruction is extremely effective for all students in the initial stages of new learning, and is of particular help to students with disabilities (Turnbull et al., 2019). The method is discussed fully in Chapter 14.

Preparation for work

Transition from school to adult life and work requires extremely careful planning for intellectually disabled students in the adolescent age range (Carter et al., 2014; Liu et al., 2018). In the past, senior special schools usually rose to the challenge of developing students' readiness for employment by providing a strong emphasis on practical skills, work routines, reliability, punctuality, and work experience. It is proving to be much more difficult to provide these opportunities for senior students in inclusive mainstream schools. This problem is yet to be resolved—which may explain why many intellectually disabled students of secondary school age have remained in senior special schools in the UK, rather than entering the mainstream (Black, 2019).

Specific approaches for students with severe intellectual disability

Several unique approaches have been developed to meet the special needs of students with severe and complex intellectual disabilities in special schools. Many of these students have no speech and some have restricted mobility. The approaches described below also have some application with students with severe autism.

Applied behaviour analysis (ABA)

Applied behaviour analysis is a broad term that encompasses several different approaches that can be used within special education (e.g., behaviour modification; discrete trial training; pivotal response training; task analysis) (Pitts et al., 2019; Stahmer, 2014). The underlying principle is *operant conditioning*, and the belief that new skills and behaviours can be taught, shaped, and reinforced by rewards or eliminated by negative consequences from the environment. As a teaching technique, ABA involves setting clear behavioural objectives for a student, and devising a schedule for rewarding him or her at every incremental step when moving successfully toward that objective (Alberto & Troutman, 2013). The approach has been extensively researched and found to be effective in teaching new behaviours to children with intellectual disability, autism, and students with behaviour disorders (Trump et al., 2018). The topic is discussed in much more detail in Chapter 8.

It should be noted that while the traditional form of ABA involves setting extremely detailed and specific behavioural objectives that could be used to measure accurately the effectiveness of an intervention, more recent applications (as used with severely disabled students) have found that general objectives are more functional because they are flexible and adaptive to individual rates of progress (Lacey, 2014).

Discrete Trial Training

Discrete Trial Training (DTT) is an ABA method for teaching a skill or behaviour using simple and structured steps, with practice and reinforcement provided for all correct responses at each and every step (Elder, 2018; Peterson et al., 2019). It is an approach to building a more complex skill by practising each small step on the way. DTT is used in domains such as speech and language training, self-help skills, discriminating among colours or shapes, and recognising letters and numbers. Task analysis has usually been conducted first to identify the best sequence of steps necessary to master any given skill or process.

Many therapists suggest that DTT is a particularly effective strategy for teaching skills to children with intellectual disability and autism; but it is difficult to implement in anything other than one-to-one teaching situations (Rabideau et al., 2018). It is an approach that can be taught to parents of children with intellectual disability or autism (Ünlü et al., 2018).

Constant time delay

Often, in one-to-one teaching situations, a teacher or tutor tends to step in too quickly after asking a question or giving an instruction. It has been found more effective if the tutor waits for a response for around 5 seconds before praising the student for a correct response or before providing a correction or prompt. A meta-analysis of this approach has indicated that it is simple to apply and more efficient than many other commonly used instructional practices (Horn et al., 2020). Constant time delay also has a part to play in remedial reading tuition at Tier 3 intervention.

Intensive interaction

A method known as *intensive interaction* has been developed for use with individuals who have severe and complex disabilities, lack verbal communication and have limited social interaction with others (Hewett, 2018; Nind & Hewett, 2005). The interactive approach tries to ensure that much of the informal teaching that takes place is based directly on the individual's *self-initiated* actions and reactions (no matter how small) rather than on any pre-planned curriculum.

The approach was first developed in England in the 1980s by teachers working in long-stay residential institutions for children and adults with severe and complex disabilities. It evolved from a technique known at that time as 'augmented mothering'—a term that sums up the essence of the interactions involved. In many ways, the method is similar to the natural approach used instinctively by parents when responding to a baby's actions. Something the child does spontaneously leads the adult to react, rather than the adult imposing communication on the child. For example, responding to the child by smiling, reaching out, touching, stroking, and vocalising–and by doing so, reinforcing the child's behaviour. There is a vital ingredient of natural warm social interaction and communication involved. Often playing very simple touching or laughing games, or using sensory or tactile equipment, will create a context for this to happen.

The approach has been adopted by several other countries, including Australia, for use with severely intellectually disabled and autistic individuals. Research findings suggest that intensive interaction has most positive effect with individuals who do not display very high levels of emotional disturbance and challenging behaviour (Tee & Reed, 2017).

For more information on intensive interaction visit: http://integratedtreatmentservices. co.uk/wp-content/uploads/_mediavault/2015/01/intensive-interation.pd.

Preference-based teaching (PBT)

This approach has similar theoretical underpinnings to intensive interaction, and the two can be used in a mutually supportive manner. PBT is based on the belief that students enjoy engaging in learning activities much more, and attention is more effectively gained and maintained, if the mode of teaching and the materials used are compatible with their personal preferences. For example, a child may enjoy engaging in sand play rather than water play, or singing with caregiver rather than listening to a story (Watkins et al., 2019). When a child is engaged in this way there are fewer behaviour problems. This is a very important consideration when working with children with severe disabilities and challenging behaviour. Cerveny (2016) conducted a study to determine if PBT embedded as a part of discrete trial training led to more learning than discrete trial training alone. It was found that learning occurred in both conditions, and there was no clear difference between PBT alone and the combined version.

Snoezelen multisensory environments

For many years it has been believed that severely disabled children can be helped most by methods that incorporate sensory awareness and sensory stimulation. The *Snoezelen* approach developed in Holland uses structured multisensory environments containing lights, textures, aromas, sounds, and movement for therapeutic and educational purposes (Russell & Cohn, 2012). Snoezelen approach provides both sensory stimulation and relaxation for severely or profoundly disabled individuals (including adults) and has been adopted in a number of special schools in Europe and Australasia (Toro, 2019).

Snoezelen is reported to have particular benefits for calming intellectually disabled or autistic individuals who also have emotional and behavioural problems. In some cases, Snoezelen has proved useful for reducing self-injurious behaviour (SIB). When working with the most severely disabled individuals, it is suggested that an assessment should be made of that person's preference for certain stimuli rather than others in order to tailor a Snoezelen sensory environment to that person's preferences (see preference-based teaching above). It is also useful to identify what types of stimuli (colour, lights, music, tastes) can be used most effectively as reinforcers in other learning situations (Fava & Strauss, 2010; Grattan & Demchak, 2014).

Information on Snoezelen can be located at: www.snoezelen.info/

The next chapter provides an introduction to children with autism spectrum disorder.

They comprise a very diverse group, with a range of mild to severe difficulties that span learning, communication, socialisation, self-regulation, and independent functioning. Those students with moderate to severe autism are often regarded as the most difficult to place successfully in inclusive classrooms.

Online resources

- Information on intellectual disability at: www.mentalhelp.net/poc/view_doc.php?type=doc& id=10365.
- University of Hertfordshire [UK]. (2020). Intellectual disability and health. www.intellectualdisa bility.info/intellectual-disability.
- Vise, A. (2019). Teaching students with intellectual disabilities: Tips and strategies. www.bright hubeducation.com/special-ed-inclusion-strategies/9893-teaching-students-with-intellectual-disabilities/.
- Reynolds, T., Zupanick, C.E., & Dombeck, M. (2019). Effective teaching methods for people with intellectual disabilities: www.mentalhelp.net/articles/effective-teaching-methods-for-people-with-intellectual-disabilities/.
- Information on Intensive Interaction Approach can be found at: http://integratedtreatment services.co.uk/wp-content/uploads/_mediavault/2015/01/intensive-interation.pd.
- Discrete Trial Training is described clearly at: www.educateautism.com/applied-behaviour-analysis/discrete-trial-training.html.

Print resources

Baum, S. (2018). *Intellectual disabilities: A systemic approach* (3rd ed.). Abingdon, Oxon: Routledge.

Bhaumik, S., & Alexander, R. (Eds). (2020). *Oxford textbook of the psychiatry of intellectual disability.* Oxford: Oxford University Press.

Browder, D.M., Spooner, F., & Courtade, G.R. (2020). *Teaching students with moderate and severe disabilities* (2nd ed.). New York: Guilford Press.

Hugh, M.L., Conner, C., & Stewart, J. (2018). *Intensive Intervention Practice Guide: Using visual activity schedules to intensify academic interventions for young children with autism spectrum disorder.* Washington, DC: Office of Special Education Programs, US Department of Education.

Matson, J. (Ed.). (2019). *Handbook of intellectual disabilities.* New York: Springer International.

Chapter 3

Students with autism spectrum disorder (ASD)

Autism spectrum disorder (ASD): defined and described

The 5th edition of the *Diagnostic and Statistical Manual of Mental Disorders* (DSM-5) (APA, 2013) contains a very detailed description and definition of ASD. It is not necessary to reproduce that description in full here (see Online Resources listed at the end of the chapter). Drawing on the DSM-5 definition and description, the main characteristics of an individual with ASD can be summarised as:

- *persistent deficits in social communication and social interaction*: may include deficits in social-emotional reciprocity; deficits in non-verbal communicative behaviours; abnormalities in eye contact and body language; deficits in understanding and use of gestures; lack of facial expressions; deficits in developing, maintaining, and understanding relationships
- *restricted, repetitive patterns of behaviour, interests, or activities:* may include stereotyped repetitive movements or speech; insistence on sameness and adherence to routines; fixated interests that are abnormal in intensity; hyper- or hypo-reactivity to sensory input such as sounds or lights.

Of course, any individual with ASD may show some but not all of these difficulties and deficits, and will display them at different levels of severity from mild to severe. When an individual with ASD is officially diagnosed by a suitably qualified professional, the diagnosis must specify whether there is also an accompanying intellectual impairment, and whether the individual has any language impairment. The severity of the disorder is reflected in the specified level of support that the individual requires, ranging from 'very substantial support' (level 3) to 'requiring some support' (level 1).

Autism (as it was first termed) was originally identified in the 1940s and was regarded at first as a single disability that affects communication, emotional development, and social competence. The condition is now referred to as *autism spectrum disorder* (ASD) to reflect the fact that it is not a single syndrome with clear-cut characteristics but actually manifests itself along a continuum with varying degrees of severity and marked differences in behaviour patterns (APA, 2013; Casanova & Casanova, 2018). Some children with autism may also have an intellectual disability that impacts their ability to learn.

Most high-functioning individuals with only mild ASD receive their education in mainstream schools, where their unusual behaviour patterns can often cause them to be regarded as strange (quirky) by peers and teachers, and they may have difficulty making friends. While lack of friends may not bother some ASD students, others appear to experience deep loneliness (Mazurek, 2014). Some high-functioning autistic students benefit from personal counselling and social training that focuses on helping them understand the feelings of others, how to initiate and maintain social interactions, dealing with their own problems or frustrations, and how to avoid trouble with other students and with teachers.

Among the group of high-functioning individuals with autism are those previously referred to as having Asperger syndrome. The fifth edition of the *Diagnostic and Statistical Manual of Mental Disorders* no longer classifies Asperger syndrome as a distinct category (APA, 2013). These individuals are now regarded as simply located somewhere on the upper end of the autism spectrum. They have some of the behavioural and social difficulties associated with other degrees of autism, but they tend to have language and cognitive skills in the average or even above average range. A few may even exhibit a talent or deep knowledge in areas such as music, art, mental calculation, or can recall factual information with amazing accuracy. Examples of individuals at this high-functioning level of autism were portrayed well by actors in the film *Rain Man* and the TV series *The Good Doctor*.

While children with mild autistic tendencies can usually be accommodated in the mainstream, those with severe degrees of autism tend to function at a level that is too low to cope with the demands of even an adapted mainstream curriculum. In the most severe cases, the individual may not use speech and may be virtually unresponsive to social contact. It is common to find the individual displays ritualistic habits (*stereotypic behaviours*) such as constant body rocking or self-stimulation, and many are highly sensitive to any change in their routine or immediate environment.

Early detection remains the top priority for providing appropriate intervention for ASD. To be diagnosed as autistic, a child must show symptoms of abnormal social and interpersonal development during early childhood, and must meet criteria listed in the *Diagnostic and Statistical Manual of Mental Disorders* (APA, 2013). In DSM-5. a new category, *social communication disorder* (SCD) was been added, to identify individuals who have no speech disorder but display significant difficulties using spoken language to communicate with and respond to others in socially appropriate ways. They may also have difficulty interpreting non-verbal communication cues used by others (smiles, frowns, gestures). This difficulty can make it harder for a child to make and keep friends. These students do not, however, display the same repetitive and stereotypic behaviours or obsessions evident in some individuals with more severe forms of autism spectrum disorder.

Prevalence

Autism spectrum disorder has been identified in all parts of the world, so the disorder does not appear to be in any way culturally determined. It is regarded as a low-incidence disability with approximately 4 to 10 cases per 10,000 in the population. The lower figure represents the most severe cases, and the upper figure represents children with only mild autistic tendencies. The ratio of males to females is 4 or 5 to 1. There has been a reported increase in the number of identified cases of ASD over the past two decades, but this may be due to improved assessment procedures and greater awareness in the community rather than any actual increase in prevalence.

Causes

The underlying cause of autism spectrum disorder is unknown, and current opinion is that there may be several contributory factors. Studies have tended to suggest a possible genetic factor, perhaps affecting the brain systems necessary for normal social and communicative development. It is unclear whether genetic susceptibility is interacting with environmental influences; and if so, what those environmental factors may be (National Autistic Society, 2018). Several theories have been put forward—such as the possible negative effects of vaccinations in childhood—but these theories have all been refuted. The National Health Service in the UK has declared that autism is not caused by bad parenting, vaccines, diet, or infection.

Intervention for autism

Many approaches have been used to help children with autism become more responsive to teaching and management by increasing their communication skills and reducing negative behaviours (McCollow & Hoffman, 2019). Definite gains are reported from intervention programmes, but there is considerable variability in response among individuals, with some children (usually those with milder autism) making much more progress than others. A few children with the most severe forms of autism and with accompanying emotional disturbance often appear to make minimal gains despite many hours of careful stimulation and teaching.

Interventions have included pharmacological (drug) treatments, diet control, psychotherapy, music therapy, play therapy, preference-based play activities, facilitated communication, behaviour modification, and cognitive self-management training. It is generally considered that behaviour modification (applied behaviour analysis) has produced the best results to date and tends to be the most widely used approach (Leaf et al., 2018). In some studies, after one year of consistent implementation of ABA strategies (setting of clear behaviour goals and consistent reinforcement of required responses), many children with autism spectrum disorder demonstrate gains in communication skills, social interaction, and self-control (Pitts, Gent, & Hoerger, 2019).

Some approaches and 'treatments' advertised online are regarded as highly controversial and of doubtful value (Worley et al., 2014). Often these programs are recommended on websites that provide information for parents of autistic children, but give no evidence at all of the *proven* efficacy of the programme.

Teaching, training, and management: general principles

Teaching, training, and managing children with moderate to severe autism is almost always complex, and has to be ongoing and multidisciplinary. It has been said that effective intervention is characterised by structure, intensity of treatment, low adult-to-child ratio, and individualised programming (Hampshire & Hourcade, 2014). To create the optimum situation for teaching, the environment and routines must always be consistent, and teaching sessions for the children need to be implemented according to a predictable schedule. Each child's programme must be based on a very detailed appraisal of his or her current developmental level and existing skills, so that goals can be set that help build on any existing strengths and capabilities. New information, skills, or behaviours need to be taught in small increments.

There is general agreement that the focus of any intervention programme should attempt to:

- stimulate cognitive development;
- facilitate language acquisition;
- promote social interactions;
- use visual cues as supplements to all verbal instructions and requests.

All teachers, parents, and caregivers must know the precise goals of the programme and must collaborate closely on the methods to be used with the child. The most effective interventions involve the child's family as well as teachers and therapists. It is essential that parents and caregivers also be trained in the teaching and reinforcement strategies to be used in any intervention programme, because the child spends more time at home than at school (Mazurek et al., 2019). Home-based intervention programmes (or home programmes combined with clinic-based intervention) produce better results than purely clinic-based programmes.

For non-verbal autistic children, intensive use of alternative communication methods and visual cues (hand signing, pointing, gesture, pictures, and symbol cards) is usually necessary in most teaching situations. One approach to helping a student improve in self-regulation is the use of visual activity schedules, with pictures or symbols depicting what he or she must do at particular times during the school day (e.g., wash hands; dress for PE) (Hugh et al., 2018). Such systems can also operate at home. For higher-functioning students, an electronic hand-held planner can be useful for storing the daily schedule and for sending appropriate prompts at given times. Some forms of assistive technology (see Chapter 4) have also proved valuable for engaging the attention of a child with ASD and for facilitating communication.

Specific programmes and methods

TEACCH

One approach that has developed in recent years is TEACCH (*Treatment and Education of Autistic and Communication-handicapped Children*) (Mesibov et al. 2005). This approach is based on the need for a high degree of structure in the day for children with ASD. It uses a combination of cognitive and behavioural-change strategies, coupled with direct teaching of specific skills. Importance is placed on training parents to work with their own children and to make effective use of support services. A meta-analysis of studies involving TEACCH has suggested that it is effective for increasing social behaviour (Virues-Ortaga et al., 2013). A study by Park and Kim (2018) has also demonstrated that the structured nature of TEACCH is effective in enhancing a child's active engagement and reducing disruptive behaviour.

An important feature of this approach is that it capitalises on autistic children's preference for a visual system of communication rather than auditory-verbal mode. Several studies support using visual cues, prompts, and schedules to hold a child's attention and to represent information in a form that is easily interpreted (Hugh et al., 2018).

TEACCH approach for autism spectrum disorders is explained at: www.saceaz.org/treatment-and-education-autistic-and-related-communication-handicapped-children-teacch

Lovaas: Young Autism Program

One very intensive programme for autistic children devised by Lovaas (Lovaas & Smith, 2003) is also referred to as *Early Intensive Behavioral Therapy* (EIBT). The programme begins with the child at age two years and involves language development, social behaviours, and the stimulation of play activity. The programme contains elements of applied behaviour analysis and discrete-trial training, with skills broken down into their most basic components, and consistent rewarding of every positive performance with praise and other reinforcement. Excessive ritualistic behaviour, temper tantrums, and aggression are gradually eliminated. The second year of treatment focuses on higher levels of language stimulation, and on cooperative play and interaction with peers.

Lovaas claimed high success rates for the programme, with almost half of treated children reaching normal functioning levels. However, the fact that this programme takes up to 40 hours per week using one-to-one teaching over two years, makes it very labour intensive and expensive. While the general principles are undoubtedly sound, it is difficult, if not impossible, to replicate the approach in the average special preschool or kindergarten.

For more information, visit the Lovaas Institute website at: http://lovaas.com/

Pivotal response training (PRT)

This approach, developed by Robert and Lynn Koegel and associates (2006) is based on the principle that intervention in autism should focus heavily on strengthening particular behaviours that have wide and beneficial effects on learning. Examples of pivotal behaviours are focusing and maintaining attention, responding to multiple cues, self-regulation, and the initiation of social interaction. By targeting these key areas, it is hoped that improvements will generalise across areas of sociability, communication, behaviour and academic skills. Pivotal response training employs applied behaviour analysis techniques, and has been used effectively in improving play and social behaviours (Brock et al., 2018; Stockall & Dennis, 2014).

An important example of a specific pivotal behaviour is *selective attention*. If a child with ASD has major difficulty coping with distractions in the environment, training will seek to increase selective attention and reduce distractibility. Many benefits then occur, such as improved ability to engage in a learning task, use working memory, and process information more effectively.

For more information on PRT visit the Autism Speaks website at: www.autismspeaks.org/pivotal-response-treatment-prt-0

SCERTS Model

Detailed information on SCERTS can be found in the two-volume manual by Prizant et al. (2006). The acronym SCERTS is derived from *Social Communication, Emotional Regulation, Transactional Support*; these are the areas of development prioritised within this approach. The designers of this trans-disciplinary and family-centred model stress that SCERTS is not intended to be exclusionary of other treatments or methods. It attempts to capitalise on naturally occurring opportunities for teaching that occur throughout a child's daily activities and across social partners, such as siblings, parents, caregivers, and other children.

The overriding goal of SCERTS is to help a child with autism become a more competent participant in social activities, by enhancing his or her capacity for attention, communication, reciprocity, expression of emotion, and understanding of others' emotions. There is some evidence that SCERTS can indeed improve social communication and emotional regulation in children with ASD (Yu & Zhu, 2018).

The Son-Rise Program®

This training program for parents and caregivers of children with autism is offered in face-to-face version and online by the Autism Treatment Centre of America. In some respects, this home-based intervention uses some principles of the Intensive Interaction Approach for severely intellectually disabled individuals as described in the previous chapter —for example, by building upon a child's existing abilities (no matter how small), personal preferences, and self-initiated responses as starting points for intervention and change. A basic aspect of Son-Rise is that the facilitator (adult) joins the child in his or her world, and the activities and pace of any session are directed by the child rather than by the adult. Importance is placed on having a distraction-free environment in which to interact with the child, so that attention can be maintained.

Details of Son-Rise can be found online at: www.autismtreatmentcenter.org/essentials.php

Social stories and social thinking

Interventions for children with ASD frequently focus on improving their social awareness and social skills. These interventions aim to teach autistic individuals why they and others react socially in the ways that they do, how their own behaviours affect the way others perceive and respond to them, and how this affects their own emotions and relationships with others in different social contexts.

One approach used mainly by school counsellors that appears helpful in developing autistic children's awareness of normal codes of behaviour is the use of *social stories* (Goodman-Scott et al., 2017; Gray, 2015). These are simple age-appropriate narratives supplemented by simple illustrations, and personalised to suit the child's behavioural needs. The theme and context of the story help an autistic child interpret and respond more appropriately to typical social situations–for example, sharing a toy, taking turns, or standing in line. It has also been found that simple comic strips with stick figures can be used to create situations where a child with ASD is led to think about the actions, reactions, and feelings of others (Gray, 2015).

Another promising approach is *Children's Friendship Training*, a 12-week parent-assisted social intervention that targets the knowledge and skills for forming relationships (Mandelberg et al., 2014).

Picture Exchange Communication System (PECS)

Picture Exchange Communication System was developed in 1984 and used in the Delaware Autistic Program. Since then, PECS has been implemented with learners of all ages who have cognitive and communication challenges. The approach has been found particularly useful when working with individuals who have severe intellectual disability and lack speech.

There is a six-stage teaching protocol based on applied behaviour analysis techniques, including prompting and reinforcement strategies and systematic error correction. The effectiveness of this intervention depends heavily on the adequate professional training of teachers or other adults involved (Chua & Poon, 2018). The goal of PECS is to teach a person with autism and very limited communication skills a self-initiating communication system. Children using PECS are taught to communicate their wishes, needs, requests, opinions, or ideas to another person by give them a picture that represents the topic (e.g., picture of a cup if a drink is being requested; picture of playground equipment if the child wishes to go outside to play). PECS works well in the home or in the classroom; and it is reported that some learners using PECS also develop speech.

The next chapter provides coverage of students with physical disabilities or health conditions that may affect their learning and development. Chapter 5 extends this coverage to explore the needs of students with impairments of vision or hearing.

Online resources

- Detailed information on autism: www.intellectualdisability.info/diagnosis/autistic-spectrum-disorders.
- The DSM-5 definition of autism spectrum disorder can be found at: https://images.pearsonclinical.com/images/assets/basc-3/basc3resources/DSM-5_DiagnosticCriteria_AutismSpectrumDisorder.pdf.
- What is autism? www.nhs.uk/conditions/autism/.
- Autism spectrum disorder. www.nhsinform.scot/illnesses-and-conditions/brain-nerves-and-spinal-cord/autistic-spectrum-disorder-asd.
- Autism spectrum disorder in children. https://childmind.org/topics/disorders/autism-spectrum-disorder/.
- Teaching students with autism spectrum disorder. www.scholastic.com/teachers/articles/teaching-content/teaching-students-autism-spectrum-disorder/.

Print resources

Boucher, J.M. (2017). *Autism spectrum disorder* (2nd ed.). London: SAGE.
Carter, K. (2020). *Autism from A to Z*. Sirenia Books.
Castellon, S. (2020). *The spectrum girl's survival guide: How to grow up awesome and autistic*. London: Jessica Kingsley.
Fletcher-Watson, S., & Happé, F. (2019). *Autism: A new introduction to psychological theory and current debate* (2nd ed.). London: Routledge.
Ganz, J.B., & Simpson, R.L. (2019). *Interventions for Individuals with Autism Spectrum Disorder and Complex Communication Needs. Augmentative and Alternative Communication Series*. Baltimore, MD: Brookes.
Iyama-Kurtycz, T. (2020). *Diagnosing and caring for the child with autism spectrum disorder*. New York: Springer International.

Chapter 4

Students with physical disabilities and health issues

Physical disability is a relatively low incidence category of special educational need, but these students comprise a very diverse group. Data collected in 2017 from Australian schools suggest that approximately 3 students in every 100 have a physical disability and receive some form of additional support (ACARA, 2019). Similar prevalence is reported in the UK (GOV.UK, 2014b) and is probably also found in other developed countries. A higher figure will certainly pertain in countries with poor standards of health care and pre-natal services, and in countries engaged in ongoing wars and conflict.

The education for children with physical disabilities must focus on providing them as far as possible with the same range of social interactions and learning experiences as those available to other students. For all students with a physical disability, their greatest need is help in accessing resources and facilities, and in moving around easily within the learning environment (Beauchamp et al., 2018; Dominica, 2019). In order to function successfully and maintain a good quality of life, some may also need support from outside services that can provide treatment, therapy or counselling (Tracy-Bronson et al., 2019).

It is beyond the scope of this chapter to provide details of each and every physical disability or health problem. Attention here will be given only to the most commonly occurring conditions, namely cerebral palsy (CP), spina bifida (SB), epilepsy, hydrocephalus, and traumatic brain injury (TBI). Brief discussion will also include health issues such as asthma, obesity, and allergies, as these conditions can also affect learning and development.

Learning and development

Many students with a physical disability are of average or better than average intelligence, and can cope well with the mainstream curriculum if accommodations are made and if any necessary assistive technology is provided. Typical accommodations that may need to be provided include seating arrangements, space for a wheelchair, extra time on assignments and during examinations, and provision of peer assistance for some students in areas such as note-taking or collecting materials for a lesson (Logsdon, 2019).

It is essential for teachers to recognise that a physical disability does not automatically impair a student's ability to learn. Assumptions should never be made about an individual's capacity to learn on the basis of a physical condition. While it is true that a disability or acquired injury that involves neurological damage can affect cognition, there are many other disabilities that do not affect intellect or learning aptitude. Teachers' expectations must always be optimistic concerning how much these students can accomplish when given appropriate access, support and opportunity.

Many students with a physical disability have no problems developing friendships and interacting socially. This is particularly the case if the individual has a pleasant personality and can communicate well. However, students who lack mobility, have communication difficulties, or who have high support needs, may experience much greater difficulty with socialisation. Some of the strategies described later in Chapter 9 will be applicable to assist with the social development and acceptance of these students.

Assistive technology

Assistive technology (AT) plays a major role in the effective education of students with physical and other disabilities by enhancing movement, participation, and communication, and facilitating access to the curriculum (Redford, 2019; Satsangi et al., 2019). The complexity of AT ranges from 'very low tech' equipment such as adjustable slant-top desks, pencil grips, modified scissor grips, specially designed seating, wedges to help position a child for optimum functioning, walking frames, standing frames, and head-pointers—through to 'high-tech' adaptations such as electric wheelchairs operated by head movements or by breath control, modified computer keyboards, touch screens, voice output communication aids (VOCA), and switching devices. Common devices such as smart phones and iPads have also usefully supplemented the more complex equipment needed by these students.

Augmentative and alternative communication (AAC)

Many students with severe and multiple disabilities, whether congenital or acquired, may lack an oral–verbal method of communication. This can lead others to judge them, wrongly, as functioning at a low cognitive level. The priority in intervention for severely disabled persons without speech is to develop an alternative method of communicating. The ultimate aim of any augmentative or alternative communication system is to allow the child to converse about the same range of things that other children of that age would discuss.

Alternative communication modes include:

- sign language, finger-spelling, cued-speech, and gesture;
- picture and symbol systems that a person can use by pointing or by eye glance on a communication board, screen, or book;
- computer-aided communication.

The simplest form of alternative communication is a communication board comprising a small set of pictures or symbols that are personally relevant to the child's life and context. For example, the board may have pictures of a television set, a glass, a knife and fork, a toilet, a toy, and X for 'no' and a green tick for 'yes'. The child can communicate his or her wishes or basic needs by pointing to or looking at the appropriate picture. Other pictures and symbols are added as the child's range of experiences increases.

Waller (2019) has observed that augmentative and alternative communication has been transformed in recent years by the social media revolution and the emergence of mobile technology. The immediate need now is to encourage developers of this technology to devise systems that are very easy to operate and do not require high levels of cognition and aptitude.

Cerebral palsy

Cerebral palsy (CP) is one of the more frequently occurring physical disabilities, with a prevalence rate of approximately 2 cases per 1000 live births. There has been no significant decline in the prevalence rate of this disorder over recent years, even though there have been major advances in prenatal care. CP is a disorder of posture, muscle tone and movement resulting from damage to the motor areas of the brain occurring before, during or soon after birth (Howard et al., 2014). The disability may affect one side or both sides of the body. CP exists in several forms (*spasticity, athetosis, ataxia,* and *mixed forms*) and at different levels of severity from mild to severe. Type and severity of the condition are related to the particular area or areas of the brain that have been damaged and the extent of that damage. Students with CP often have additional disabilities, with at least 15 per cent of cases having impaired hearing or vision defects. Epilepsy is present in up to 30 per cent of cases of CP, and a significant number of these children are on regular medication to control seizures. This medication can often have the side effect of reducing the individual's level of alertness and span of attention, thus adding to potential problems in learning. Epilepsy is discussed in more detail later.

CP is not curable, but its negative impact on the individual's physical coordination, mobility, learning capacity, and communication skills can be reduced through appropriate intensive therapy, training, and education. It is anticipated that future brain imaging studies (fMRI) may help to throw more light on the ways in which damage to specific areas of the brain affect the functioning in individuals with CP (Weierink et al., 2013).

It is reported that approximately 60 per cent of individuals with moderate to severe CP also have some degree of intellectual impairment and additional complications (Turnbull et al., 2019). It must be noted, however, that a few persons with quite severe CP are highly intelligent, and there is a danger that the potential of these non-verbal CP students is not recognised because of their inability to communicate. One of the main priorities for these individuals is to be provided with an alternative method of communication (Heller & Bigge, 2010).

Some children with severe CP may not develop intelligible speech, although their receptive language (understanding) may be in the normal range. They may also be unable to control jaw and face muscles, resulting in facial contortions and drooling. These physical problems are totally beyond that individual's control but do represent potential barriers for easy social integration and acceptance.

There have been many suggested treatments and therapies for CP, but few of these have been subjected to really rigorous evaluation. Even *conductive education,* a once popular and comprehensive approach originating from Hungary (Pawelski, 2007) actually produces very mixed results. It appears that only the children who have normal intelligence and milder forms of CP are likely to benefit greatly. The results produced with severely disabled persons are not impressive.

Details of conductive education can be found online at: www.conductive-ed.org.uk/index.htm *or at*: www.smallsteps.org.uk/about-small-steps/conductive-education/

Instructional needs of students with cerebral palsy

Academic instruction for children with CP will depend upon their cognitive ability, their range of functional movements, and their attention span. Students with mild cerebral palsy and normal intelligence may simply be slower at completing assignments and only need more time and encouragement. Allowance may need to be made for poorly coordinated handwriting or slow keyboarding. For some students, devices such as adapted pencil grips, modified keyboards and page-turners may be required, and papers may need to be taped firmly to the desktop while working. A few students may use computers with modifications such as touch panels or voice activation rather than a keyboard or mouse.

In addition to problems with movement and speech, many children with severe CP tend to:

- tire easily and have difficulty attending to tasks for more than brief periods of time;
- take a very long time to perform physical actions (e.g., pointing at or picking up an object; eating meals);
- require the teacher or an aide to lift and move them, and place them in a particular position for work, using padded wedges that enable them to apply their limited range of movements to best advantage;
- need to be placed and supported in a 'standing frame' with desk-top attached;
- need to be fed and toileted by an aide.

Epilepsy

Epilepsy is a fairly frequent additional problem that may accompany physical disabilities that stem from neurological damage or dysfunction (McGeehan, 2018). Epilepsy is due to abnormal electrical discharges within specific areas of the brain. Severity can vary from very mild loss of awareness (mental absences lasting a few seconds) through to severe seizures in which the individual falls to the ground, convulses and may lose consciousness (*tonic-clonic seizures*). Some instances of epilepsy that are evident in preschool or primary school years may disappear spontaneously by adolescence or adulthood; but for some individuals the condition remains and requires a lifetime regimen of medication and management. Medication with anti-epileptic drugs is usually successful in controlling seizures in at least 80 per cent of cases.

Teachers need to know details of the child's condition, and how to manage him or her in the event of seizures. All seizure events should be reported to parents. Information on how to treat a student who has a seizure can be located at: www.epilepsy.org.uk/info/firstaid/what-to-do

Spina bifida

Spina bifida (SB) is a congenital disorder, possibly of genetic origin, and occurs when certain bones in the spine fail to seal over correctly before birth to protect the spinal cord. SB presents with different degrees of severity and affects approximately 1 in every 1000 live births. The milder forms of SB have no significant influence on learning and mobility, and it is estimated that approximately 80 per cent of individuals with spina bifida have intelligence within the normal range. There is no reason why the majority of students with mild SB cannot be placed in inclusive classrooms and follow the common curriculum.

Greater difficulties in learning occur with increasing severity of the disability, and learning problems are common in the remaining 20 per cent, with major deficits in sustained attention, visual perception, memory and number skills (Dennis, 2012). A study by Gaintza et al. (2018) found that successful inclusion of children with moderate to severe SB depended upon schools, teachers and families working very closely with medical and psychological professionals to provide all necessary support.

The most serious form of spina bifida, with the greatest impact on the individual's life and development, is *myelomeningocele*. In this condition, a small part of the spinal cord protrudes from a gap in the spine. The cord is usually damaged and bodily functions below this point may be seriously disrupted, including use of lower limbs and control of bladder and bowel. The individual may need to use a wheelchair or leg braces, and must observe a careful diet and a strict toileting routine. The management of incontinence presents perhaps the greatest personal and social problem for students most severely affected by SB.

Approximately 60 to 70 per cent of children with myelomeningocele may also have *hydrocephalus*. In this condition, normal circulation and drainage of cerebrospinal fluid within the skull is impaired, resulting in increased intracranial pressure. Treatment for hydrocephalus involves surgical implanting of a permanent catheter into a ventricle in the brain to drain the excess fluid continually to the abdominal cavity. A valve is implanted below the skin behind the child's ear to prevent any back flow of fluid. Teachers need to be aware that shunts and valves can become blocked, or the site can become infected. If the child with treated hydrocephalus complains of headache or earache, or if he or she appears feverish and irritable, medical advice should be obtained immediately.

Children with spina bifida and hydrocephalus tend to be hospitalised at regular intervals during their school lives for such events as replacing shunts and valves, urinary tract infections or controlling respiratory problems. This frequent hospitalisation can significantly interrupt a child's schooling, and can seriously fragment the coverage of curriculum content. Subjects that depend most upon carefully building sequential knowledge and skills (such as mathematics) are most affected by lost instructional time. Students in this situation require intensive 'catch up' assistance with their schoolwork in order not to fall far behind others.

Traumatic brain injury

The term *traumatic brain injury* (TBI) is used to describe any acquired damage to the brain resulting from events such as vehicle accidents, unsuccessful suicide attempts, serious falls, blows to the head, sports injury, the 'shaken infant syndrome', and recovery after near-death drowning. The actual incidence of TBI in the population is uncertain, but many school-age students with this acquired disability are regularly recorded among those receiving special education either short term or long term (Blankenship & Canto, 2018). An increasing number of school-age individuals acquire brain injury from falls, car accidents, and partial drowning.

The detrimental effects of TBI can include:

- memory problems;
- attention difficulties;
- slow information processing;
- inability to solve everyday problems and plan ahead;
- speech and language functions disrupted temporarily or permanently;

- impairment of motor coordination;
- onset of epilepsy;
- vision problems;
- severe headaches;
- unpredictable and irrational mood swings or behaviour (aggressive, restless, apathetic, depressed).

Students with TBI often improve dramatically in the first year following injury, but after that progress is usually much slower. Turnbull et al. (2019) indicate that for some individuals with TBI there is a slight to moderate decline in functional intelligence, with skills such as reading comprehension and mathematical problem solving presenting as areas of particular difficulty. Some individuals begin to have difficulty remembering a word or name (*anomia*) and this can slow down their communications, and also cause great frustration. Many children with TBI express great irritation in knowing an answer to a question in class but being unable to retrieve the necessary words at the right time.

Given the complexity of the problems that can occur with TBI, it is common to find that individuals affected usually require ongoing personal counselling as well as an adapted learning programme. The main challenges for a teacher are:

- finding ways of maximising the individual's engagement and attention in a learning task by reducing distractions, providing prompts and cues, limiting the amount of information presented, and giving frequent positive feedback;
- keeping instructions clear and simple, and not overloading the student with information or tasks;
- breaking down lesson content into manageable units of work with goals that are achievable within the individual's attention span;
- helping to compensate for memory loss by presenting visual cues and graphic organisers;
- rehearsing information more than would be necessary with other learners;
- teaching self-help strategies such as keeping reminder notes in your pocket, and regularly checking the daily schedule on a hand-held electronic planner;
- helping the individual plan ahead by setting personal goals and then working towards them;
- accepting the student's poor ability to concentrate and to complete the work that is set.

Additional information on TBI can be located at: www.headway.org.uk/about-brain-injury/individuals/types-of-brain-injury/traumatic-brain-injury/

Foetal Alcohol Spectrum Disorder (FASD)

Over the past decades there has been a marked increase in the number of children diagnosed with *foetal alcohol spectrum disorder* (Gill & Thompson-Hodgetts, 2018). It is likely that children with this syndrome had been present in classrooms long before the disorder was identified, and the children were simply regarded as slow learners.

FASD is caused by a mother having consumed significant amounts of alcohol during pregnancy, causing impairment to the child's developing brain. FASDs range in severity from mild to moderate, and manifest themselves in attention deficits, lowered intelligence, poor attainment in school, hyperactivity, behaviour problems, and poor self-regulation. It is not possible to reverse the damage done to the brain, but carefully planned and implemented intervention—particularly focused on improving basic literacy skills, strengthening self-management and behaviour control—can help these children develop their abilities as far as possible. An appropriate approach will employ the same basic principles as described in Chapter 1 for students with learning problems, but could include some strategies listed above for students with TBI.

One programme that has been recommended for children with FASD is the *Alert Program* ® (Mac Cobb et al., 2014). This programme is designed to teach children better self-regulation—so they can listen, learn and participate. For details see: www.families onlinemagazine.com/alert-program/

Childhood obesity

While childhood obesity is not classified as a physical disability, its effects can be disabling. Children who are significantly overweight risk a number of health problems as they get older, and their social life and self-esteem are also negatively affected. For example, obese children are more likely than others to suffer from asthma (Thompson, 2013). Certain students with disabilities are particularly prone to weight problems, including those with a disability that restricts their mobility and those with an intellectual disability or autism who spend a great deal of passive and sheltered time at home (McConkey et al., 2019).

The growing number of overweight children is an issue of concern in schools (and in society generally) (McMullan & Keeney, 2014; Powell, 2018). A study by Rouse et al. (2019) found that children's obesity rates increase from kindergarten through to Grade 8, and they recommended that children's Body Mass Index (BMI) should be routinely recorded in schools to help identify those at risk. The increase in obesity is mainly associated with a contemporary lifestyle of sedentary occupations, such as sitting at a computer for hours at a time, easy access to fattening foods, and advertising that actively promotes such activities and foods.

Children seem now to engage less in 'running about' and playing in vigorous games at recess time in the school yard, so it is essential that schools do all they can to increase children's awareness of the benefits of exercise, a good diet and a healthy lifestyle. Where possible, a school curriculum or extra-curricular activities should increase the amount of time devoted to physical education and fitness (Larson et al., 2013). Children with physical and intellectual disabilities should be included fully in all such activities, as indicated in Chapter 2.

Asthma and allergies

Asthma has become a very common condition affecting school-age children and it can result in frequent periods of absence from school (Everhart et al., 2018). It is necessary to provide remedial teaching and 'catch up' homework for these children when they return to school. Asthma is due to inflammation of the bronchial airways, resulting in severe breathing problems. Parents must always notify the teacher if their child has asthma, and discuss the response that needs to be made if the child has an asthma attack while at school.

Allergies are causing problems for an ever-increasing number of students, and teachers need to be alert to any child who may have an extreme reaction to particular food, pollutants, chemicals, medicines, insect bites, or other agents (Sauer et al., 2018). The most extreme reaction is referred to as *anaphylactic shock*, which can be life threatening. Schools need to have a list of all students with allergies, together with emergency telephone contact numbers, and a response plan that is known to all teachers.

General points for mainstream teachers

It is not surprising that many teachers lack experience in working with physically disabled students. The following list provides some of the basic information they need to know.

- It may be necessary to rearrange the classroom desks and chairs to give easier access and a wider corridor for movement for students in wheelchairs or walking with sticks.
- Some students with physical disabilities will need to use modified equipment and assistive devices, so it is the teacher's responsibility to ensure that the student does use these items.
- Secondary school students with physical disabilities may have great difficulty taking notes. The teacher could establish a peer support network to assist with this, and allow the student to photocopy notes of other students or use a scribe.
- Assignments could be submitted as an audiotape rather than an essay.
- Some students with physical disabilities have a high absence rate due to therapy or treatment appointments during school hours, or due to frequent health problems. The teacher will need to provide short-term catch-up work (e.g., textbook reading or a video to watch) for the student to do at home.
- Some students with epilepsy are likely to be on medication that tends to lower their level of responsiveness in class. If seizures appear to increase in severity or frequency, check that the student is actually taking the medication. Report all cases of seizure to parents.
- While applying all commonsense safety procedures, teachers should try not to overprotect students with physical disabilities. Whenever possible, these students should be encouraged to take part in the same activities enjoyed by other students. Teachers of PE and sport need to get practical advice on ways in which physical activities can be adapted to include students with physical disabilities.

The following chapter extends the coverage of disabilities by presenting information on students with sensory impairments (vision and hearing).

Online resources

- The website of the National Institute of Neurological Disorders and Stroke (NINDS) provides information on a number of physical disabilities.
- Cerebral palsy at: www.ninds.nih.gov/Disorders/Patient-Caregiver-Education/Hope-Through-Research/Cerebral-Palsy-Hope-Through-Research.
- Traumatic brain injury at: www.ninds.nih.gov/Disorders/All-Disorders/Traumatic-Brain-Injury-Information-Page.

- Epilepsy at: www.ninds.nih.gov/Disorders/All-Disorders/Epilepsy-Information-Page.
- Spina bifida at: www.ninds.nih.gov/Disorders/Patient-Caregiver-Education/Fact-Sheets/Spina-Bifida-Fact-Sheet.
- Tips for teaching students with physical disabilities can be located at: www.thoughtco.com/physically-handicapped-students-3111135.
- More about teaching students with physical disabilities: www.brighthubeducation.com/special-ed-physical-disabilities/51778-teaching-strategies-for-students-with-physical-disabilities/.
- Tips for supporting students with physical disabilities in further education at: www.accessible campus.ca/tools-resources/educators-tool-kit/teaching-tips/teaching-students-with-physical-disabilities/.

Print resources

Asola, E., & Hodge, S.R. (2019). Special education for young learners with physical disabilities. In F.E. Obiakor & J.P. Bakken (Eds). *Advances in Special Education*, v. 34. Ch.11. Bingley, West Yorkshire: Emerald Group Publishing.

Bellon, M. (Ed.) (2014). *Sensory, physical and multiple disorders.* French's Forest, NSW: Pearson Australia.

Brock, M.E. (2016). *A teacher's guide to adapted physical education.* Baltimore, MD: Brookes.

Hull City Council [UK]. (2016a). *Supporting children with cerebral palsy* (2nd ed.). London: Taylor & Francis.

Hull City Council [UK]. (2016b). *Supporting children with dyspraxia and motor-coordination difficulties.* London: David Fulton/NASEN.

Pike, M. (Ed.) (2013). *Disorders of the spinal cord in children.* London: MacKeith Press.

Wicks, B., & Walker, S. (2018). *Educating children and young people with acquired brain injury.* Abingdon, Oxon: Routledge.

Chapter 5

Students with sensory impairments

Students with sensory impairments comprise a varied group within the population of those with special needs, covering a broad range of cognitive ability, aptitude, and behaviour. These students often require adaptations to be made to teaching approaches, resource materials, and methods of communication in order to learn most effectively.

The majority of students with sensory impairments are now included in regular classes and taught by mainstream teachers; but many teachers lack sufficient knowledge of effective strategies for supporting them (Fast & Wild, 2018). Most mainstream teachers need professional guidance on how best to accommodate a student with impaired vision or hearing loss within the curriculum, and how to assess their learning (Rosenblum et al., 2018).

Vision impairment

In some countries the term *vision impairment* is replacing the older term *visual impairment*. When a child is described as vision impaired, it does not necessarily mean that he or she is blind, it means that the child has a serious defect of vision that cannot be corrected by wearing spectacles. In the population of children with impaired vision, there are those who are totally blind, those who are 'legally' blind, and those with low vision (partial sight). Taken together, these categories represent between 2 per cent and 3 per cent of individuals below the age of 18 (Ruderman, 2016), but the actual prevalence in any particular country or region depends greatly on factors such as quality of health care and availability of early assessment and intervention.

While impaired vision is a low incidence disability, it is important to note that it also occurs as a secondary condition in many cases of severe and multiple disabilities. For example, many students with cerebral palsy also have serious problems with vision, as do some individuals with traumatic brain injury. There is also a very small population of students who are both deaf and blind, and who therefore require extremely skilled teaching.

Impaired vision has many causes, including structural defects or damage to the retina, lens, or optic nerve, inability of the retina to transmit images to the brain, or inefficiency in the way the brain processes visual information. Prematurity and very low birth weight are often associated with vision problems in childhood, with *retinopathy of prematurity* (ROP) being reported as one of the most common causes of impaired vision in newborn children. Some vision problems are inherited, including those associated with *albinism*, congenital cataracts, and degeneration of the retina; others may be due to disease or to medical conditions such as diabetes.

Special educational needs of children with impaired vision

Early years

Blind children and those with very low vision may often be delayed in acquiring basic motor skills such as crawling, walking, and feeding, because vision is important for observing and imitating the actions of others. Young children with impaired vision benefit from physical activities that help them develop body awareness, movement and coordination. From an early age these children need to be encouraged, within the realms of safety, to explore and interact with their immediate environment.

Absence of sight can also lead to delays in cognitive development and concept formation. Early sensory stimulation is vital for young blind children, and they should be given different objects to explore through touch in order to build relevant concepts such as shape, texture, weight, moving parts. These experiences need to be accompanied by constant verbal input from the parent or caregiver —for example, supplying concept words like 'soft', 'hard edges' 'bigger than', 'next to', 'inside', 'heavier than.' Children with impaired vision are obviously much less able to acquire knowledge and skills through observation, so the environment and events happening within it must be described by others to increase the child's awareness of things he or she cannot see. Auditory skills need to be strengthened through activities that involve careful and focused listening and responding.

Social and emotional development

Impaired vision can affect an individual's confidence to move about and interact with the wider environment, and this in turn can reduce willingness to initiate social contacts. This is partly due to lack of opportunity to mix and interact with other children from an early age—and thus observe and acquire social behaviours. It is also due to the fact that blind children can't see important non-verbal aspects of social interaction and communication such as nodding in agreement, looking surprised, smiling, and respecting personal space when engaging in conversation (Martins et al., 2019; MacConville & Rhys-Davies, 2007). Lack of social interaction with peers can negatively affect a blind student's self-esteem and emotional well-being. Teachers can be proactive in helping blind and partially sighted students become more involved in the social groups within the classroom.

For vision impaired students who are able to learn in the mainstream, inclusion can be extremely beneficial for social development. However, for some students, socialisation in the classroom and in the playground can be problematic. Social development is further restricted if members of the peer group lack confidence to interact with a fellow-student who is blind or partially sighted. It is sometimes helpful to foster better understanding in the peer group by discussing openly with the class the problems that a person with impaired vision may have in dealing with schoolwork and with the physical environment. Obviously, if such discussion is attempted, it must be done with due sensitivity and should only be done with the student's agreement.

Accessing curriculum and environment

There are several areas in which blind children and those with seriously impaired vision need to be taught additional skills. These areas include mobility, orientation, the use of

Braille, and assistive technology. Mastery of mobility and orientation are two of the main goals in helping a blind student move towards increased independence. Studies have indicated that individuals who successfully achieve independent orientation and mobility manifest higher levels of well-being and increased social interaction (Idawati et al., 2020; Malik et al., 2018).

Mobility

Increased mobility adds significantly to the quality of life for persons with impaired vision (Idawati et al., 2020). Blind students and those with very low vision need to be taught mobility skills to enable them to move safely and purposefully in their environment, including such abilities as crossing the road, catching buses or trains, and locating shops. In special schools for blind students, a mobility-training specialist usually carries out the detailed planning and implementation of the programme; but classroom teachers and parents can certainly assist with development of mobility skills, including:

- *self-protection techniques*—for example, holding the hand and forearm loosely in front of the face for protection, while trailing the other hand along the wall or rail in unfamiliar environments; checking for doorways, steps, stairs, and obstacles; finding one's position in a room by using auditory information (e.g. air-conditioner, pot boiling on a stove, an open doorway with traffic noise).
- *long-cane skills*—moving about the environment with the aid of a long cane swept lightly across the ground ahead to locate hazards and to check surface textures;
- *using electronic travel aids*—for example, 'sonic spectacles' with a built-in device that emits a sound warning to indicate proximity to objects;
- *using public transport*—teaching the individual how to use and negotiate buses and trains.

Orientation

Orientation is the term used to explain the awareness a person with impaired vision has of his or her own exact position in relation to objects in a particular environment, such as furniture, barriers, open doors, or steps—'knowing where I am, and where things are'. For the safety and convenience of students with vision impairment, the physical class-room environment should remain reasonably constant and predictable. If furniture has to be moved or some new static object is introduced into the room (e.g., a fish tank on a stand, a large television) the blind student needs to be informed of that fact and given the opportunity to locate it in relation to other objects. In classrooms it is necessary to make sure that equipment such as boxes, books, gym apparatus are not left on the floor, and doors are not left half open with a hard edge projecting into the room.

Braille

Braille, the tactile method of communication that replaces print, is of tremendous value as a medium for those students who are blind or whose remaining vision does not enable them to perceive enlarged print. In recent years there has been debate around whether communication technology such as screen-to-speech and speech-to-text applications for computers has made Braille obsolete. Persons in the blind community have expressed varied opinions, but most believe that Braille is still very important because it provides an independent means of accessing, recording, storing, and revisiting information at any time. It is deemed more effective for deep study than relying on audio recordings.

Braille is a complex code, so its use with students who are below average in intelligence can present difficulties. Obviously if an individual's cognitive level is such that he or she would experience difficulty learning to read and write with conventional print, Braille is not going to be an easier code to master. However, if a child's intelligence is adequate, the younger he or she begins to develop some Braille skills the better, as this will prepare the child to benefit from later schooling and university study. There is some evidence to suggest that employing an enlarged size of Braille can result in faster learning in the youngest children (Barlow-Brown et al., 2019).

A simplified system similar in principle to Braille is called Moon. It is reported to be easier to learn, particularly for children who have additional disabilities. Moon uses only 26 raised shapes, based on lines and curves, to represent the standard alphabet, plus ten other symbols.

Assistive technology

It is evident that many mainstream teachers are still unaware of the importance of assistive technology in advancing disabled students' abilities, and more attention should be given to this issue in pre-service teacher training (Wong & Law, 2016). In the same way that students with physical disabilities can be helped to access the curriculum and participate more effectively in daily life through the use of assistive technology, children who are blind or with low vision can also be greatly assisted (Satsangi et al., 2019b). Many devices have been designed to enable partially sighted students to cope with the medium of print. *Low vision aids* are magnification devices or instruments that help the individual with some residual sight to work with maximum visual efficiency. The devices include a variety of hand-held or desktop magnifiers, and closed-circuit television or microfiche readers (both can be used to enlarge an image).

Despite the value of this technology, many students try to avoid using these devices in mainstream class because they feel that it draws unwanted attention to their disability. This emotional sensitivity to assistive technology as a marker of disability can begin in the primary school years, but occurs most frequently among vision impaired students in secondary schools. Teachers in mainstream classes may need actively to encourage a student to overcome this avoidance behaviour, because the assistive device is of very great benefit to them.

Other forms of technology

The use of 'talking books' technology has been found to benefit blind students and has application in most areas of the curriculum (Argyropoulos et al., 2019). Calculators and clocks with audio output, dictionaries with speech output, compressed speech recordings, and thermoform duplicators used to reproduce Braille pages or embossed diagrams and maps are all of great value. Despite the potential value of using ICT and other technology with vision impaired learners, evidence to date suggests that schools in some countries are not yet employing the medium to its maximum potential (Ramos & de Andrade, 2016).

In subjects such as science, teachers have devised methods for helping blind students understand physical changes that can occur that sighted students can observe by eye—for example what happens when you switch on an electric current and produce light, or filling a flask to a certain level—by supplementing the visual event with an accompanying sound (a buzzer or bell) or tactile effect (Kizilaslan, 2019; Okcu & Sozbilir, 2019).

It is increasingly evident that digital technology in the form of hand-held devices, although not specifically designed as assistive in a narrow sense, are being welcomed and used by individuals who are vision impaired. McLaughlin and Kamei-Hannan (2018) have suggested that students with low vision benefit from the use of electronic tablets that allow them to adjust font size, style, color, and contrast. Similarly, Beal and Rosenblum (2018) found that using an iPad app in the context of learning mathematics resulted in students answering more mathematics problems correctly and they were more motivated than during their traditional approach. One important new area of technology with great potential for learners who are blind is 3D printing (Jo et al., 2016; Karbowski, 2020). This can be used for making tactile and 3D instructional materials (e.g., relief maps, models, figures and embossed diagrams) to accompany lessons in science, history, geography, and the arts.

Teaching students with impaired vision

Teachers in the mainstream with no prior experience of vision impairment in children may wrongly tend to hold fairly low expectations of what these children can accomplish. Having a problem with vision should not exclude any children from access to normal classroom experiences, although significant modifications to materials and methods often need to be made. The following general advice may help mainstream teachers provide vision impaired students in their classes with the best opportunities to learn.

- Use very clear verbal descriptions and explanations, because words must compensate for what the student cannot see.
- Read written instructions aloud to students with impaired vision to reduce the amount of time required to begin a task, and to ensure that the work is understood.
- Almost all students with impaired vision in mainstream classes will have *low vision* (partial sight) rather than total or legal blindness, and it is essential to encourage them to use their residual vision.
- Seat the student in the most advantageous position to be able to see the whiteboard, computer or large screen.
- Ensure that your material written on the whiteboard, PowerPoint, or computer screen is neat and clear, using larger script than usual. Always keep the whiteboard surface clean to ensure clarity of text.
- Enlarge the font used in all notes, on-screen material, and handouts to one of the following point sizes: 24 36
- Use a photocopier when necessary to make enlarged versions of notes, diagrams and other handouts.
- Avoid overloading worksheets with too much information.
- Allow partially sighted students to use a thicker black-tip pen that will produce clear, bold writing.
- When necessary, prepare exercise paper with darker ruled lines.
- Allow much more time for students with impaired vision to complete their work.

- Use concrete materials for early number work (counters, abacus, models) to facilitate manipulation and touch.
- Train other students and the classroom aide to support the student with impaired vision when necessary—for example, by taking notes during the lesson, repeating teacher's explanations and clarifying points.
- Call on blind students frequently by name during lessons to engage them fully in the group-learning processes. Verbally acknowledge and value their contributions.
- Call upon other students clearly by name so that the blind student knows who is responding.
- Make sure that any specialised equipment is always at hand and in good order. If the student with impaired vision uses magnification or illumination aids or other devices, make sure that you know when and how the equipment needs to be used, and ensure that the student does not avoid using it.
- Some forms of vision impairment respond well to brighter illumination, but in some other conditions bright light is undesirable. Obtain advice on illumination from specialist support service personnel who are aware of the student's vision characteristics.
- If the student has extremely limited vision, make sure that any change to the physical arrangement of the room is explained and experienced by the student to avoid accidents. The student needs to develop fresh orientation each time an environment is changed.
- Try to help the student establish a network of friends within the class because social interaction is often not easily achieved without assistance.

Transition to work or further study

Helping vision impaired students prepare for post-secondary school transition to work or further study requires careers teachers and counsellors to familiarise themselves with possible barriers that may exist. The following strategies are regarded as important when preparing vision impaired students for transition.

- Discuss with the student his or her strengths, interests, and aspirations, and provide appropriate career counselling and informed advice.
- Encourage and facilitate a student's increasing independence, self-confidence, resilience, and assertiveness.
- Assist the student directly by arranging suitable job placements and trial internships.
- Give adequate time to teaching 'interview skills', so that they can present themselves well during interviews for employment or university.
- For students contemplating tertiary study, help them explore the support services that will be available for them in that setting.
- Ensure that the student leaves school or college with an up-to-date knowledge of all forms of assistive technology that may continue to help him or her function.

Hearing impairment

Hearing impairment is a general term used to describe all degrees and types of hearing loss and deafness. Many students with impaired hearing have no other disability, but hearing impairment can often be present as a secondary problem in children with intellectual disability, cerebral palsy, or language disorders. Having impaired hearing does not mean that an individual cannot detect any sounds. He or she may simply hear some frequencies of sound much more clearly than others. Individuals are usually referred to as *deaf* if they are unable to detect speech sounds and if their own oral language development is disordered. In some countries, those who can hear some sounds and can make reasonable use of their residual hearing are often termed *partially hearing*. In the USA, the most widely used term is *deaf* or *hard of hearing* (DHH).

Hearing impairment is often accompanied by speech difficulties. Many factors—time of onset, severity, type of hearing loss and exposure to speech models—interact to produce large variations in deaf children's spoken language. The speech of many children with impaired hearing often has an unusual quality and can be difficult to understand. Any improvement in language will allow each child to make better use of his or her intellectual potential, understand much more of the curriculum, and develop socially and emotionally.

In some situations, speech and auditory training sessions are advocated for hearing-impaired students. Speech therapists may use forms of phonological and articulation coaching that involve modelling, imitation, reinforcement and shaping. In recent years, however, speech therapists and teachers have placed much more importance on trying to stimulate language development through the use of naturally occurring activities in the classroom (*milieu approach*). Such teaching is thought to result in the best transfer and generalisation of vocabulary and language patterns to the child's everyday life. Clinical one-to-one training rarely transfers as effectively to everyday natural settings.

Many hearing-impaired children are now included in mainstream classes where accommodation and adjustments to teaching need to be made (Alasim, 2018; Allman et al., 2019). It is argued that in mainstream classrooms they have an opportunity to mix with other students who provide good models of natural spoken language. At the same time, students with normal hearing can develop improved understanding and empathy for individuals who have difficulty hearing.

Types and degrees of hearing loss

Most hearing loss can be classified as either *conductive* or *sensori-neural*. The key features of each type of are summarised below.

Conductive hearing loss

Conductive hearing loss occurs when sounds do not reach the middle ear or inner ear (cochlear) because of some physical malformation, blockage or damage. Common causes are excessive build-up of wax in the ear, abnormality of the ear canal, a ruptured eardrum, dislocation or damage to the tiny bones of the middle ear, or infection in the middle ear (*otitis media*). Hearing loss due to middle-ear infection is usually temporary and will improve when the infection is treated. If infections are allowed to continue untreated, damage may be done to the middle ear, resulting in permanent hearing loss. The use of a hearing aid may significantly help an individual with conductive hearing loss.

Sensori-neural loss

Sensori-neural hearing loss is related to the inner ear and the auditory nerve. The most serious hearing losses are often of this type. As well as being unable to hear many sounds, even those that are heard may be distorted. The problem of distortion means that the wearing of a hearing aid may not always help, because amplifying a distorted sound does not make it any clearer. Some individuals with sensori-neural loss are particularly sensitive to loud noises, perceiving them to be painfully loud.

Level of hearing loss

Hearing is measured in units called decibels (dB). Zero dB is the point from which people with normal hearing can begin to detect the faintest sounds. Normal conversation is usually carried out at an overall sound level of between 40 and 50dB. Loss of hearing is expressed in terms of the amplification required before the individual can hear each sound. The greater the degree of impairment, the less likely it is that the child will develop normal speech and language, and the more likely it is that they will need special education services. Individuals with a hearing loss above 95dB are usually categorised as 'deaf' or 'profoundly deaf', while losses between 15–40dB are classified as slight to mild. The difficulties experienced by children with slight to moderate hearing loss often remain undetected for several years, placing the child at risk of failure in school. This is particularly the case if the hearing problem is intermittent and related, for example, to head colds or middle ear infections.

Impact of moderate to severe hearing loss

Social and emotional development

According to Luckner and Movahedazarhouligh (2019), children who have a hearing impairment are at risk of lagging behind their peers in age-appropriate social and emotional development. Their communication difficulty makes it awkward for them to mix effectively with their peers and be accepted and understood. Their lack of easy comprehension in a verbal environment can lead to frustration and result in inappropriate behaviour. It is also acknowledged that their problems with social-emotional development can be linked with poor academic performance (Harris, 2014). Much learning in school and in the world outside depends on having a system with which to communicate with and comprehend others; helping children improve their understanding and use of language is therefore a priority in the early years.

Helping a deaf child acquire intelligible speech can be a long and difficult process, so early intervention with active parental involvement is essential (McLean et al., 2019; Scott et al., 2019). Even before a child reaches primary school age, preschool teachers need to work closely in collaboration with outside experts such as speech therapists in order to implement the most effective support for language development (Donne et al., 2019; Dorn, 2019). During the school years, effective inclusion of students with impaired hearing relies heavily on the continuing availability of expert advice from visiting teachers and regional hearing-support services.

Basic academic skills

It is frequently reported that the academic attainment level of children with impaired hearing in areas such as reading, spelling, and number skills lags well behind that of their hearing peers. It is typical of these students that as they progress through the primary school years, they fall three to four years behind in reading ability. This lag then has a detrimental impact on their performance in all subjects across the curriculum.

With hearing-impaired children in early primary school, careful attention must be given to the explicit teaching of reading and spelling skills (Scott et al., 2019). While the beginning stages of reading instruction can focus on building a basic sight vocabulary by visual methods (recognising words by sight), later teaching must embody explicit instruction in decoding skills. Although it may seem counterintuitive, phonics-based instruction is viable for these students if it is supplemented by visual materials and, in some cases, by cued speech (ICLI, 2014). Without decoding skill, students' ability to read and spell unfamiliar words will remain seriously deficient. It is also essential when providing reading instruction for hearing-impaired children that due attention be given to developing effective comprehension strategies.

Instruction in spelling needs to be direct and systematic rather than incidental. For deaf children it is likely that more than the usual amount of attention will need to be given to developing visual memory, to enable them to store word images and check words 'by eye' as well as by ear. The 'look–say–cover–write–check' strategy is particularly helpful and needs to be taught thoroughly (see Chapter 12).

The written expression of deaf children is also often problematic, with syntax and vocabulary being major weaknesses (Strassman & Schirmer, 2013; Yan & Li, 2019). Difficulties include inaccurate sentence structure, incorrect verb tenses, difficulties representing plurals correctly, and inconsistencies in using correct pronouns. The written work of older deaf students has many of the characteristics of the writing of younger children.

Modes of communication

Oral–aural approach (oralism)

The belief underpinning an oral–aural approach is that in a hearing world you need to be able to communicate through oral–verbal methods in order to be accepted socially and to succeed. Students relying on an oral–aural approach often require and benefit from speech training from a speech therapist. The approach stresses the use of residual hearing, supplemented by lip reading. Teachers should note, however, that the ability of many hearing-impaired students to lip read is often greatly overestimated—it is actually very difficult.

While listening and speaking remain the preferred methods of communication for students with mild and moderate degrees of impairment, for those who are severely deaf, alternative manual methods may be needed. Manual methods include natural gesture, sign language, cued speech, and fingerspelling.

Sign language

There are different forms of sign language, all sharing obvious characteristics in common but also having some unique features (e.g., British Sign Language, Signed English, Auslan, American Sign Language). Deaf children from deaf families will almost certainly have been exposed to, and become fairly competent in, manual communication even before entering formal education. Experts suggest that sign language should be respected as a language system in its own right, with its own vocabulary and syntax that contribute to cognitive development. It should be valued and encouraged as an effective mode of communication (Beal-Alvarez & Huston, 2014).

Fingerspelling

Fingerspelling is usually used as a supplement to sign language, to spell out terms for which there is no clear hand sign. Fingerspelling is also incorporated into certain other signals to help convey exact meaning. Illustrations of a typical fingerspelling alphabet can be found at: www.british-sign.co.uk/fingerspelling-alphabet-charts/

Cued speech

A manual system known as *cued speech* was developed to help resolve the many visual ambiguities inherent in 'reading the lips.' Cued speech uses eight hand signs in four positions of the hand alongside the mouth of the speaker to differentiate between similar sounds or words. More information and illustrations can be located at: www.cuedspeech.co.uk/what-is-cued-speech/

Total communication approach

The relative popularity of signing versus oralism ebbs and flows from decade to decade. In response, *total communication* (TC) or *simultaneous communication* (SC) deliberately combines gesture, signing, fingerspelling, and oral–aural methods to help deaf children comprehend and express ideas and opinions. A combination of oral and manual training at an early age appears to foster optimum communicative ability (Turnbull et al., 2019).

Assistive technology

Hearing aids

Hearing aids are designed to amplify sound, and are of various types, including the typical 'behind the ear' or 'in the ear' aids and radio frequency (FM) aids. A hearing aid is prescribed by an audiologist to suit the individual's sound-loss profile. The aid is adjusted as far as possible to give amplification of the specific frequency of sounds needed by the child. No hearing aid fully compensates for hearing loss, even when carefully tailored to the user's characteristics. The great limitation of the conventional hearing aid is that it amplifies all sound, including background noise in the environment.

The advantage of the radio frequency (FM) aid is that it allows the teacher's voice to be received with minimum interference from environmental noise. The teacher wears a small microphone and the child's hearing aid receives the sounds in the same way that a radio receives a broadcast transmission. The child can be anywhere in the classroom, and does not need to be near to or facing the teacher, as with the conventional aid. Childress (2015) describes the 'induction loop system'—a perimeter of wire that surrounds a designated area like a classroom and sends auditory information to a T-coil setting on either a hearing aid or a cochlear implant.

Many hearing-impaired students do not like to be seen wearing a hearing aid, especially in mainstream secondary schools; and students with intellectual disability often neglect to wear the aid (Nipe et al., 2018). Some students take every opportunity to hide an aid away and not use it. Some report that they feel more socially at ease, and thus able to fit in more easily with their peers, if they do not wear the aid. Teachers thus have a responsibility to make sure a hearing aid is used during lessons and is maintained in good order.

Cochlear implants

A cochlear implant is a device used to produce the sensation of sound by electrically stimulating the auditory nerve. The device has four parts: processor, transmitting coil, receiver, and electrode array. The implant is able to bypass the functions of the hair cells in the inner ear that are often damaged or defective in cases of sensori-neural loss.

Many developed countries now carry out the surgery required to implant this form of assistive device at a very young age. Cochlear implants are normally recommended only for children who are profoundly deaf and cannot benefit at all from a hearing aid. While the child can begin to perceive the electrical stimulation soon after surgery, it normally takes at least a year for gains in the child's language skills to become evident. The child's effective adaptation to the cochlear implant needs much support and encouragement from parents.

Many children with implants still rely on supplementary sign language or gesture to understand fully what is said, but the general consensus is that having an implant is beneficial. For example, a study by Michael et al. (2019) indicated that parents of children with a cochlear implant report that their children exhibit lower levels of hyper-activity and inattention and higher levels of pro-social behaviour compared to children with a traditional hearing aid.

Other forms of technology

There is increasing evidence that integrating various forms of technology and software into teaching of students with impaired hearing can bring positive results. For information on various devices and apps that have relevance for assisting those with impaired hearing see: www.osspeac.org/wp-content/uploads/2017/08/childress.connectanddiscover.100817.pdf

Teaching students with impaired hearing

The following strategies for teaching hearing-impaired students may also be helpful for teaching students with other learning difficulties in the classroom.

- The student with impaired hearing should be seated where he or she can see you easily, can see the whiteboard, and can observe the other student.
- Do not seat the student with impaired hearing near to sources of noise (e.g., open window, air-conditioner, over-head fan, generator).
- Involve the hearing-impaired student in the lesson as much as possible.
- Make sure a deaf student can see the other students who are speaking or answering questions when group discussion is taking place.

- Repeat the answer that another student has given in class if you think the hearing-impaired student may not have heard it.
- Check frequently that the student is on task and has understood what he or she is required to do.
- Make greater use of visual methods of presenting information whenever possible (whiteboard, overhead projector, computer screen).
- Do not give instructions while there is noise in the classroom.
- Write any important instructions as short statements on the whiteboard whenever possible.
- Always attract students' full attention when you are about to ask a question or give out information.
- Repeat instructions clearly while facing the class.
- Use simple language and clear enunciation when explaining new concepts.
- Do not talk while facing the whiteboard—a deaf student needs to see your mouth and facial expression;
- Do not walk to the back of the room while talking and giving out important information.
- Teach all new vocabulary by writing new words on the whiteboard, ensuring that students with hearing impairment see the word and say the word.
- Revise new vocabulary regularly, and revise new language patterns (e.g. 'Twice the size of ...', 'Mix the ingredients ...', 'Invert and multiply ...').
- Provide senior students with printed notes when possible, to ensure that key content from the lesson is available for later study.
- Encourage other students to assist the hearing-impaired student complete any work that is set—*but* without doing the work for the student.
- Make sure that you check the student's hearing aid on a daily basis.
- Modify assessment and testing procedures when necessary (e.g., more time; assistance with reading a question).
- Seek advice regularly from the regional advisory service and from the visiting support teacher, and integrate such advice into your programme.

The following chapter provides an overview of the characteristics and needs of gifted and talented students. Some of these students may also have sensory impairments or a specific learning disability, and in their case much of the advice above also applies.

Online resources

- Information on blindness and vision impairment is available from the National Dissemination Center for Children with Disabilities, Fact Sheet 13 at: www.parentcenterhub.org/wp-content/uploads/repo_items/fs13.pdf.
- Suggestions for modifying the learning environment of vision impaired students can be found at: https://visual-impairment.weebly.com/at-school.html.
- Newcastle University has notes on teaching students with vision impairment at: www.ncl.ac.uk/students/wellbeing/assets/documents/SuggestedTeachingStrategiestousewithBlindandPartiallySightedStudents.pdf.
- The Statewide Vision Resource Centre at Nunawading in Victoria, Australia, as information on educational support for students with impaired vision at: http://svrc.vic.edu.au/wp-content/resources/PLvi_additional-booklet.pdf.

- Information on deaf and hearing-impaired students available from: www.myschoolpsychology. com/wp-content/uploads/2014/02/nichcy.org-Deafness_and_Hearing_Loss.pdf.
- The issue of including hearing impaired students in the mainstream is addressed in a paper at: www.brighthubeducation.com/special-ed-inclusion-strategies/42913-hearing-impairment-tea ching-strategies-for-an-inclusive-classroom/.
- There is no shortage of websites online that offer hints for teaching deaf and hearing-impaired students. Two useful sites are:
  - ➢ https://therapytravelers.com/strategies-teaching-hearing-impaired-deaf-students/.
  - ➢ www.ncl.ac.uk/students/wellbeing/assets/documents/SuggestedTeachingStrategiestouse withDdeafandhardofhearingStudentsv2.pdf.

Print resources

Dispenza, F., & Martines, F. (Eds). (2019). *Sensori-neural hearing loss.* Hauppauge, NY: Nova Science.

Eggermont, J.J. (2017). *Hearing loss: Causes, prevention and treatment.* Amsterdam: Elsevier.

Griggs, V. (2020). *Vis-ability: Raising awareness of vision impairment.* Kibworth, Leicester: Troubador.

Knoors, H., & Marschark, M. (Eds). (2018). *Evidence-based practices in deaf education.* New York: Oxford University Press.

Rosemeyer, M. (2018). *Orientation and mobility training program for the visually impaired.* [Classic reprint]. London: Forgotten Books.

Chapter 6

Gifted and talented students

The previous chapters have given attention to the characteristics and needs of students with various forms of learning difficulty or disability. This chapter explores the special needs of a group of students often assumed to have no problems in learning—namely those of high intellectual ability and those who possess a specific aptitude or talent. It is now accepted that these students do require additional consideration and support, both in terms of academic programming and their social and emotional needs (Hébert & Smith, 2018; Montacute, 2018). In an ideal world there would be a comprehensive approach to identifying gifted students in schools; but most countries have a laissez-faire approach. Unfortunately, this approach tends to result in many students with good potential but only average classroom performance, falling through the net.

Many intellectually gifted students—but by no means all—are high achievers in most academic subjects across the school curriculum. Many may display exceptional ability and creativity in a specific area such as art and design, the sciences, technology, music, drama, dance, sports, gymnastics, and interpersonal skills or leadership. These talented students also require special attention to enable them to develop their talent to the full.

The nature of giftedness, talent, and creativity

Over the years, experts have debated the nature of giftedness and whether it stems entirely from innate potential or arises as a result of hard work. The consensus is that giftedness, talents, and creativity do have a genetic component that represents a potential for advanced development, but such development only occurs if many factors combine in positive ways. These factors include helpful attributes in the individual such as motivation, perseverance, and resilience, and a context that provides good opportunities and resources for learning. The evidence suggests that an individual's giftedness and specific talents will only develop as a result of opportunity, sustained personal effort and long-term commitment (Hattie & Yates, 2014).

Some definitions of giftedness suggest that *creativity* is always a component in all forms of giftedness and talent. Renzulli (2005) for example, proposed that giftedness arises from a positive interaction among three human traits—above average ability, a high degree of task commitment (motivation, persistence and effort) and creativity. Others have suggested that creativity, while clearly essential in some fields, is not a necessary ingredient in *all* forms of outstanding ability or talent. Certain intellectually and academically gifted students are not necessarily highly creative in the artistic or performance sense, although they may be extremely creative in solving problems and in generating new ideas. What is generally agreed now is that creativity, when it is present, is a multifaceted and valued attribute that merits specific support and encouragement within the school curriculum (Hines et al., 2019).

Prevalence

It is generally agreed that when measured intelligence is used as the criterion for giftedness, between 3 per cent to 5 per cent of the school population can be regarded as intellectually gifted. In Britain these students are referred to now as '*highly able students*' or students with '*high learning potential*' (Smithers & Robinson, 2012). Within this population there are said to be varying degrees of giftedness, ranging from 'moderate' to 'profound'. Less than one child in every 100,000 would be classed as 'profoundly gifted', with an IQ above 180. Taken together, intellectually gifted and other talented students comprise some 10 to 15 per cent of the school population.

Separation or inclusion?

One of the enduring debates in education concerns the appropriate placement for gifted and talented students within the school system. The current policy of inclusive education has called into question their placement into specialist schools or full-time classes for the gifted. These options are often frowned upon now because they separate gifted students from their mixed-ability age-group. Instead, it is argued that gifted students should remain in the mainstream and receive a suitably differentiated programme to match their learning rate, abilities, and talents (Kaplan, 2019). A gifted student's programme would be one of several alternative programmes operating in a mixed-ability classroom under the system known as 'tiered instruction'. It is envisioned that an ideal programme for a gifted student would involve a mix of teacher-directed instruction accompanied by learning activities with personalised goals that embody opportunities for independent study, extension, and enrichment (Altintas & Özdemir, 2015; VanTassel-Baska, 2015). The potential benefits claimed for a differentiated approach are that students of high ability remain as members of a mixed-ability class and are able to interact socially and intellectually with other students of differing abilities and interests. The high-achieving students also act indirectly as role models for other students in the class in terms of study habits, work output, and motivation.

The potential disadvantage of attempting differentiation (and it is a serious disadvantage) is that many teachers find it almost impossible to sustain these different levels of activities operating at the same time within the classroom (Abu et al., 2017; Hertberg-Davis, 2009). As a result, studies have found that very little differentiation of instruction actually occurs for gifted students in many typical classrooms (e.g., McGrath, 2019). When these students finish assignments quickly, they tend to be given 'more of the same' or 'busywork', rather than extension and enrichment. Delisle (2006, p.52) has commented, 'This error of inclusion and its ragtag "solutions" of differentiation and cooperative learning have done enormous harm to the appropriate education of gifted children.'

It must be recognised that differentiation is indeed a very complex task, and most teachers have not been trained to work efficiently in this way (Van Geel et al., 2019). The larger the class size, the more difficult multi-tasking and multi-tier programming become. These points are made here not to suggest that adopting a differentiated approach is not worthy, but rather to indicate that almost all teachers require far more training and supervised practice in differentiated teaching strategies than they currently receive (Reid & Horváthová, 2016; Sayi, 2018).

In contrast to those who advocate for full inclusion with differentiation in the mainstream as the ideal model for students of high ability, educators and researchers working specifically in gifted education believe that there must be a *continuum of placement* and delivery options, ranging from staying in a regular class to being in a special group (Smithers & Robinson, 2012; Vogl & Preckel, 2014). It is argued, for example, that gifted students can be in a mainstream class for much of the time and not require differentiation; but at other times they benefit greatly from working in a special group or with a mentor. When special groups operate, it is argued that teachers can be more effective in designing a challenging curriculum and enabling a faster pace of learning. Grouping by ability at certain times also allows gifted and talented students to work closely and productively with others of similar or higher ability. It has been found in at least one study that students in gifted classes exhibit more interest in school and report better student–teacher relationships than similar students retained in regular classes (Vogl & Preckel, 2014).

Identifying gifted learners

There is general agreement among experts in gifted education that identification should combine relevant information from parents and teachers, evaluation of work samples and curriculum test results, and formal psychological assessments of intelligence and aptitude. In reality, identification of giftedness and talent usually occurs through recognising high standards in a student's classroom work and test results, appreciating their valuable contribution to class discussions, and their higher-than-average interest in and commitment to learning.

In the USA and in Australia there is no national mandate that all states must identify their gifted and talented students and make special provision for them. It is left to individual states to determine their own policy and practices—and many have done so (Walsh & Jolly, 2018). In the UK, the Department for Education and Employment introduced a gifted and talented education policy in 1999, and gifted education was given a higher profile. At that time the Government requested all schools to prepare a written policy on gifted and talented students, with details of how these students would be identified and what provisions would be made for them. However, it was not made mandatory that a specific support system must be established in a school; and two decades later concern continues to be expressed that many very capable students are still not being identified and fully supported by their schools (Koshy et al., 2018).

In an effort to combat this weakness, it was determined that regular school inspections in the UK should in future include a focus on how well a school is meeting the needs of highly able students. To assist with this process the Department for Children, Schools and Families issued guidelines under the title *Identifying Gifted and Talented Learners* (updated 2008). This publication suggested criteria and processes for schools to use when reviewing their existing provisions for gifted learners. The document is available online at: https://webarchive.nationalarchives.gov.uk/20110907134700/https://www.education.gov.uk/publications/eOrderingDownload/Getting%20StartedWR.pdf.

There is growing evidence that high-ability students from lower socio-economic families are less likely than students from higher socio-economic families to be identified for access to enriched academic opportunities (Plucker et al., 2018). A high priority in preparing teachers for working in disadvantaged schools should be an improvement in their expertise in identifying capable students and in implementing a differentiated approach to meet their needs (Burrell et al., 2017). In the USA, the influential National Association for Gifted Children (NAGC) and the Council for Exceptional Children (CEC) have attempted to address this problem by recommending standards for the training of all teachers in gifted education (NAGC-CEC, 2013).

Studies have shown that teachers in general are fairly poor at identifying gifted students who are *underachieving* (Bennett-Rappell & Northcote, 2016). Gifted underachievers tend not to be recognised as such because they produce classroom work and test results that are satisfactory, but not outstanding. Their high potential remains unrecognised, so nothing is done to vary their programme. Underachievement is often associated with early dropping out from school—which in turns can affect long-term life prospects for the individual.

Underachievement

There are many reasons why some high-ability students may underachieve in school. Among the most common reasons are:

- *Boredom*: The curriculum is not sufficiently challenging to hold the student's interest and attention. The pace at which topics are covered in the mainstream programme may be much too slow for students who are able to learn at a much faster rate. There may also be too much time devoted to revising material they have already mastered. Even in early childhood education settings there is evidence that the daily programme contains too little of intellectual challenge for young children of high ability (OECD, 2006). Inattention is a major problem for some gifted students who have attention deficit hyperactivity disorder (ADHD) (McCoach et al., 2020).
- *Personal or emotional problems:* The student may be experiencing difficulties at home or within the peer group, and these problems can severely undermine the ability to concentrate and devote effort to study. Some highly gifted individuals are also prone to experience stress, anxiety and depression (Gaesser, 2018). A few students of high ability are obsessed with producing results that are always perfect, and are constantly fearful of failure. This *perfectionism* can have very negative long-term effects on their school progress and mental well-being (Wilson & Adelson, 2018).
- *Peer pressure*: A few students of high ability may underachieve by concealing their talents from classmates in order not to stand out as 'different'. For example, they may be reluctant to hand in work of a high standard, or ask questions and contribute to class discussions, even though they have much to offer. Both boys and girls may deliberately underachieve so as not to be thought 'too smart'. This is especially true during adolescence (Coleman & Cross, 2014).
- *Poor study habits:* Some gifted students are not naturally inclined to work hard, to set themselves goals, to make a commitment, and devote the necessary effort. The fact that a student has high potential does not in any way ensure that he or she is motivated to develop that potential through hard work. In addition, a few gifted students lack effective study strategies, so they do not always tackle assignments efficiently or successfully.

- *Disability:* It must be recognised that some students with physical or sensory disabilities may also be gifted and talented, but their disability often hides their potential. A few students who are very talented and of high intelligence may have a specific learning disability in areas such as reading, spelling, writing, or mathematics, or they may have attention deficit hyperactivity disorder (Assouline et al., 2010). These students with a specific learning disability are often referred to as 'twice exceptional', and some may experience problems securing peer group acceptance because of their learning difficulties or behaviour (Ronksley-Pavia et al., 2019b). Dyslexic students, for example, may be intellectually gifted but have chronic problems with writing assignments and reading comprehension. The danger is that gifted students with these basic skill difficulties may be thought by the teacher to be low-achievers, and may even be placed in a low-ability group.
- *English as a second language:* Gifted students whose first language is not English can have difficulty performing to the best of their ability in schools where English is the medium of instruction. The problem relates not only to difficulties with understanding spoken and written language but also to a reluctance (sometimes related also to cultural differences) to participate actively and ask and answer teachers' questions in class or to request additional help and explanations.
- *Socio-economic disadvantage:* Some potentially gifted students may underachieve for a variety of reasons related to social disadvantage. For example, poverty leading to lack of resources in the home, dysfunctional family, low expectations, and lack of support for learning are all factors associated with underachievement in school.

Addressing underachievement must always be an important aim within gifted education. It has been found that interventions for underachievement can be effective in increasing motivation for learning, improving self-regulation, and finding school more meaningful (Steenbergen-Hu at al., 2020). One approach that appears to be useful in this respect is the *Achievement Orientation Model* (Ritchotte et al., 2014; Siegle et al., 2017). The principle underpinning this model is that in order to do well and achieve their potential, learners need to recognise the value of an activity, put in the required effort, and build confidence in their own ability to achieve (self-efficacy). An explanation of the model can be found at: https://thegraysonschool.org/wp-content/uploads/The-Achievement-Orientation-Model.pdf

Meeting the needs of gifted and talented students

Effective education for gifted learners relies heavily on selecting a viable organisational model for delivery. As indicated already, the options range from full-time inclusion in the mainstream, through to full-time attendance at separate schools or separate classes for students who have been identified as gifted. Other options include part-time withdrawal programmes, promotion to a higher age group, modifying the curriculum so that a gifted student moves through the content more rapidly, independent study programmes, and the use of mentors. Some schools also enroll students in special after-hours or summer programmes for gifted and talented learners. Designing appropriate teaching for students of high ability, regardless of where are taught, involves three main considerations—acceleration, extension, and enrichment (Yuen et al., 2018).

Acceleration

Acceleration refers to any method adopted to cater for a gifted student's faster pace of learning, and to avoid students having to repeat material they already know. Studies have shown unequivocally that acceleration can contribute greatly to gifted students' motivation and academic achievement; and in most cases has no negative effect on their social adjustment (Crawford, 2018; Steenbergen-Hu et al., 2016). Acceleration can be a feature within a gifted student's differentiated programme in the regular classroom, or it can be achieved through some of the practices described below.

- *Grade skipping:* Gifted students can work with an older group or class for certain lessons; or a student may be permanently promoted to a higher age group. A study by Gronostaj et al. (2016) found that grade-skipping in most cases was beneficial to the students, intellectually as well as socially, but that eventually further intervention such as a specialised class with a tailor-made gifted programme was needed to provide sufficiently challenging opportunities for learning. It should be noted that moving to a higher grade will not help a gifted student at all if the programme into which the student is promoted is of poor quality. Promotion to higher grades each year is also a difficult system to sustain over several years of schooling, particularly when a student moves to another school. Early admission to university represents another extreme example of this acceleration model. While useful for some exceptionally advanced students, the model does require a certain degree of maturity and social adaptability in the students, and it does not necessarily suit all.
- *Curriculum compacting:* In this approach to differentiation, the teacher omits certain topics or exercises in a course of study and modifies assignments so that a student of high ability can skip work already known, work on new topics, and achieve learning objectives in a shorter period of time. If the teacher is well-informed on the content of online programmes, e-learning represents one way that the curriculum can be adapted for gifted learners. For this compacting approach to be effective, it is essential that the teacher adapting the curriculum has deep command of subject matter, so that condensing and restructuring a course can still achieve the desired learning outcomes. It is not an easy option, and seems to be seldom used in any methodical way in the average classroom.
- *Independent learning contracts:* An individualised work plan is designed for the student of high ability, allowing him or her to work fairly independently or with a mentor for specific periods each week. The teacher and student together negotiate and agree upon the details of the contract such as what is to be the product, when it is to be completed, and what resources are needed (Newbould, 2018). Such contracts usually involve more challenging learning objectives and the provision of relevant learning resources (texts, computer software, Internet connection, hyperlinks for e-learning).

Extension

Extension activities enable high achievers to go much more deeply into an area of study (Henshon, 2018). This can be achieved in part by compacting the curriculum to save time, and then using that time to work on more challenging and open-ended assignments.

E-learning in all its forms has opened up many new possibilities for doing this in recent years. The extension approach tends to involve students in more first-hand investigation and problem solving, with an emphasis on development of critical and creative thinking. Students may need first to receive direct teaching in the use of particular researching and data processing skills. Extension activities often rely heavily on students' ability to learn independently and self-regulate.

Enrichment

Enrichment can be thought of as an approach that seeks to broaden a field of study to include more applications and additional examples or problems—but not necessarily more difficult concepts. The purpose is to encourage deeper knowledge through original creative or exploratory activities related to the topic or theme. Enrichment is often achieved through computer-assisted learning, project work, individual or cooperative study contracts, and the use of classroom learning centres. Enrichment is also often the main function of the extra-curricular activities organised by many schools. Often, these activities serve the purpose of encouraging growth and talent development in areas other than academic subjects.

Mentoring systems

Both extension and enrichment goals can also be facilitated through *mentoring systems*. Mentoring can be provided for gifted students with an interest and aptitude in a particular field. Use is made of adults or older students with expertise in that particular area as tutors, guides, or critical friends. The area of study may be academic or may be related to fine arts, performing arts, recreation, sports or technology. Often these mentoring sessions take place as extra-curricular activities. In recent years, *online mentoring* of individuals or small groups has proved to be effective as a means of providing coaching for gifted and talented learners (Stoeger et al., 2017).

General principles of teaching

No matter whether gifted and talented students are taught within the mainstream or in ability groups, their curriculum needs to be suitably comprehensive and challenging. The activities provided must engage students in knowledge acquisition, higher-level thinking, problem solving, investigation, and creation of new ideas. It is also important to promote students' independence in learning by encouraging their curiosity, persistence, and willingness to share ideas.

Effective teaching and learning for students of high ability must include at least the following components:

- individualised goal setting;
- opportunity to progress rapidly;
- access to challenging topics, problems and materials (e.g., online resources)
- direct teaching and application of age-appropriate study skills and strategies;
- activities that require deep study, reasoning, critical thinking, and creativity;
- opportunities to pursue personal interests and develop talents.

Specific implementation models

Many different programmes and curricula have been devised to serve the needs of gifted and talented students. It can be seen that although the programmes have different names, they all tend to share some similar features. The main aim in all cases is to provide a more challenging and motivating approach to meets the learning needs and interests of students of high ability. Some of these models are most easily implemented in situations where gifted and talented students are gathered together as a separate group, rather than in mixed-ability classes.

Enrichment Triad Model and Schoolwide Enrichment

The *Enrichment Triad Model* (ETM) and the *Schoolwide Enrichment Model* (SEM) (Renzulli & Reis, 2014) are examples of well-designed approaches to foster and support gifted students and other learners through differentiation in the mainstream. Various adapted versions of *Enrichment Triad Model* and *Schoolwide Enrichment Model* have emerged in different countries and for application with different age groups.

The *Enrichment Triad Model* presents students with a variety of activities that enable them to explore a given topic from different perspectives and at different levels of complexity. All students first engage in a range of introductory activities (Type I enrichment) to become generally conversant with the topic and to identify interesting issues worth investigation. All students are then taught necessary investigative and data processing skills required to explore and report on these issues in greater depth and breadth: e.g., online searches, interviewing, note-taking, summarising, tabulation, producing graphics (Type II enrichment). Finally, students can focus on specific issues or personal interests related to the central theme and study these in much greater depth through independent or collaborative study (Type III enrichment). It is Type III enrichment in particular that takes students of high ability beyond the regular curriculum objectives, to explore new areas of interest in greater depth.

Enrichment Triad Model is part of the *Renzulli Learning System* that assists teachers and students to meet the *Common Core State Standards* in the USA (Renzulli et al., 2014). For example, the resources used in the system place a strong emphasis on problem solving, creativity, and critical thinking. Students develop important skills that enable them to analyse informational texts, research and integrate information from multiple sources (including ICT), use mathematics and literacy skills to investigate, solve, and describe real-world problems. More information, including research findings, can be found on the *Renzulli Learning System* website at: https://renzullilearning.com/

Parallel Curriculum Model

The Parallel Curriculum Model (PCM) evolved from earlier work on curriculum adaptation by Carol Tomlinson in the USA. PCM is based on the premise that every learner is somewhere on a path towards gaining expertise in a particular subject. The parallel curriculum sets out to develop further the existing abilities of all students and to extend the specific talents of students who perform at advanced levels (Hathcock, 2018; Irving et al., 2016). Four parallel components are provided, comprising (i) a *core curriculum* of key knowledge, concepts and skills related to the subject; (ii) *connections*, helping students relate new content to prior knowledge in this and other subject areas, and apply skills across disciplines; (iii) *practice*, to help students function effectively in a particular discipline; and (iv) *identity*, helping students identify personally with the subject more deeply by connecting it with their own lives, interests, and aspirations. These four curricular components are used by teachers as a framework when they plan units of work around a central theme. Teachers must determine each student's current ability level, and from this information develop activities that will move him or her along a continuum towards greater expertise (Kaplan et al., 2009; Tomlinson et al., 2008). Leppien and Purcell (2011) applied the model to produce an effective science curriculum for students in Grades 6 to 12.

The *Parallel Curriculum Model* is explained at: https://presentlygifted.weebly.com/parallel-curriculum-model.html

Autonomous Learner Model

The Autonomous Learner Model (ALM) recognises the need for gifted students to become self-directed learners, able to take responsibility for implementing and reflecting upon their own learning processes (Betts, 1985; Betts & Kercher, 2009). The model focuses on gifted and talented students across the school age range and is flexible enough to be used in the regular classroom, in small group settings (pull-out programmes), or as an individual course. Among the basic principles of the model are emphases on fostering self-understanding, and making full use of a student's personal interests and aptitudes. The approach is entirely compatible with the preference of many gifted students to be independent in their learning—but also able to call upon a mentor when necessary.

ALM has five major dimensions:

- *Orientation*—understanding one's own abilities, aptitudes, aspirations, interests; and comprehending the scope and purpose of ALM in relation to self-development.
- *Individual development*—acquiring powerful study and research skills needed for independent life-long learning; use of technology; career path awareness; working collaboratively with others.
- *Enrichment*—enhanced opportunities to explore topics or problems that are not necessarily components of the core curriculum; participating in cultural activities, community service, excursions, and camps.
- *Seminars*—individual or group presentations of topics that have been studied. Small discussions, sharing advanced knowledge.
- *In-depth study*—individual projects, group research, mentorships.

A manual prepared by Betts et al. (2016) provides useful activities that teachers can use to implement principles of ALM. These activities are all geared to help advance the emotional, social, and cognitive development of students on the road to becoming more autonomous in learning and motivation.

The *Autonomous Learner Model* is described at: https://presentlygifted.weebly.com/autonomous-learner-model.html

The CLEAR Curriculum Model

This model integrates three approaches that have proved to be effective in gifted education, namely: differentiation, increasing depth and complexity of the curriculum, and

Schoolwide Enrichment (Azano, 2013; Foster et al., 2011). The acronym CLEAR is derived from Continuous assessment, Learning goals, Experiences, Authentic products, and Rich curriculum. The curriculum content and activities are designed so that all students are fully engaged and appropriately challenged to facilitate higher achievement. Evaluation of the effectiveness of CLEAR Curriculum indicates that it provides a viable option to enhance students' learning and that teachers are able to implement it with moderate to high fidelity (Oh et al., 2012). A comprehensive overview of this model (with specific examples) can be found at: https://eric.ed.gov/?id=ED535658

The Purdue Three-Stage Model

The purpose of this model is development of thinking skills and strategies that are used in creative problem solving. The model has had most application with gifted learners in pull-out programmes, but the general principles are applicable for teaching in a regular class setting. At Stage 1 students are instructed in specific strategies that will be needed to solve particular problems. Stage 2 involves practice in applying these strategies to routine problems; and at Stage 3 students apply their skills to investigate real-life non-routine problems (Feldhusen & Kolloff, 1988; Moon et al., 2009).

Information on the *Purdue Three-Stage Model* can be found online at: https://sites.google.com/site/modelsforthegifted/customization/purdue-three-stage-model-eval

The next three chapters consider important personal, social, emotional, and behavioural attributes of students with learning difficulties or disabilities. Topics explored include how students manage their own learning, how teachers manage behaviour in the classroom, and factors that influence students' social and emotional development.

Online resources

- In the USA the National Association for Gifted Children provides much useful information. www.nagc.org/.
- Also based in the USA, the Center for Creativity, Gifted Education, and Talent Development is a good source and has several research programs in operation. https://gifted.uconn.edu/.
- The Department for Education and Skills in the UK prepared a guide titled Effective provision for gifted and talented children in primary education. Available online at: http://webarchive.nationalarchives.gov.uk/20130401151715/http://www.education.gov.uk/publications/eOrderingDownload/GTPrimary.pdf.
- The Ministry of Education in New Zealand has published a document titled Gifted and talented students: Meeting their needs in New Zealand schools. Available online at: www.gifted.tki.org.nz/.
- A clear description of the Enrichment Triad Model can be found at: https://enrichmenttriadmodel.weebly.com/what-is-triad.html.

Print resources

Jolly, J.L., & Jarvis, J.M. (2018). *Exploring gifted education: Australian and New Zealand Perspectives.* London & New York: Routledge.

Mofield, E., & Phelps, V. (2020). *Collaboration, coteaching, and coaching in gifted education: Sharing strategies to support gifted learners.* Waco, TX: Prufrock Press.

Rimm, S., Siegle, D., & Davis, G. (2018). *Education of the gifted and talented* (7th ed.) Boston: Pearson Merrill.

Rinn, A. (2020). *Social, emotional, and psychosocial development of gifted and talented individuals.* Waco, TX: Prufrock Press.

Taber, K.S., Sumida, M., & McClure, L. (Eds). (2019). *Teaching gifted learners in STEM subjects.* London & New York: Routledge.

Winebrenner, S. (2018). *Teaching gifted kids in today's classroom: Strategies and techniques every teacher can use* (4th ed.). Golden Valley, MN: Free Spirit Publishing.

Chapter 7

Self-management and autonomy

Self-management (self-regulation) is an essential competency that all students need to develop if they are to become autonomous learners. This is particularly important now that schools are tending to use more student-centred approaches, independent studies, and e-learning, all calling for good self-direction (Lee, 2019; C.H. Wang et al., 2013). Studies have yielded data indicating that students who have the capability to self-regulate tend to do well in school, and are more confident, diligent and resourceful (Lawrence & Saileella, 2019; Oppong et al., 2019; Rhodes, 2019).

One of the common observations concerning students with special needs or disabilities is that they are often passive learners, unable to make good decisions or regulate their own learning processes and behaviour appropriately. One of the goals of education must therefore be to help these students achieve a higher level of self-management and self-efficacy (Kulakow, 2020). In particular, they need to become better at monitoring and controlling their own responses and reactions in the classroom (Lawson et al., 2019). In the case of students with intellectual disability, autism, emotional disturbance, learning disability, and behaviour problems, it is often necessary to teach explicitly the behaviours that enable self-monitoring and self-management (Hoff & Ervin, 2013; Regan & Martin, 2014). When the students acquire this capability, it is much easier for them to be engaged effectively in inclusive classrooms and to improve in their learning. Teaching self-management must therefore be a high priority when working with these students.

Definition of terms

Several important terms are used in discussions on students' self-regulation, some overlapping in meaning but each used in a specific context. In the field of psychology each has its own precise meaning.

- *Self-regulation* is the general term commonly used in relation to an individual's ability to monitor his or her own behaviour and modify responses and reactions as necessary. Self-regulation in learning usually involves the ability to 'think about one's own thinking' (*metacognition*) and control processes such as selective attention, strategy application, and self-correction. Self-regulation also includes the ability to manage one's emotions, to control anger or frustration, and to cope with stress (Ennis & Jolivette, 2014). Self-regulation and metacognition in the context of classroom learning are discussed more fully later in the chapter.

- *Self-determination.* Self-determination refers to a person's autonomy to plan, set goals, make decisions, and take appropriate action to achieve one's goals (Wehmeyer et al., 2018). Too often, the life of persons with disabilities is largely controlled by others, and they are given very few opportunities to exercise self-determination. The American Association on Intellectual and Developmental Disabilities (AAIDD, 2019) has remarked:

  > People with intellectual and/or developmental disabilities have the same right to, and responsibilities that accompany, self-determination as everyone else. They are entitled to opportunities, respectful support, and the authority to exert control in their lives, to direct their services, and to act on their own behalf.

- *Self-directed learning.* Self-directed learning means that students are made responsible for monitoring and managing their own learning processes to achieve desired outcomes (Ohashi, 2018). The approach requires students to be intrinsically motivated and to exercise personal management over all actions taken in tackling a particular learning task. Interest has grown in recent years in promoting this self-directed learning, particularly in the final years of secondary school and in tertiary education, where it has major importance in relation to all forms of e-learning.
- *Classroom self-management* is a specific aspect of self-regulation that refers to a student's ability to function effectively in a classroom environment, without the need for constant supervision or direction from others. This capability relates to such behaviours as organising one's lesson materials, knowing what to do when work is completed, recognising when to seek help from the teacher or a peer, understanding how to check one's work for careless errors, how to maintain attention to task, how to observe well-established routines such as ordering lunch, having sports equipment or books ready for a specific lesson, knowing when a change of lesson or room is to occur, and so on. All these skills are easily acquired by students without learning problems or disabilities, but can be difficult for some students with special needs.

The importance of classroom self-management

Self-management by a student with a disability seems to be one of the most important factors contributing to successful inclusion. Some students—for example those with intellectual disability or with social, emotional or psychological disorders—frequently exhibit very weak self-management, having become overly dependent on control from others. It is essential that all students with special needs, whether placed in special settings or in the regular classroom, be helped to develop adequate levels of independence in their work habits, self-control, and readiness for learning. When students are able to manage routines in the classroom and look after their own needs during a lesson, the teacher is able to devote much more time to teaching rather than managing the group.

Teaching self-management

Evidence is accumulating to indicate that specific training in self-management and self-regulation can be effective in promoting students' autonomy (Schulze, 2016; Hoff & Ervin, 2013). Intervention studies involving self-management training at various age levels have suggested that there are strong positive effects from such training (e.g., Sandjojo et al., 2019; Thompson, 2014). One approach that is receiving attention is the structured *Alert Program*® that uses the analogy of an 'engine' that has to be controlled in order to run on high, low, or appropriate power for the task in hand. Mac Cobb et al. (2014) found that students undertaking the programme gained a better understanding of their own behaviour and could identify self-management strategies for use in class. Other studies (e.g., Gill et al., 2018) have also supported the use of the *Alert Program*® in school settings for improving children's self-regulation.

The specific self-management skills required by a child in school will tend to differ slightly from classroom to classroom according to a particular teacher's management style, routines and expectations, and according to the nature of the curriculum. The self-management skills required in an informal classroom setting tend to be very different from those needed in a more formal or highly structured setting. For example, in some secondary school classrooms a premium may still be placed upon passive listening, note-taking, and sustained on-task behaviour, while in other classrooms it is groupworking skills and cooperation with others that are essential prerequisites for success. Knowing how to respond to the demands and constraints of different lessons and settings is an important aspect of a student's growth towards autonomy. To encourage students' self-management, teachers need to consider precisely which skills or behaviours are required in order to function independently in their particular environment—for example, it may be that in a certain lesson the prerequisites are staying on task without close supervision, resisting distractions, and using resource materials and technology independently. In another situation, the ability to work closely with peers, share ideas, and show initiative are the required behaviours.

For students with special educational needs, a five-step procedure can be used to teach self-management.

- *Explanation*—Discuss with the student why a specific self-managing behaviour is important. Help the student identify and observe other students exhibiting that target behaviour.
- *Demonstration* – Teacher clearly explains and models the behaviour.
- *Role play* – The student imitates the behaviour, with feedback from the teacher or peer.
- *Cueing* – In the natural classroom setting, the student is reminded and prompted when necessary to carry out the behaviour.
- *Maintenance* – It is important to teach and reinforce the particular behaviour to the point where the student no longer needs to be prompted. When the student displays the behaviour spontaneously without prompting, he or she is rewarded.

For additional advice, see Online Resources at the end of the chapter.

Locus of control and self-efficacy

Self-management links quite closely with two important personality constructs known to influence academic achievement—namely, *locus of control* and *self-efficacy* (Hwang et al., 2016; Kumaravelu, 2018). To understand locus of control it is necessary to recognise that individuals attribute what happens to them in any particular situation either to internal factors (e.g. their own ability, effort, decisions, or actions) or to external factors (e.g. luck, chance, something outside their control) (Fournier, 2018). Students with an internal locus of control recognise that they can influence events by their own actions, and believe that they do to some extent control their own destiny. At classroom level, an example of internality might be when students recognise that if they really concentrate on the task at hand and work carefully, they get much better results. Appreciating the fact that outcomes are under one's personal control is a key component of one's feelings of 'self-efficacy' and a strong defence against passivity.

Internalisation of locus of control usually increases steadily with age if a child experiences normal success and reinforcement from his or her efforts in school and in daily life outside school. However, it has been found that many children with learning problems and others with negative school experiences remain markedly external in their locus of control in relation to school, believing that their efforts have little impact on their progress because they lack ability to change outcomes. Young children enter school with positive views of their own capabilities, but this confidence rapidly erodes if they experience too many early failures and frustrations.

The child who remains largely external in locus of control is likely to be the child who fails to assume normal self-management in class and is prepared to be controlled by others such as the teacher, parent, classroom aide, or more assertive peers. There exists a vicious circle wherein the child feels inadequate, is not prepared to take a risk, seems to require support, gets it, and develops even more dependence upon others. This can be described as *learned helplessness* (Filippello et al., 2018; Hwang, 2019). The teacher's task is one of breaking into this circle and causing the child to recognise the extent to which he or she has control over events and can influence outcomes. It is natural for a teacher, tutor, or aide to wish to help and support a child with special needs, but it should not be done to the extent that all challenge and possibility of failure are eliminated. Failure must be possible and children must be helped to see the causal relationship between their own efforts and the outcomes. Children will become more internal in their locus of control, and much more involved in learning tasks when they recognise that their effort and persistence can overcome failure.

It is important that teachers and parents publicly acknowledge and praise children's positive efforts, rather than emphasising lack of effort. In general, teachers' use of *descriptive praise* has a strong positive influence on children's beliefs about their own ability and the importance of making an effort. When praise is perceived by children to be genuine and credible, it appears to enhance their motivation and feelings of control. Teachers' use of praise has been well researched, and it seems that praise is particularly important for students *provided that it is genuine and deserved*, and that the praiseworthy aspects of the performance are specified. For example: 'Good work, David! You used your own words instead of simply copying from the reference book.' 'Well done Joanne. I like the way you have used a different colour to show the higher ground.' A child should know precisely why he or she is being praised if appropriate connections are to be made in the child's mind between effort and outcome. Trivial or redundant praise is very quickly detected by children and serves no useful purpose.

Attribution retraining

A markedly external locus of control (as in learned helplessness) usually has a negative impact upon a student's willingness to persist in the face of a difficult task. It is easier for the child to develop avoidance strategies rather than persist if the expectation of failure is high. *Attribution retraining* is an approach designed to redirect students' self-blaming causal explanations for their difficulties (e.g., 'I lack academic ability'; 'I just don't understand big numbers') by encouraging them instead to attribute poor performance to controllable factors, such as the amount of effort they put in and the time they devote to the task (Chodkiewicz & Boyle, 2016). When a task is completed successfully, students are taught to appraise carefully the results of their own efforts, and encouraged to verbalise their conclusions aloud: 'I did that well because I took my time and read the question twice'; 'I listened carefully and planned my answers.' Verbalising in this way helps students focus their attention on the real relationship between effort and the observed outcomes. In most cases, attribution retraining seems to have maximum value when it is combined with *cognitive behaviour modification* (Bosnjak et al., 2017; Haynes-Stewart et al., 2011).

Cognitive behaviour modification

Cognitive behaviour modification (CBM) involves training students to gain better control over their own thoughts and actions by using inner self-talk. When used in clinical settings to modify maladaptive behaviours or emotions (e.g. phobias, anxiety disorders, stress, anger, and aggression) the approach is often referred to as *cognitive behavioural therapy* (CBT). The approach has been used successfully with a wide range of individuals who present with learning or behaviour difficulties (Cooney et al., 2018; Garvik et al., 2014).

In a school situation, a student with a behaviour or attitude problem in class is taught to memorise and use a mental 'script' that enables them to monitor and regulate their own behaviour in a particular situation. An example might be a student who has great difficulty staying on task and who often gets out of her seat to disturb others during the lesson. A small timing device with a beeper might be placed on her desk and she would be taught to monitor her own on-task behaviour every time the beeper sounds. If she is on task, she praises herself: 'Good! I am working. I am finishing the task.' At the end of each lesson the teacher rewards the student in some way if she has achieved the set goal by remaining seated and on task. It is usual for a teacher to implement a CBM programme with advice from the school psychologist, who is able to assess the particular characteristics of the student and then recommend appropriate strategies (Weeks et al., 2017).

Metacognition

Metacognition refers to the ability to monitor one's own thinking processes and exercise control over them (Rhodes, 2019). Metacognitive processes enter many aspects of cognition and the development of self-regulation and autonomy. It has been suggested that metacognition is one of the most significant predictors of academic performance, possibly even more influential than intelligence (Ohtani & Hisasaka, 2018). Metacognition helps a learner in school recognise that he or she is either doing well or is having difficulty with a particular learning task. The learner who is monitoring his or her own ongoing performance will detect the need to pause and check, perhaps begin again before moving on, weigh up possible alternatives, or seek outside help. This is clearly an important ability in almost all areas of the curriculum.

Metacognitive training focuses on assisting a learner to monitor the appropriateness of his or her thoughts when faced with a particular task or problem. This involves self-questioning and analysis that can lead to a more considered plan of action. Teachers should provide modelling of this process by thinking aloud, to reach a decision on what action to take. Metacognitive training has to utilise authentic topics, problems, or tasks as the focus of instruction, and curriculum areas such as reading comprehension, mathematical problem solving, and planned essay writing have been popular topics for research. The Education Endowment Foundation in the UK has stated that metacognition and self-regulation training approaches have yielded consistently high levels of impact for all learners, and are particularly effective for low-achieving students (EEF, 2019).

Cognitive strategies and strategy-based instruction

A cognitive strategy can be thought of as a 'mental plan of action' that enables a student to tackle a particular task or assignment systematically. Strategy training involves a teacher providing a clear demonstration of exactly how to approach that task. The teacher who says: 'Watch and listen. This is how I do it – and this is what I say to myself as I do it', is providing the learner with a secure starting point. The teacher who simply says, 'Here is the exercise. Get on with it', is providing an invitation to failure and frustration for some students.

Although most teachers are aware of the value of implementing strategy training, too few manage to do this as a routine part of their approach. They tend to be more concerned with covering curriculum content than with helping students become more efficient at learning that content (Magnusson et al., 2019). If cognitive strategies are not taught explicitly, many students fail to discover them incidentally.

It was noted in Chapter 1 that many students with general or specific learning difficulties appear to lack appropriate strategies for tackling schoolwork. They do not seem to understand that these tasks can be completed effectively if approached with a plan of action in mind. *Strategy-based instruction* (SBI) involves teaching students to apply effective thinking procedures to guide their actions and self-monitoring when approaching a particular task or problem. For example, attempting to solve a routine word problem in mathematics usually requires careful reading of the problem, identification of what one is required to find out, recognition of the relevant data to use, selection of the appropriate process, completion of the calculation and a final checking of the reasonableness of the answer. This approach to solving the mathematical problem involves metacognition, application of a cognitive strategy, and utilisation of procedural knowledge (how to carry out the steps in a specific calculation). There is clear evidence that teaching students with learning difficulties in mathematics how to apply this type of cognitive strategy can improve their achievement (Adani et al., 2012). An Effect Size of.69 has been reported for strategy training (Hattie, 2012). Any Effect Size above.40 is regarded as a very positive effect.

The typical teaching procedure used in strategy-based instruction usually has the basic structure described below.

- *Modelling*—teacher performs the task or carries out the new process while thinking aloud. This may involve self-questioning, giving self-directions, making overt decisions, changing one's mind, and evaluating the results.
- *Overt external guidance*—students copy the teacher's model and complete a similar task, with the teacher still providing any necessary prompting and verbal directions.

- *Overt self-guidance*—students repeat the performance with a similar task while using self-talk.
- *Covert self-instruction*—students perform several similar tasks while using inner speech to monitor their actions, guide their responses, and make decisions.

In a mathematics lesson, typical self-questions, statements, and directions a student might be taught to use when attempting to solve a problem would include:

> What exactly do I have to do? Where do I start?
> Don't rush.
> OK, I need to multiply these two numbers and then subtract the answer from 100.
> That's good. I know that answer is correct.
> I'll need to come back and check this part. Does this make sense?
> I think I made a mistake here, but I can come back and work it again. I can correct it.

These self-monitoring statements cover focusing attention, goal setting, planning, checking, self-reinforcement, self-appraisal, error detection and self-correction. These statements are applicable across a fairly wide range of academic tasks.

Students with learning difficulties tend to take very much longer than other students to adopt a new learning strategy, so abundant practice needs to be sustained until independent use is finally established. Maintenance of strategy use can be assisted by frequent discussion with students about how and when to apply the strategy, and by the use of descriptive praise when a student remembers to use a strategy without prompting.

Students find most relevance in strategies they can use to complete classroom assignments and homework more successfully. Sometimes the steps involved in tackling a specific task can be printed on a cue card to be displayed for as long as is necessary on the students' desks. The students can also be taught a mnemonic for remembering the strategy. Examples of mnemonics are provided later in the chapters on literacy and numeracy.

Generalisation of taught strategies has always been problematic, particularly for students with learning difficulties. The students may learn how to apply the strategy successfully to one specific task, but not recognise how the same approach could be used in other contexts. To help students overcome the problem of limited generalisation, teachers might:

- provide training from the beginning that deliberately requires the strategy to be applied in a variety of different authentic tasks from across the curriculum;
- review a particular strategy quite often to discuss the situations in which it could be applied.

This chapter has presented concepts and practices that relate to ways of making students more autonomous in their approach to learning, and in monitoring and regulating their own responses. The next chapter looks at issues concerned with classroom behaviour more generally.

Online resources

- Virginia State University (2019). Developing responsibility and self-management in young children: Goals of positive behavior management. Available at: www.pubs.ext.vt.edu/content/dam/pubs_ext_vt_edu/350/350-052/350-052(FCS-132P).pdf.

- National Center on Intensive Intervention. https://intensiveintervention.org/sites/default/files/Self_Management_508.pdf.
- Center on the Social and Emotional Foundations for Early Learning, Helping Children to learn to manage their own behavior at: http://csefel.vanderbilt.edu/kits/wwbtk7.pdf.
- Transforming Education Website. Teaching self-management: Practical ways to help students develop skills in this key component of social-emotional learning. Available at: www.slideshare.net/TransformingEducation/teaching-self-management.
- How to improve metacognition in the classroom. Inner Drive Website at: www.innerdrive.co.uk/improve-metacognition/.

Print resources

Chapin, B., & Penner, M. (2012). *Helping young people learn self-regulation.* Chapin, SC: Youth Light Inc.

Cleary, T.J. (2018). *The self-regulated learning guide.* Abingdon, Oxon: Routledge.

Shanker, S. (2020). *Reframed: Self-reg for a just society.* Toronto: University of Toronto Press.

Strosnider, R., & Sharpe, V.S. (2019). *The executive function guidebook: Strategies to help all students achieve success.* Thousand Oaks, CA: Corwin.

Chapter 8

Managing behaviour

Managing students' difficult behaviour is a matter of concern for teachers worldwide, as evidenced by the large number of behaviour management research studies conducted each year. Challenging behaviour is not necessarily a characteristic of students with learning difficulties and disabilities, but in a few cases—for example, students with emotional disturbance and others with poor self-control—behaviour problems can accompany learning and socialisation difficulties. There are, of course, many students without a learning difficulty or disability who exhibit problem behaviour, stemming from a variety of causes. This chapter explores problem behaviour and reviews some of the proactive and responsive strategies that teachers can use to address the problem.

A well-managed classroom with a minimum of problem behaviours is conducive to positive learning opportunities for all students. Teachers in primary and secondary schools place great importance on managing students' behaviour and helping them gain control over their own conduct. Many teachers report that one of their main concerns in the classroom is the child who disrupts lessons, cannot work cooperatively with others, and seeks too much attention from teacher or peers (Landers et al., 2013; MacSuga-Gage et al., 2018). A teacher may know what the child needs in terms of basic instruction and support, but it proves impossible to deliver appropriate teaching because the child is unreceptive.

The effects of misbehaviour

There are always numerous negative outcomes from behaviour problems in school, both for the students and their teachers. Students who are creating the problems usually miss out on many important learning opportunities by spending huge amounts of time off task. They also tend to have poor quality of life in school because their social acceptance is negatively affected when they alienate members of their peer group. The general classroom climate is also affected, because the teacher is unable to relax and use methods which do not require tight control.

One of the main factors contributing to teachers' stress and burn-out is students' challenging behaviour. Teachers need the support of the school principal and the understanding from colleagues that a student's challenging behaviour is not due to their own inability to exercise effective classroom control. When a school fails to adopt a collaborative and supportive approach to the management of difficult and disruptive behaviour, certain problems tend to arise:

- individual teachers feeling that they are isolated and unsupported by their colleagues;
- teachers feeling increasingly stressed by daily conflict with some students;
- the problem becoming worse over time.

Preventing behaviour problems

The fundamental requirement for preventing problem behaviour is to provide students with a safe, secure, and predictable environment in which learning can take place. Lessons and the activities within them need always to employ teaching methods, activities, and resources that engage students fully in the learning process, and that help them feel successful (Egeberg & McConney, 2018; Nagro et al., 2019a; Vukovic, 2019). This often requires tasks and activities to be differentiated to match the various ability levels of the students. A common cause of inappropriate behaviour or total disengagement from learning is when students are expected to undertake work that is too difficult, too easy, or boring. Teachers who are most effective in classroom management and maintaining student engagement tend to set interesting and achievable tasks for students to attempt. They also avoid 'dead spots' in lessons, and check students' progress regularly to provide timely and constructive feedback and encouragement.

The underlying principle for managing students' behaviour today is to be positive rather than punitive. An example of this is the proactive approach known as *School-wide positive behaviour support* (SWPBS), which seeks to improve students' academic and behavioural outcomes by targeting the school's organisational and social culture (Adamson et al., 2019; Reimers, 2020; Wienen et al., 2019). Under a proactive and preventive approach, teachers are encouraged to 'catch students being good' and to praise them descriptively for their appropriate behaviour, rather than waiting for bad behaviour to occur and having to react to it. Too often, teachers give far more attention to students who are not behaving appropriately compared to the positive attention given to the other 95 per cent of well-behaved members of a class (Dix, 2017). Studies in mainstream schools have supported the application of SWPBS, with reports of significantly lower truancy rates and higher reading and math proficiency (Noltemeyer et al., 2019; Pas et al., 2019). In the context of students with special needs (including those with autism) this positive approach is reported to be linked to improved outcomes for the students and their teachers (Alter & Vlasak, 2014; Vukovic, 2019; Wang & Kuo, 2019).

Behaviour management policy

At school level, it is essential to have a clear policy on behaviour management to ensure uniform and consistent implementation by all staff. This document should have been drawn up and negotiated with input from all teaching and support staff (and often also from parents) to describe ways in which matters of classroom control and discipline should be approached (Sprick & Knight, 2018). Ideally, a policy will also make specific reference to the management of students with diagnosed behavioural disorders, and how the school may involve outside agencies to assist. In the case of any student with chronic behaviour problems, it is essential to involve his or her parents fully in the implementation of any behaviour change programme. The parents and school staff should together agree on the goals and strategies for a behaviour management plan, and then be consistent in applying the same strategies in school and at home.

It is always necessary to establish rules for behaviour in the classroom that are clearly understood by students and accepted by them as reasonable. At the core of any behaviour management policy should be the stated aim of teaching all students effective and responsible ways of managing their own behaviour. A good policy in action will help all students recognise the personal and group benefits that self-control and responsible behaviour can bring. In many ways, a school policy on student behaviour should be seen as dealing more with matters of social harmony, welfare, and safety, rather than a list of procedures for enforcing discipline. This is in keeping with the belief that schools must be safe and friendly environments in which to work, play, and socialise with peers.

A three-tier model of intervention

In the same way that support for difficulties in learning is best delivered through a three-tier model (see Chapter 1), it is now accepted that managing behaviour also needs to be implemented at three levels (Sayeski & Brown, 2011; Stanton-Chapman et al., 2016). Tier 1 involves establishing for all students an environment in which expectations and rules for behaviour are clear to all students, and all students are helped to acquire appropriate self-management. Estrapala et al. (2018) indicate that Tier 1 involves teaching pro-social behaviours to prevent problems arising, implementing evidence-based classroom management strategies, and openly acknowledging (reinforcing) students when they display positive behaviours. Tier 2 provides additional targeted guidance for some students who at times display poor behaviour. Tier 3 involves intensive behaviour change intervention targeted at any individual student with ongoing challenging behaviour (Bradshaw, 2013; Jenkins et al., 2013). Methods used most frequently at Tier 3 in special schools are based on principles derived from *applied behaviour analysis* (ABA), with clear goal setting, modelling, reward systems, and practice (Pitts et al., 2019). Other strategies for working with students at the three tiers are described in the following sections.

Pas et al. (2019) report that this three-tiered model is now implemented in nearly 26,000 schools in the USA. Evaluations in primary and secondary settings indicate lower suspension rate (small effect size) and higher reading and math proficiency rates (small to large effect sizes) in the primary years. In secondary schools there has been a decrease in truancy rate as well as higher reading and math proficiency.

The need for a team approach

At school level, behaviour problems are best dealt with through a team approach. All teachers who have contact with a student receiving Tier 3 intensive intervention need to collaborate and use a consistent approach when dealing with the problem behaviour. Occasionally of course it is necessary to seek outside expert advice when a child's behaviour does not respond to standard forms of effective management; but in many cases behaviour can be modified successfully within the school setting. In some schools, *behaviour support teams* have been created to assist in this process and to ensure that all personnel who have contact with a problem student share a common goal and are consistent in their approach. These teams also have the roles of assisting with staff development, implementing behaviour policy, encouraging positive approaches to classroom management, and helping to solve specific problems related to behaviour and learning. In several countries, regional or district services have also established similar behaviour support teams or units, to work with parents as well as schools.

Modifying behaviour

It should be understood that changing a student's behaviour is difficult, because a behaviour we regard as inappropriate has often proved to be quite effective for that student in responses—for example, to approach another student in a friendly rather than confrontational manner; to ignore a teasing remark rather than respond to it with aggression.

Recent years in Britain have seen the introduction of 'isolation booths' in some primary and secondary schools (Weale, 2020). These are small closet-size spaces or cubicles set apart from the main classroom to which an unruly or aggressive student may be sent for time out. These isolation areas are variously referred to as exclusion units, consequence booths, time-out spaces, and calm rooms. This type of provision has come in for harsh criticism, based on the lack of evidence that they are effective in modifying behaviour and that they are a breach of the UN Charter on the Rights of the Child.

Students with learning difficulties or disabilities

There is a misguided belief that all students with special needs have some form of behaviour problem. It was this erroneous belief that caused many teachers in the beginning to have serious doubts about the feasibility of introducing inclusive education. The belief is of course entirely untrue, because many of these students are well behaved in class, cooperative, friendly, and create no problem at all for classroom management.

It is true, however, that *some* students with autism and others with intellectual disability have inappropriate ways of responding to frustration, anxiety, or stress. They may withdraw into themselves (internalising behaviour), or instead may respond aggressively to teacher and peers (disruptive externalising behaviour). In addition, there are a few students who are diagnosed as having an *emotional or behavioural disorder* (EBD) and who require a behaviour intervention plan (BIP).

Emotional or behavioural disorders

Students with EBD comprise a diverse group, with a wide range of intellectual and academic abilities. Their social interaction with other students is often problematic, making it difficult to include them easily in mainstream classes. They tend to do best in smaller units with a structured and predictable routine, and where they can receive intensive Tier 3 intervention and support. This usually combines an ABA approach to reinforce positive pro-social behaviours and eliminate undesirable responses, while at the same time providing individual guidance and counselling of a therapeutic nature. As stated earlier, students with an autism spectrum disorder, and others with intellectual disability, also sometimes require and benefit from a similar Tier 3 approach. In all other cases of disability or sensory impairment, the students concerned can participate in and benefit from all of the approaches described in this chapter.

Autism

One approach that has proved to be useful for children with autism, to help them understand events from the perspective of others, is *Social Stories*™ (Karal & Wolfe, 2018). These simple stories can focus on skills such as sharing and cooperating, how to make friends, how to cope with changes to routine, what to do when you are angry or unhappy. They are useful also for preschool children who often need help to understand codes of behaviour, social interactions, and relationships. Haggerty et al. (2005) explained that social stories can be presented using pictures of children engaging in desirable and undesirable behaviour. The children are then guided to observe and reflect upon the behaviour and the reaction it gets from others. For example, a first picture might show children lining up in front of a cake stall at the school Open Day. One child is pushing another out of the line in order to take his place. The children on each side are looking very unhappy. In the next picture, two of the other children are beginning to push the naughty child away from the line and a fight starts. In the third picture the lady in charge of the cake stall says that she will stop selling the cakes unless children line up in a neat queue. The final picture shows a neat queue of children with happy faces, each paying in turn for a cake. Simple stories of this type can also be presented in an active form, through video and virtual reality programs (Ghanouni et al., 2019).

More information on social stories can be found at: https://carolgraysocialstories.com/social-stories/

Dealing with disruptive behaviour

Teachers can lose almost half of their teaching time in some classrooms due to students' unruly behaviour. An analysis of data from the *Programme for International Student Assessment* (PISA) found that in some countries (particularly Western countries like the UK, Australia, and the USA), around 40 per cent of students report that their lessons have too much noise and disorder, and that students do not listen to their teachers (Thomson et al., 2017). This type of behaviour upsets the orderly conduct of teaching and prevents achievement of the objectives for a particular lesson. Frequent disruptive behaviour may also impair the quality of personal and social interaction within the group by destroying a positive class-room climate. Sometimes, simple changes such as modifying seating arrangements, restructuring working groups, reducing noise level and monitoring more closely the work in progress will significantly reduce the occurrence of disruptive behaviour.

Analyses of various interventions used to decrease disruptive behaviour have found that the use of group rewards (group contingency interventions) can be effective (Bolt et al., 2019; Pokorski, 2019). Under this arrangement, when behaviour in a class improves, all members are rewarded. This also has the advantages that it is easier to administer than individual reward systems, and it involves the whole class of students in monitoring and improving behaviour.

Good Behaviour Game

The Good Behaviour Game (GBG) has existed in various forms for many years, but has seen an increase recently in its application. It is an approach that rewards students for displaying appropriate on-task behaviours during lessons. The class is usually divided into two teams that include any students with special needs, and points are given to a team for all appropriate behaviours displayed by its members. The team with the most points at the end of the session (or end of the week) wins a group reward. Obviously, this approach needs to be used frequently enough to have the desired impact. GBG has been found effective for reducing disruptive behaviour, increasing on-task behaviour, and increasing teachers' use of praise relative to reprimands (Fallon & Kurtz, 2019; Rubow et al., 2018). Adapted versions of GBG have even proved useful in the preschool age range (Foley et al., 2019; Wiskow et al., 2019). Combining deliberate social skills train-ing with GBG approach has been found effective for bringing about improvements in the engagement and behaviour of primary school students diagnosed as having emotional and behavioural disorders (Meredith-Murphy et al., 2020).

ClassDojo and tootling

Technology has provided a new medium for monitoring behaviour and providing reinforcement that can improve classroom climate. One example is the use of 'tootling', in which students report positively and pro-socially on their peers' behaviour via ClassDojo technology. ClassDojo is a widely used school-based social media platform that can provide an effective system for behaviour monitoring and control (Manolev et al., 2019). Teachers can also provide on-time feedback and reinforcement to students regarding individual and group behaviour (Çetin & Çetin, 2018). When students' tootles are recorded using ClassDojo and displayed via a projector, appropriate behaviour can be reinforced for the group or the individual. Results from a study with primary school students indicate substantial decreases in class-wide disruptive behaviours and increases in academically engaged behaviour (Dillon et al., 2019). A study with older special education students also suggested that ClassDojo monitoring produced a reduction in problem behaviour for the classroom as a whole and for most individual students (Lipscomb et al., 2018). A similar result was obtained with high school students using tootling via hand-written notes rather than technology (Lum et al., 2019).

Behaviour contracts

Often it is necessary to supplement any whole-class approach to behaviour management by addressing the particular problem behaviour of an individual student. A behaviour contract is a written agreement signed by all parties involved in a behaviour-change programme, including the student (Webster, 2018). After discussion and negotiation, the student agrees to behave in certain ways and carry out certain obligations. In return the staff and parents agree to do certain things—for example, the student may agree to arrive on time for lessons and not disrupt the class. In return the teacher will sign the student's contract sheet indicating that he or she has met the requirement in that particular lesson, and add positive comments. The contract sheet accompanies the student to each lesson throughout the day. At the end of each day and the end of each week, progress is monitored and any necessary changes are made to the agreement. If possible, the school negotiates parental involvement in the implementation of the contract, and the parents agree to provide some specific privileges if the goals are met for two consecutive weeks, or loss of privileges if it is broken. When behaviour contracts are set up in a secondary school, it is essential that all subject teachers who have the student in their classes are informed of the details.

Many websites provide examples of Behaviour Contract templates. For example, see: www.freeprintablebehaviorcharts.com/behavior_contracts.htm

Aggressive behaviour

Aggression can manifest itself in many forms—physical aggression, verbal aggression, violence against persons and property, online abuse, and sexual aggression. Teachers are bothered most by aggressive behaviour in children (Nields, 2014) and increases in work-related stress among teachers are related in part to increases in acting-out and aggressive behaviour among their students. Teachers need to acquire some effective strategies for dealing with students' anger and potential aggression.

A cognitive behavioural approach described earlier can be effective in helping students monitor and control their own anger—although the students must genuinely want to change their own behaviour if the approach is to work. Often aggression has proved in the past to be a useful response for a student, helping him or her establish a 'tough persona' that he or she may be reluctant to lose. It is worth noting that students with a history of aggressive responses are often not particularly proficient in using language to argue their point of view, and sometimes the aggressive behaviour is used to compensate for their inability to win an argument or convey their feelings (Chow & Wehby, 2019). Intervention for these students may need to focus on improving communication competencies as well as modifying overt behaviours.

What really needs to be taught is how to resolve threatening situations by negotiation and compromise and not by aggression (Neale, 2019). In typical cognitive approaches participants explore the following issues:

- the nature of anger;
- when anger can be justified;
- when anger becomes a problem;
- things that trigger our anger;
- how to take control when we are becoming angry (anger management);
- how to use self-instruction to and control to choose alternative responses.

It is reported that less aggression is found in schools where a caring and supportive environment has been nurtured and where curricular demands are realistic. Schools where there is constant frustration and discouragement seem to breed disaffection and stimulate more aggressive and anti-social behaviour in students (Levin & Nolan 2014).

Bullying

Traditional forms of face-to-face school bullying, and more recently cyberbullying, are causing growing concern worldwide (Chan & Wong, 2019). According to Connell et al. (2019) an estimated 30 per cent of school children experience bullying by their classmates—but studies suggest that many more students are bullied but do not report it. Both boys and girls engage in bullying, and the number of girls involved appears to have risen. The lives of too many children are made miserable when they become victims of bullying. Known outcomes include absenteeism, psychosomatic illnesses, low self-esteem, a feeling of isolation, depression, and in extreme cases, suicidal tendencies (Landstedt & Persson, 2014). From the number of adults who report the severe impact that bullying at school had on them, it is clear that it has long-lasting effects.

Bullying may take several different forms—direct physical assault, verbal attacks, or indirect attacks such as spreading hurtful rumours verbally or online, or by excluding someone from a social group. In physical bullying, bullies pick their targets very selectively, and there are often characteristics of victims that make them targets for bullies. Victims are often students who appear to be vulnerable, weaker, shy, nervous, overweight, of different ethnic background, or a 'teacher's pet.' Unpopular children and those with behaviour disorders, or poor personal and social skills, students with a specific learning disability, and those with an intellectual disability or autism are more likely than others to be victimised (Griffin et al., 2019; Ronksley-Pavia et al., 2019a, 2019b).

Many bullying incidents tend to occur in the schoolyard, the bathrooms, and cloak-rooms, particularly if supervision is poor. Increased out-of-class supervision is one step that schools can take to reduce bullying. When bullying is carried out by gangs of students, factors come into play such as the importance of status within the group. Some individuals feel that they are demonstrating their power by repressing the victim. Even those who are not themselves bullies get carried along with the behaviour and do not object to it or report it. Few would ever intervene to help the victim.

School climate appears to be an influence on prevalence of bullying, with schools that have poor teacher-student relationships and a 'non-inviting' atmosphere exhibiting more cases (C. Wang et al., 2013). Within a school's behaviour management policy there should be due attention given to creating an ethos of consideration and respect for others and the right of every student to feel safe. There must also be agreed procedures for handling incidents of bullying and procedures for collaborating with parents, so that all approach the problem with similar strategies. School-wide procedures also need to be in place for providing support and counselling for victims of bullying, and methods for working to modify the behaviour and attitude of the bully (Gage et al., 2019).

Cyberbullying

Data from many countries suggest an alarming increase in cyberbullying in the form of derogatory comments, malicious gossip and lies posted on social network websites, instant messaging, emails, and by mobile phone (Nordahl et al., 2013). The use of cyberbullying is found not only in schools, but also in colleges and universities. Kyriacou and Zuin (2018, p. 99) have commented that 'cyberbullies are finding more opportunities to express their aggression towards others as social networks become technologically more sophisticated'. In the case of older adolescents, the bullying can also take the form of sending embarrassing photographs involving the victim. It is known that all forms of cyberbullying result in anxiety and depression for the victim (Hinduja & Patchin, 2019). Victims of extensive cyberbullying have been found to display poor mental well-being and are under constant emotional distress and can even contemplate suicide (Mark, Värnik & Sisask, 2019).

Unfortunately, as with other forms of bullying, children often do not report such bullying to their parents. In his advice to parents, Beane (2008) suggests that signs of cyberbullying to watch for include the child seeming to be constantly upset, anxious, or secretive, particularly after spending time on the computer or mobile phone, and spending more time than usual in online chat rooms. Beane's book also provides a number of helpful hints for parents and teachers on how to monitor a child's use of information and communication technology and how to deal with problems of cyberbullying.

Teachers should discuss with their classes what cyberbullying is and its effect on the person targeted. They need in particular to talk about the role that other students play in passing on rumours, lies, false accusations, and fake stories to others, thus contributing to the harm that is done. Students should be encouraged to avoid joining in online attacks on a victim and to report the matter to a teacher. It is suggested that issues of bullying and cyberbullying should become the focus of attention within the school curriculum—perhaps under the general heading 'human relationships'—and should certainly be part of a safe, socially-aware, and caring school environment (Bhat, 2018).

In 2014, the Department for Education in the UK produced a publication titled *Cyberbullying: Advice for headteachers and school staff*. This document stated that schools should develop policies and practices designed to combat bullying, including cyberbullying. The policy should also provide clear guidance to help protect every member of the school community, and to ensure that any sanctions are appropriate and consistently applied (DfE, 2014b). Advice for parents and caregivers was also issued at the same time. In 2018, the DfE published *Approaches to preventing and tackling bullying: Case studies*, available for download at: www.gov.uk/government/publications. In the USA, the Department of Health and Human Services has produced guidelines and information. These can be accessed online at: www.stopbullying.gov/prevention/index.html. In Australia, the *Bullying: No Way!* website for Australian schools is managed by the Safe and Supportive School Communities Working Group. Available online at: https://bullyingnoway.gov.au/PreventingBullying/InvolvingTheSchoolCommunity

Attention deficit hyperactivity disorder

Some students (estimated at between 5 per cent and 10 per cent) display problems maintaining attention to any learning task and are easily distracted. They may also exhibit impulsive behaviour and hyperactivity. These students are classified now as having *attention deficit hyperactivity disorder* (ADHD) and are frequently referred for psycho-educational assessment. A few of these students may also be diagnosed with *conduct disorders*—defined as a disregard for age-appropriate social norms and rules, lack of empathy and respect for others, and persistent violations of their rights (APA, 2013). ADHD can accompany certain other disabilities such as cerebral palsy, traumatic brain injury, autism, specific learning disability, and emotional disturbance. Even students who are identified as potentially gifted can exhibit distractibility and hyperactivity. Morrill (2018) rightly points out that accurate diagnosis of ADHD in children is difficult, because the symptoms of inattentiveness and hyperactivity can be exhibited at times by any child.

The fifth edition of *DSM* divides ADHD into two main categories: *inattention* (failure to listen or pay attention to details, distractibility, difficulty staying on task) and *hyperactivity and impulsivity* (excessive fidgeting, random movement, an inability to remain seated, excitability, and excessive talking) (APA, 2013). In many cases, both inattention and impulsivity are present. *DSM-5* has also placed increased emphasis on the fact that ADHD is not limited to the childhood years and may be diagnosed in some adults.

Most authorities now agree that the ADHD syndrome has multiple possible causes and no single factor has been identified. The following influences have all been put forward as possible explanations: genetic factor, central nervous system dysfunction, subtle forms of brain damage too slight to be confirmed by neurological testing, allergy to specific substances (e.g., food additives), adverse reactions to environmental stimuli (e.g., bright lights, noise), maternal alcohol consumption during pregnancy, and inappropriate management of the child at home. Some studies have found that there are gender differences in the age at which symptoms of ADHD begin, and the ways in which they change across the age range (Murray, Booth et al., 2019).

Students with ADHD, while not necessarily below average in intelligence, usually exhibit poor achievement in most school subjects. Weak concentration and restlessness associated with the syndrome have usually impaired the child's learning during the important early years of schooling. Many ADHD students also have problems developing social competence and peer relationships. Some seem to lack an understanding of the emotional reactions and feelings of others, resulting in many negative confrontations and other inappropriate social interactions.

Interventions for ADHD

It is not surprising to find that many different forms of treatment and intervention are advocated. Treatments have included diet control, medication, psychotherapy, behaviour modification and cognitive therapy. There have also been other 'alternative' treatments of doubtful value. Experience seems to show that what works for one child may not work for another. The most effective treatment seems to require a behaviour management plan, parent counselling, home management programme, and (possibly) medication. In the USA, almost 60 per cent of students with ADHD are taking medication such as Ritalin or Adderal to reduce their hyperactivity and to help them focus attention on schoolwork. In Britain and Australia, the use of medication as a first resort is a little less common, with the focus being more on behavioural interventions. The use of medication remains a controversial issue, and teachers often express doubts about the ethics of using drugs to control behaviour.

There is strong agreement among experts that children with ADHD need structure within the teaching used in the classroom. The programme must be effective in motivating and engaging the student and holding their interest and attention (Webb, 2019). Enhancing the learning of these children may also need to involve:

- providing strong visual input and hands-on activities to hold attention;
- using guided computer-assisted learning (CAL);
- teaching the students better self-management skills;
- giving the students specific roles, responsibilities, and duties in the classroom;
- monitoring them closely during lessons to find many opportunities to praise and reinforce them descriptively when they are on task and productive.

The following chapter explores how students with learning difficulties or disabilities may be helped to develop more effective social skills alongside better self-management, and thus gain greater acceptance in inclusive classrooms.

Online resources

- Classdojo website at: www.classdojo.com/.
- Zook, C. (2020). The 8 best classroom strategies for 2020. www.aeseducation.com/blog/wildly-successful-classroom-management-strategies.
- Association for Positive Behavior Support, Positive Behavioural Support Competence Framework. http://pbsacademy.org.uk/pbs-competence-framework/.
- A plan of action for developing a school-wide behaviour management system can be located at: http://behavioradvisor.com/SchoolWideSystem.html.
- A policy for behaviour and anti-bullying can be found at: www.marywebbschool.com/wp-content/uploads/2018/11/Behaviour-Anti-Bullying-Policy.pdf.

- Information concerning ADHD can be found on the Attention Deficit Disorder Association website at: www.understood.org/en/learning-attention-issues/child-learning-disabilities/add-adhd/adhd-fact-sheet.

Print resources

Anderson, M. (2019). *What we say and how we say it matter: Teacher talk that improves student learning and behavior.* Alexandria, VA: Association for Supervision and Curriculum Development.

Barkley, R.A (Ed.) (2018). *Attention-Deficit Hyperactivity Disorder: A handbook for diagnosis and treatment* (4th ed.). New York: Guilford Press.

Bates, B., Bailey, A., & Lever, D. (2019). *A quick guide to behaviour management.* London: Sage.

Plevin, R. (2019). *Take Control of the noisy class: Chaos to calm in 15 seconds (super-effective classroom management strategies for teachers in today's toughest classrooms).* Penrith, Cumbria: Life Raft Media.

Shotton, G., & Burton, S. (2018). *Emotional wellbeing: An introductory handbook for schools* (2nd ed.). London: Routledge.

Webb, E. (2019). *Teach for attention! A tool belt of strategies for engaging students with attention challenges.* Golden Valley, MN: Free Spirit Publishing.

Chapter 9

Social skills and peer group acceptance

In order to cope well in inclusive schools and be accepted into the peer group, students with learning difficulties or disabilities must possess adequate social skills for mixing and working with other students. Any student is at risk in school if he or she lacks age-appropriate social behaviour, and as a result is marginalised, rejected, bullied, or in some other way victimised by other students. It is for this reason that one of the most important goals for inclusive education is helping all students develop skills that enable them to engage in positive social interactions (Knopp, 2019).

It is evident that poor peer relationships during the school years can have a lasting detrimental impact on an individual's confidence and competence in later years. Problems gaining acceptance in a social group can be just as debilitating in school as constant academic failure. Students who leave school with significant deficits in social skills are at risk for negative interactions in the community, delinquency, unemployment, and mental health problems. On the other hand, individuals with adequate social skills are much less likely to engage in problem behaviour, are better at making friends, are able to resolve conflicts peacefully, and develop effective ways of dealing with persons in authority.

Research has found that the loneliness that can occur when individuals do not make lasting relationships often affects their personality development and quality of life during adolescence and into adulthood (Mund & Neyer, 2019). This is not to say that all persons who are not gregarious must therefore be lonely and unhappy—people differ greatly in their desire or need for constant company. This is as true of children of school age as it is of adults who are quite happy with their own company.

Children with learning difficulties or disabilities

Inclusive education settings create the potential opportunity for children with special needs to engage in many more social interactions with their peers–but their acceptance does not occur spontaneously (Broomhead, 2019; Schwab, 2019). Most studies of inclusion have shown that merely placing a child with a disability in the mainstream will not automatically lead to his or her social integration into the peer group. The reasons for lack of acceptance include:

- many children without disabilities do not readily initiate friendly contact with those who have a disability or choose them as a partner;
- children with disabilities do not automatically initiate friendly contact with other students, nor do they observe and copy positive social models that are around them;

- some teachers do not recognise the need to intervene to help promote students' positive social interactions (Sutherland et al., 2019).

Lack of social skill is often reported, particularly in children with emotional or behavioural disorders, autism, and ADHD, and these students are often marginalised in the peer group (Atkinson-Jones & Hewitt, 2019; Ducic et al., 2018; Grenier & Yeaton, 2019; Sullivan & Sadeh, 2014). These students clearly need targeted support to help them acquire the social skills necessary to maintain effective communication and interactions with others. One approach that seems to be promising for building self-esteem and social confidence is to engage these students in activities that require them to take responsibility for helping others, as for example in tutoring or acting as a leader for younger students (Watts et al., 2019).

Certain social skills need to be developed before children reach school age and are placed in regular classrooms. McCollow and Hoffman (2019) suggest that parents must therefore take a very active role in teaching preschool children essential behaviours they will need later to facilitate their social acceptance in school. Among the parent-implemented strategies they recommend are using social stories that depict various children interacting positively, helping others, sharing, and 'being a nice person'. It is also important to teach and practice specific pro-social skills such as friendly greeting, active listening, and following an adult's directions. These behaviours all represent important pivotal responses (see Chapter 3) that are effective in many situations and that facilitate further social development.

As well as possessing appropriate social skills, a socially competent student must also avoid displaying negative characteristics that impede easy acceptance by others—for example, a high level of irritating behaviour, impulsive reactions, aggression, temper tantrums, ignoring rules during play, and using abusive language. In many cases, these undesirable behaviours need to be eliminated or significantly reduced by behaviour modification and cognitive self-management (see Chapters 7 and 8).

Creating opportunities

A positive and supportive school environment is fundamental for the social development of all students, and provides the foundation that enables them to feel 'connected' to the school community (CDC, 2019). Students feel connected to their school when they perceive that adults and peers in the school care about them and value them as worthy individuals. Creating classroom environments where cooperation rather than competition is a dominant element is the first step in encouraging social development.

At least three conditions must be present in the classroom for positive social interaction and development of friendships among children with and without disabilities. These conditions are opportunity, continuity, and support.

- *Opportunity:* Children need to work and play in close proximity to other children frequently enough for meaningful contacts to be maintained. Inclusive classrooms provide proximity and frequency of contact, and opportunities are increased when the teacher uses cooperative learning methods and groupwork as an adjunct to teacher-directed instruction. Students must be involved on a daily basis in group activities that encourage social cooperation and mutual support. These arrangements create the best chances for children with disabilities to interact positively with their peers and imitate social behaviour of others.

- *Continuity:* When children are placed together as a class unit over a reasonable period of time (school term, school year) there is continuity from day to day in getting to know and like one another.
- *Support:* Some children need more help than others to make good quality contact with members of the class in order to work and play with them. Teachers' observation of their own classes will reveal which children need this extra support—for example, noticing any children who appear to be without friends at recess and lunch breaks and who seem unable to relate closely with classmates during lessons.

Facilitating social interaction

The following strategies can be used to increase the chances of positive social interaction for students with disabilities.

- Use cooperative groupwork frequently and ensure that any student with a disability is appropriately paired with a supportive classmate. Each student needs to understand clearly his or her area of responsibility—for example, 'John, you can help Craig with his writing, then he can help you with the lettering for your title board.' More is said in the next section concerning the composition of groups.
- Sometimes, make increased use of non-academic tasks because a student with special needs can more easily contribute at his or her own level of competence (e.g., painting, table games, dressing-up, pretend play, model-making).
- Use the class activity called *Circle Time* (Bustamante et al., 2018) as an opportunity for children to discuss age-appropriate aspects of social behaviour, such as how to make friends, helping one another, working together, preventing bullying or teasing, building self-esteem, looking for strengths in other people, and showing interest in the ideas of others.
- Encourage other students to help any classmate with special needs—if that student welcomes such assistance. Often, young students are unaware of the ways in which they can help. The support they give should not be so great that it causes the student to become overly dependent and passive. The goal is not to do everything for the student, but rather help him or her become more confident and competent. Using *Circle of Friends* as a peer-group support strategy can be beneficial (O'Connor, 2016). The system operates by involving a small group of classmates as a natural source of support to help a student with difficulties solve any problems that may arise during the school day.
- Establish after school-hours clubs and activities that students with special needs can also join. This also has the benefit of helping taught social skills to be extended beyond the classroom setting (Smith et al., 2018).

A difficulty that can arise with any attempt to improve social interaction is that some students actually resent obvious intervention by a teacher to 'fix them up' with a friend. This is particularly the case with adolescents who are ultra-sensitive to peer group opinion. The reality is that teachers cannot really 'force' friendships to be established between students with special needs and others; they can only establish the conditions under which this may occur spontaneously.

Groupwork

Working and playing in groups is one natural way that students of any age and ability can mix socially and acquire important social and communication skills (Forslund & Hammar-Chiriac, 2018). Careful planning is always required if groupwork is to achieve the desired educational and social outcomes. The success depends on the composition of the groups and the nature of the tasks set for the students.

When utilising groupwork as an inclusive strategy alongside teacher-directed instruction, it is important to consider the following basic principles.

- Groupwork must be used frequently enough for the students to become familiar with the skills and routines. Infrequent groupwork results in children taking too long to settle down and a lesson can become chaotic.
- The size of the group is important. Often children working in pairs (for example at the computer) is a good starting point. Select the pairs carefully to avoid incompatibilities. The teacher may need to intervene to help a particular child gain a partner or to enter into a larger group activity.
- Seating and work arrangements are important. Group members should be in close proximity but still have personal space to work on materials without getting in each other's way.
- It is not enough merely to establish groups and to set them to work. Group members may have to be taught how to work efficiently together. There is great value in discussing openly with a class the best ways of working as a team, and identifying the skills necessary to cooperate productively—listening to the views of others, following instructions, sharing, praising each other, and offering help. In the early stages, many groups can be helped to function efficiently if the teacher (or classroom assistant or a parent helper) works as one group member without dominating or controlling the activity. Helping each other and sharing materials are behaviours that must be modelled and reinforced.
- Choice of tasks for group work is extremely important. It is essential that all tasks have a very clear structure and purposes that are understood by all. When tasks are poorly defined or too complex the session can become chaotic. Tasks have to be selected that actually require students to work collaboratively. Initially there is merit in having all groups working on the same task or activity at the same time. This makes it much easier to prepare resources and manage time effectively. When several groups are undertaking quite different tasks it becomes a major challenge for the teacher to control the lesson.
- Teachers should monitor closely what is going on during group activities and must intervene when necessary to provide guidance, prompts, and suggestions, and to praise examples of good teamwork (van de Pol et al., 2019).
- When groups contain students with special needs, it is vital that the specific tasks to be undertaken by these students are clearly delineated. It can be useful to establish a system whereby the results are rewarded and praised for the way in which they have *worked together* positively and supportively. Under this structure, group members

have a vested interest in ensuring that all members participate and learn, because the group's success depends on the achievement of all.

New opportunities for students to work together in pairs or groups but without face-to-face contact have been created by information and communication technology. In what has become known as *technology-enhanced learning spaces* students can collaborate to study topics, without even being in the same classroom (Chang & Kang, 2016; Mendini & Peter, 2019). At the moment, this form of collaborative learning at distance has been adopted mainly in tertiary education—but it has relevance also for the senior school years, particularly for extending gifted students and for involving students with disabilities that prevent them from attending school or university. Through the medium of a website, apps, emails, and online chat rooms dedicated for a particular course of instruction, students can join discussions, ask and answer questions, work on a common activity, seek and share information, make suggestions, and assist one another with understanding a topic.

Social skills training

It is evident that early social skills training can be instrumental in reducing problems in later years. Social skills training involves explicit teaching of positive pro-social behaviours and social problem-solving skills to individuals who experience difficulties with social relationships (Mansour & Wiener, 2019). The aim of intervention is to strengthen existing skills and teach new behaviours that can be maintained and generalised to everyday situations. These skill training approaches are usually based on cognitive behavioural principles. Social skills training needs to be intensive and long-term in nature, and promote maintenance, generalisation and transfer of new skills into the individual's daily life.

The teaching of social skills involves setting out to establish the following behaviours. Each behaviour should be considered relative to its appropriateness for the particular child's age and specific needs in their current social environment. Typical skills and responses that may need to be taught include:

- making eye contact
- greeting others by name
- gaining attention in appropriate ways
- knowing when to talk, what to talk about and when to hold back
- initiating a conversation
- talking in a tone of voice that is acceptable
- maintaining conversations
- answering questions
- listening attentively to others and showing interest
- sharing with others
- saying 'please' and 'thank you'
- helping someone
- being able to collaborate in a group activity
- taking one's turn
- smiling
- accepting praise and giving praise

- accepting correction without anger or resentment
- making apologies when necessary
- coping with frustration and managing conflict.

The most meaningful settings in which to work on a child's skills are usually the classroom and schoolyard (Mathews et al., 2018). This is a good example of 'situated learning' in that it can result in more rapid and permanent learning and maintenance of new behaviours. To a large extent, functional social skills once established are likely to be maintained by natural consequences—that is, they are repeated as a result of more satisfying interactions with peers.

Many students with special needs and disabilities can make friends quite easily, if they have a pleasant personality and do not have irritating and disturbing behaviours; but others may have great difficulty due to lack of basic social skills. In some cases (e.g., students with autism spectrum disorders or those with emotional and behaviour disorders) it is necessary to provide additional intensive training beyond what is possible through normal everyday activities. This type of Tier 3 social skills intervention usually uses a combination of modelling, coaching, role playing, rehearsing, feedback, and counselling.

Intensive intervention for individual students in a clinical setting typically begins by showing the student the social skill to be taught. This may be done (according to the student's age and ability) by using video, pictures, or a simulation using puppets. Teacher and student together discuss how a particular skill or behaviour helps positive social interaction to occur. The teacher may say, 'Look at the two girls happily sharing the set of materials. Tell me what they might be saying to each other.' 'Here is a boy joining this class for the very first time. What would you say to him to make him feel welcome?' The student then role-plays that situation and receives informative and descriptive feedback from the teacher. 'Good try! But you've not quite got it yet. You need to look at him while you speak. Try it again. That's better! You looked and smiled. Well done.' Providing feedback to the student via video recording may be appropriate in some situations. It is then necessary to find authentic opportunities for the same skill to be applied in the classroom and other natural settings. Later in the week, the teacher watches for instances of the student applying the skill at other times in the day without prompting, and provides praise and reinforcement.

Training in social skills is usually not a matter of simply teaching a child something that is missing from his or her repertoire of behaviours but may also involve replacing an undesirable behaviour with a new alternative behaviour. This is often difficult, because a behaviour that society regards as undesirable may actually be regarded by the individual concerned as very rewarding—for example, winning an argument through aggression, or by taking possession of a coveted object by stealing. The negative behaviour has already proved to work well for the child, and it acts as a powerful force that militates against any new pro-social skills we attempt to teach. The residual influence of pre-existing behaviours is one reason why new skills taught during training are often difficult to maintain.

Finally, it seems clear that poor social acceptance is often an accompaniment to poor academic achievement in class. Unless achievement within the curriculum can also be improved, social adjustment and acceptance may remain problems for some students. With this in mind, attention in the chapters that follow is focused on evidence-based approaches for intervention in the area of literacy and numeracy.

Online resources

- Useful discussion on training social skills can be found at: www.minddisorders.com/Py-Z/Social-skills-training.html and https://www.verywellmind.com/social-skills-4157216.
- A list of children's books useful for teaching social skills can be located online at: www.pinterest.com/jillkuzma/books-i-love-for-teaching-social-skills/.
- Additional information on Circle of Friends can be obtained from: www.friendshipcircle.org/blog/2012/01/11/circle-of-friends-a-type-of-person-centered-planning/.
- For practical activities for classroom use see: www.thoughtco.com/classroom-activities-to-build-social-skills-3110718.
- A useful source of information on social skills is the Center on the Social and Emotional Foundations of Early Learning at: http://csefel.vanderbilt.edu/resources/strategies.html.
- 10 ways to teach social skills in your classroom: www.theinclusiveclass.com/2015/08/10-ways-to-teach-social-skills-in-your.html.

Print resources

Daniels, N. (2019). *Social skills activities for kids: 50 fun exercises for making friends, talking and listening, and understanding social rules.* Emeryville, CA: Rockridge Press.

Dundon, R. (2019). *Teaching social skills to children with autism using Minecraft®: A step by step guide.* London: Jessica Kingsley.

Fair, G., & Florell, D. (2019). Bullying, bystanders, and books. *Middle School Journal*, 50(1), 12–23.

Gueldner, B., Feuerborn, L.L., & Merrell, K.W. (2020). *Social and emotional learning in the classrooms* (2nd ed.). New York: Guilford Press.

Snowdon, S. (2018). *Anger management workbook for kids: 50 fun activities to help children stay calm and make better choices when they feel mad.* Emeryville, CA: Althea Press.

Talaee, E, (2019). Longitudinal impacts of home computer use in early years on children's social and behavioral development. *International Electronic Journal of Elementary Education*, 11(3), 233–245.

Whiren, A.P., Rupiper, M., Kostelnik, M., & Soderman, A.K. (2017). *Guiding children's social development and learning: Theory and skills* (9th ed.) Boston, MA: Wadsworth-Cengage.

Chapter 10

Intervention for reading difficulties

Learning to read is one of the most important skills that students with learning difficulties need to accomplish. Students who find reading difficult fall quickly behind their age peers in most areas of the curriculum; and failure to master reading then undermines their confidence and motivation. This situation leads eventually to disengagement from learning and a growing belief that reading is simply too difficult and to be avoided. Early identification and intervention are absolutely essential for at-risk children, so that they are helped to make better progress before detrimental feelings of anxiety and helplessness set in (Ramirez et al., 2019). For several decades in the US, Australia, and the UK, weakness in reading has remained the principal reason for the high number of referrals for additional support in schools.

Research studies over several decades have confirmed that an effective Tier 1 literacy programme for beginners must incorporate explicit instruction in listening for sounds in words (phoneme awareness), phonic decoding, recognising common words by sight, and building a rich vocabulary through listening to stories read aloud, and reading to gain information (Lombardi & Behrman, 2016; Willson & Falcon, 2018). As students move from the beginning stages of reading, decoding and sight vocabulary building will become less a focus of attention, and the higher-order processes involved in comprehending text become very important. Reading programmes must also incorporate many activities to encourage aural and oral language development and vocabulary growth. Enrichment activities should encourage careful listening, establish familiarity with language patterns, and introduce books that foster children's interest and enjoyment in reading.

The teaching method supported most by research involves instructing all beginners in letter knowledge and decoding skills, using what is known as *systematic synthetic phonics*. This method provides beginners and older students with learning difficulties with a system for identifying any unfamiliar words they encounter—proving to them that learning to read does not involve trying to store every single word image as a separate memory (Baker et al., 2018). Children cannot really become independent readers unless they master the alphabetic code, and can use it to decode new words.

For many years, general reading instruction at Tier 1 in most primary schools tended to be fairly unstructured and based on a belief that children will learn to read simply by engaging with print every day and with a little guidance from an adult. Popular approaches within this 'whole-language method' include 'shared book experience' and 'guided reading'— but these tend to rely too much on children acquiring decoding skills simply from immersion in stories. It is now recognised that most children make much better progress if early reading skills such as phonic decoding (sounding and blending) are explicitly taught and practiced.

Reading intervention at Tier 2

The research evidence supports the effectiveness of early intervention at Tier 2 for reducing the need for more intensive support (Morrison et al., 2020). Under the Response to Intervention model described in Chapter 1, students who struggle with Tier 1 reading instruction during the first year of school are soon given additional teaching in groups of up to five students. These groups are often referred to as 'booster classes'. Studies suggest that the most effective programmes at Tier 2 usually employ direct teaching methods. These methods utilise targeted activities to build phonemic awareness, establish sound–letter relationships, introduce word families, and provide daily reading practice with appropriate texts to increase fluency and comprehension (Austin et al., 2017; Marchand-Martella et al., 2015). In the UK, a report by Ofsted (2017) recommended that systematic synthetic phonics should play the critical role in teaching young children to read; and Duke and Mesmer (2019, p.12) suggest that 'the need to explicitly teach letter-sound relationships is settled science'. To this end, the Department of Education in the UK introduced a *Phonics Screening Check* for students at the end of their first year in school to identify any who required additional teaching at Tier 2 (DfE, 2012). A similar assessment has been introduced for students in Year 1 in some Australian states.

At Tier 2, a student's progress is closely monitored, and when any individual begins to read at the standard expected for his or her age, the additional support is phased out. Those who do not respond well even at Tier 2 are quickly provided with Tier 3 individual intensive instruction, as described later. These students require ongoing support if they are to make adequate progress. Intervention at Tier 2 (small groups) and Tier 3 (individual) must involve not only direct teaching of reading skills, but must also address the emotional reactions to failure that may have developed in the past. Activities must be conducted in therapeutic ways that put students at ease and build their confidence to make a new effort.

Effective Tier 2 instruction is based on the following principles.

- Daily instruction is provided for approximately 30 minutes in small groups where children are given additional teaching and reading practice to develop decoding skills, word recognition, comprehension, and fluency. This may be provided within the normal classroom or in a withdrawal room.
- Sessions should aim to motivate and interest the children because they need to perceive genuine reasons for engaging in reading and writing activities (Bates et al., 2016).
- Texts used with struggling readers must be carefully selected to ensure a high success rate —graded books with repetitive and predictable vocabulary and sentence patterns can be helpful in the early stages (Groff, 2015).
- Intervention may need to focus also on correction of any negative traits the students may display that impair their progress, such as disruptive behaviour, poor attention to task, or task avoidance (Garwood et al., 2017).
- Maximum progress occurs when parents or caregivers can provide additional support and practice outside school hours (Gerzel-Short, 2018; Kupzyk & Daly, 2017). For this reason, children should be provided with appropriate books they can read at home.

Withdrawing students for tuition in small groups can achieve a great deal, but it is also essential that the regular classroom literacy programme be adjusted (that is, *differentiated*) in terms of reading materials, skills instruction and assignments, to allow weaker readers a greater measure of success in that setting. Failure to differentiate the regular class programme frequently results in loss of achievement gains when students no longer receive extra assistance.

While decoding ability and word recognition are clearly essential for reading, children must also be able to understand the information they are decoding in a text. Any early reading programme must not only contain explicit teaching of phonic skills but also instruction in age-appropriate comprehension activities. The effective teaching of reading comprehension must encourage critical thinking to evaluate ideas and propositions within a story or factual report (Snow, 2018).

Comprehension and study-skill strategies are best taught through dialogue between teacher and student, working together to extract meaning from a text. Dialogue allows students and teachers to share their thoughts about the topic of the text and to learn from the successful strategies used by others. They may be encouraged to challenge the accuracy of stated facts and may go back to re-read a passage, or seek help from others in interpreting certain details. These are strategies that need to be taught explicitly to all students, but are particularly important for those with reading difficulties (Wang & Li, 2019).

Dialogue between teacher and student also serves a diagnostic purpose by allowing a teacher to appraise the students' existing strategies used for comprehending and summarising texts. When working with students in upper primary and secondary schools (and even in college), an approach known as *reciprocal teaching* has proved to be extremely useful in facilitating dialogue and practising specific cognitive strategies (Gilbert, 2018; Rosenshine & Meister, 1994). Reciprocal teaching can be regarded as a Tier 1 approach to use with all students, but it can also be adapted for small group work at Tier 2. The approach has been described as a 'scaffolded discussion technique' to apply strategies that good readers use to understand text (Oczkus, 2018).

The explicit teaching of comprehension strategies can best be achieved through direct explanation, modelling by the teacher, and abundant guided practice. It is preferable to apply strategy training to authentic text (books, newspaper reports, magazine articles, and online documents) rather than to contrived exercises. The effect size from interventions that teach comprehension strategies has been reported to reach 0.97 (i.e., very effective) (Stevens et al., 2019).

Essential strategies that need to be developed and expanded at Tier 1 and Tier 2 include:

- gaining an overview of a topic by previewing text and illustrations before reading;
- generating questions about the material;
- reading the text carefully, and reading it again if necessary;
- locating the main idea in a paragraph;
- making notes of key points;
- in narrative texts, predicting what may happen;
- in expository text, looking for facts and linking them; noting any new terms; relating them to prior knowledge and experience; looking for possible causes-and-effects;
- rehearsing, summarising, or paraphrasing the content.

Comprehension is naturally an across-the-curriculum competency, and all subject teachers in secondary schools should integrate 'reading for meaning' into their own subjects. Deriving meaning from different forms of text–narrative, expository, and informational–helps students acquire a broader range of cognitive strategies. Different forms and genres of text will require the teaching of specific strategies for processing the types of information and styles of language used—for example, in a science textbook vs. a history book or novel (Catts & Kamhi, 2017; Magnusson et al., 2019).

Using tutors

Skilled and experienced tutors for literacy can significantly raise students' achievement levels and confidence; and the evidence suggests that efficient tutoring yields good effects (Lindo et al., 2018). However, often through lack of resources, some schools are tending to use unqualified parent-volunteers and classroom aides who have not been specifically trained as tutors for Tier 2 or Tier 3 interventions. In this situation, the volunteer tutor must always work under the direction of the teacher and implement activities that have been selected to meet the child's diagnosed learning needs.

All tutors need to be knowledgeable about explicit teaching of decoding skills, and how to encourage reading fluency. Above all, tutors need to appreciate the vital contribution that active engagement, time-on-task, and successful practice play in facilitating students' improvement. It is also essential that tutors are aware of how to function most effectively in their role of tutor-supporter. For example, they need to know how to break a learning task down into manageable steps, how to give descriptive praise and encouragement, and how to provide corrective feedback in a positive way. A tutor must always be supportive rather than critical and didactic. Often well-meaning tutors talk too much; they need to talk less but listen more to their students. In an ideal situation, tutors should receive constructive feedback from the teacher on their tutoring skills and their tutor–student relationship (Arendale, 2018; Waltz, 2019).

There are several useful strategies that can be taught to tutors, some of which can be applied at both Tier 2 and Tier 3. One such strategy is known as 'Pause, Prompt, Praise' (PPP). When a student encounters an unfamiliar word, instead of the tutor stepping in immediately and supplying the word, he or she waits for about 5 seconds to allow time for the student to recognise or decode the word. If the student is not successful, the tutor provides a prompt, perhaps suggesting that the child sound out the letters, or think of the meaning of the passage. When the word is identified, the student is praised very briefly ('Good. You got it.'). If the student cannot read the word even after prompting, the tutor quickly supplies it, and the student re-reads the sentence.

It is important to point out that PPP can be used to good effect across a wide range of other situations where individuals are learning a new skill or behaviour. It has been used for many years in training children and adults with intellectual disability or a physical impairment when performing a new skill such as counting money or sorting shapes, as a step towards encouraging independent functioning (Da Fonte & Capizzi, 2015).

Another closely-related teaching strategy that should be used by all tutors is *constant time delay* (CTD) (Bradley & Noell, 2018). This strategy is similar to the 'pause' step in PPP described above, and is useful for teaching and consolidating basic sight vocabulary, letter or numeral recognition, learning number facts, and naming shapes. An example of time delay is when a tutor displays a word and asks the child 'Please say this word', then waits for up to 5 seconds to allow the child to think and respond. Similarly, the card might display 9–2 =. 'Please tell me the answer'. If the response is correct, the teaching sequence moves on. If incorrect, the teacher provides the correct answer, and asks the question again. The child then responds with the correct answer.

Selecting text materials for Tier 2

The use of graded readers with decodable text has been found highly appropriate in reading interventions (Clarke, 2016; Groff, 2015), and also useful when working with slightly older students learning English as a second language. During the 1980s and 1990s, books for beginners that contained a high proportion of decodable words were utterly shunned by whole-language practitioners. It was felt that the books presented unnatural language–for example, 'A dog and a frog sit on a log.' Times have changed and many publishers have returned to producing vocabulary-controlled books and programmes that help beginners build confidence and automaticity in applying decoding successfully. With this confidence, they soon become ready to read books that are not controlled for vocabulary.

Specific interventions for older students at Tier 2

Fresh Start (FS) is a Tier 2 literacy intervention for at-risk students entering secondary school with poor reading and writing skills. Students are grouped for instruction according to their level of reading ability, and they receive a very systematic and rigorous teaching of phonics, usually 3 times per week for 33 weeks. A large-scale evaluation of the programme concluded that: '*Fresh Start* shows considerable promise as an effective catch-up intervention for low-attaining readers at the transition phase from primary to secondary school' (Gorard et al., 2015, p.4).

Rapid Phonics is a synthetic phonics intervention to improve decoding skills and reading fluency in students in Grades 6 and 7. It is implemented for one-and-a-half hours of tuition per week for groups of four students. Useful classroom and home resources include *Bug Club Phonics* materials from Pearson, and *Phonics Flashcards* from Oxford University Press.

Specific programmes for intervention at Tier 3

Students with the most severe reading difficulties need to receive intensive individualised teaching on a daily basis, usually outside of the whole class setting (Bayless et al., 2018). An individualised approach enables the pace of instruction to be regulated carefully and specific techniques such as multisensory and multimedia support can be used to help a student remember letter-to-sound correspondences and sight words. One of the key benefits of Tier 3 teaching is that it greatly increases the opportunities for the student to respond during instruction and to receive feedback. Research has found that more opportunity to respond (OTR) in individual tutoring is associated with positive improvements in word identification and reading fluency (Austin et al., 2017; Martin et al., 2018; Sanchez & O'Connor, 2015).

It is, of course, possible for teachers to devise appropriate individual tutoring programmes for students with learning difficulties, after their strengths and weaknesses have been identified, However, in recent years, several structured intervention programmes have emerged. These programmes include *Reading Recovery*®, *Success for All, QuickSmart, MULTILIT* and *Reading Rescue*.

Reading Recovery®

Reading Recovery® is an early intervention programme first developed in New Zealand in the 1970s by the late Marie Clay. It is now used in many other parts of the world, including America, Canada, Australia, and England. RR is regarded as a Tier 3 intervention as it involves intensive individual tutoring, but a few schools have adopted aspects of the model for small group teaching at Tier 2. *Every Child a Reader Project* (2005–2008) in the UK utilised *Reading Recovery*® as the main intervention. Children identified as having reading difficulties after one year in school are placed in the programme to receive individual daily tuition from a teacher specifically trained in the approach. The children receive this individual support for approximately 15 to 20 weeks.

In a *Reading Recovery*® lesson optimum use is made of the available time and students are kept fully on-task. A typical session includes seven activities:

- a quick revisiting of a familiar book;
- re-reading of a book introduced the previous day;
- letter-identification activities and simple spelling using plastic letters;
- writing of a dictated or prepared short story;
- sentence building and reconstruction from the story;
- introduction of a new book;
- guided reading of the new book.

The texts selected for use in RR are graded according to the child's reading ability to ensure a high success rate. Frequent re-reading of familiar stories boosts confidence and fluency. Teachers keep detailed records of children's oral reading errors and use these to target the knowledge and strategies a child still needs to learn. The intention is that the teacher or tutor operating the RR session will provide scaffolded guidance that helps a young reader move forward in his or her zone of proximal development (Lewis, 2018).

Reading Recovery®, when correctly implemented, can be effective in raising young children's reading achievement and confidence (Institute of Education Sciences, 2013). It is claimed that at least 80 per cent of children who undergo the full series of lessons can then read at the class average level or better. A meta-analysis of data from evaluation studies has yielded an overall effect size of 0.59 (D'Agostino & Harmey, 2016).

However, children's responses to *Reading Recovery*® vary, and there are indications that the approach fails to meet the needs of children with the most severe reading problem (Serry et al., 2014). It is possible that these children have a learning disability (dyslexia) or some other disorder that causes a major problem that is very resistant to remediation. It must be noted that data from the Ministry of Education in New Zealand indicate that 9 per cent of children in RR do not make adequate progress and have to be referred for longer specialist support (Tunmer et al., 2013). Observers also question the sustainability of the success rate of those who complete all sessions, suggesting that gains made during the programme are not always maintained when the child returns to regular class (Paige, 2018). This is possibly because the reading materials provided in the regular setting are not so carefully matched to the child's ability level. More follow-up research is required (Holliman et al., 2016).

Reading Recovery® is therefore not without its critics (e.g. Cook et al., 2017; Tunmer et al., 2013). For example, it is felt that far too little attention is devoted to explicit instruction in phonics and decoding for children with major weaknesses in this area. In part, this is due to the fact that *Reading Recovery*® was created during the era when whole-language approach held sway and phonics teaching was regarded as having only a minor role in reading proficiency (Serry et al., 2014).

Other difficulties associated with *Reading Recovery*® include the need to organise time in the school day for some children to be taught individually; and the need to provide appropriately trained personnel to give the daily tuition. The high cost of such a labor-intensive one-to-one intervention remains an unresolved issue (Cook et al., 2017).

For additional information visit: http://readingrecoveryworks.org/rti/

Success for All

Success for All is an approach that has much to offer at all three tiers of the RtI model. It is a comprehensive whole-school programme intended to improve literacy teaching and prevent reading failure. The reading and language lessons operate daily for 90 minutes, providing primary students with intensive instruction and practice. One unique feature of *Success for All* is that junior classes throughout the school usually group for reading at the same time, with children going to different classrooms based on their current ability level.

The intervention aspect at Tier 3 involves intensive one-to-one teaching, using teachers or specially trained paraprofessionals to help improve the learning rate for at-risk and socially disadvantaged children. Emphasis is placed on direct phonics instruction (segmenting words, and sounding and blending phonemes). Equal importance is also placed on students reading meaningful texts and self-monitor for comprehension. In an attempt to avoid the common lack of transfer of taught skills back to the student's regular classroom, *Success for All* teachers also participate in the mainstream reading programme and assists with reading lessons in the regular classroom. This helps ensure that one-to-one tutoring is closely linked to the mainstream curriculum, not divorced from it.

Success for All was designed in the US by Robert Slavin and his associates (Slavin et al., 2009; Slavin & Madden, 2012). The programme spans school years from Kindergarten to Grade 8, and also provides training and follow-up support for teachers and tutors. The programme is widely used in the US, where the *Common Core State Standards* are now incorporated into the approach (Slavin & Madden, 2013), and it has also been adopted for use in several other countries where positive results are reported (Tracey et al., 2014). Research evidence in general has supported *Success for All* as an effective intervention model (IES, 2009; Miller et al., 2017). The *Best Evidence Encyclopedia* states that: 'Success for All has strong evidence of effectiveness for struggling readers. Across nine qualifying studies, the weighted mean effect size was +0.55' (0.55 represents a significantly positive effect).

The *What works clearinghouse* 2017 report on *Success for All* can be viewed online at: https://files.eric.ed.gov/fulltext/ED573328.pdf

QuickSmart

QuickSmart is Tier 3 intervention implemented in Australia (Graham et al., 2007). It targets middle-years students (age 10 to 13 years) who exhibit ongoing difficulty acquiring functional literacy and numeracy. The reading component focuses on improving students' automaticity in common word recognition, and on increasing fluency in reading connected text. Teaching focuses on mastery of sets of words, beginning with high-usage three-and-four letter words, and moving later to more complex and demanding words. In addition to practising the words in isolation, they are also incorporated in two or more passages of connected text on various topics. Typical activities used in the sessions include:

- flashcards;
- vocabulary building;
- repeated readings of a target text to improve fluency;
- comprehension;
- reading games;
- regular testing for mastery.

The lesson format for *QuickSmart* is designed to ensure maximum engagement in learning and a high success rate for students during each 30-minute session. Students are taught in pairs and the programme is normally implemented three times a week for 30 weeks. The guiding principle is that building fluency and confidence in the most basic reading skills enables students to devote much more cognitive effort to the higher-order processes involved in reading for meaning.

QuickSmart learning and teaching strategies are drawn from research evidence identifying effective methods for students with learning difficulties. These include explicit instruction, modelling, discussion, questioning, feedback, scaffolding, guided and independent practice, and frequent reviews. Each lesson involves brief revision of work covered in the previous session, a number of guided practice activities, independent practice, practice of memory and retrieval strategies, and games and worksheet activities—some of which are timed. Strategy instruction and concept development are seen as key components of each lesson.

The professional development component of *QuickSmart* focuses on training teachers and tutors to provide effective instruction to maximise students' engagement in learning activities during the available time, embodies abundant guided and independent practice to develop fluency and confidence, and gives positive feedback for success. The total programme is extremely comprehensive and includes preparation sessions for school principals, teachers, and instructors, professional follow-up, resource materials for teachers and students, a computer-based assessment and monitoring component, and the use of data from formal standardised measures of attainment for objective evaluation of students' progress. The programme has undergone regular evaluation and revision. Results from several studies indicate that *QuickSmart* students are able to narrow the gap between their performance and that of their higher-achieving peers (NCSiMERRA, 2009).

Details of *QuickSmart* literacy and numeracy intervention can be found online at: https://simerr.une.edu.au/quicksmart/pages/qsreading-intervention.php

MULTILIT

The name *MULTILIT* stands for 'Making up Lost Time in Literacy'. This comprehensive Tier 2/Tier 3 approach to teaching low-progress readers (aged 7 or above) addresses five key areas necessary for effective reading instruction—namely, phonemic awareness, phonic decoding, fluency, vocabulary and comprehension. It has three strands covering *word attack* (phonics), *sight words*, and *reinforced reading* (reading of meaningful text).

The teaching approach within *MULTILIT* draws on evidence from research into the most powerful strategies to help readers who are significantly behind their peers. The student is given a placement test at the beginning of intervention to ensure that he or she is placed at the correct level within the programme. It is claimed that a child undertaking *MULTILIT* can make 15 months' progress in word recognition in two terms of instruction.

The programme is tutor or teacher-led and should be delivered at least three to four times a week. The tutor and student work through each of several levels of instruction for tackling unfamiliar words, progressing to the next level once the student has mastered the current level. Sight vocabulary is targeted at the same time, with particular reference to a list of 200 key words. Rapid automatic recognition of sight words helps to develop reading fluency. The other component in the programme is termed 'reinforced reading'. During this part of each session the student is able to transfer and generalise knowledge and skills by reading books chosen carefully to be at an instructional level.

As well as providing programme and materials development, *MULTILIT* also incorporates a strong component of professional training for teachers and tutors. The designers conduct ongoing research into the overall effectiveness of the approach (e.g., Buckingham et al., 2012; Wheldall et al., 2017). Lim et al. (2018) conducted an interesting small-scale study in which children with Down Syndrome undertook selected components from *MultiLit Reading Tutor Program* and applied these skills in a shared-book situation. The researchers reported that following the intervention a significant improvement was seen in reading fluency, together with a reduced error rate during shared-book reading.

The designers of *MULTILIT* suggest that *Reading Recovery*® fails to provide the least able students with sufficient explicit training in phonemic awareness and decoding. To address this need they have also devised *MINILIT* (Meeting Individual Needs in Literacy) (Reynolds et al., 2007; Wheldall et al., 2017). This involves a 15-week tutoring programme with groups of three to six students working for one hour daily with a tutor. Each session involves time spent on phonemic awareness, sight vocabulary, word-attack skills, text reading and story time. The intervention paves the way for smooth entry into the classroom reading programme, or into *MULTILIT* for those still needing support.

Full details of MULTILIT can be found online at: http://multilit.com/ and updates on research at: https://multilit.com/research/whats-new-at-mru/

Reading Rescue™

Reading Rescue™ is a one-on-one, 30-minute literacy intervention delivered daily for elementary school students in Grades 1, 2 and 3. It also has a strong professional development component for teachers, mainly providing training in teaching phonics, vocabulary, and writing skills. The programme was developed by the University of Florida and the Literacy Trust (US) and was adopted for use in New York City public schools. In the years 2017–2018 almost 1050 students received this form of assistance. *Best*

Evidence Encyclopedia considers the approach to be as effective as Reading Recovery® and for additional data on effectiveness for the period 2015 to 2017 see: www.readingrescue.org/results

Details of Reading Rescue™ can be found online at: www.readingrescue.org/about

Supplementary tutoring strategies and activities

Repeated Reading

Repeated Reading is a well-known procedure used to increase fluency, accuracy, expression and confidence in students who are already under way with reading. The procedure is equally useful in primary and secondary schools, and has a place in adult literacy interventions. Evaluations indicate that not only does Repeated Reading increase fluency but also has a very positive effect on reading comprehension (Hammerschmidt-Snidarich et al., 2019; Zimmerman et al., 2019). The approach has been found effective with students learning English as a second or additional language, secondary school students with poor reading ability, and with various groups of students with emotional and behavioural disorders (McKenna & Bettini, 2018; Shimono, 2019; Southward, 2018).

Repeated Reading simply requires readers to practise reading a short passage aloud until their accuracy rate is above 95 per cent and the material can be read aloud fluently. The teacher first models the reading while the student follows in the text and then spends a few minutes making sure that the student fully understands the material. The student then practises reading the same material aloud, with corrective feedback from the teacher if necessary. The student continues to practise until nearly perfect, and finally records the reading on audiotape. When the recording is played back, the student hears a fluent performance, equal in standard to the reading of even the most competent student in class. This provides an important boost to the student's confidence. Greater fluency also leads to improved comprehension because the reader is expending less mental effort on identifying each word.

Multisensory approaches

For students with severe learning difficulties who cannot easily remember letters or words, it is helpful to use methods that engage them most actively with material to be studied and remembered. The multisensory approach has a long history in special and remedial education, dating back to the work of Orton (1937) and later to Gillingham and Stillman (1956).

The abbreviation VAKT is often used to indicate that multisensory methods combine visual, auditory, kinaesthetic, and tactile modalities to support learning and memory. The typical VAKT approach for beginners or for those with a cognitive disability involves the learner in finger-tracing over a word, or drawing it in the air, while at the same time saying the word, hearing the word and seeing the visual stimulus. For older learners, writing a word or using a keyboard and typing a target word while watching it appear on the screen is also a multisensory activity.

The best-known multisensory method is the Fernald VAK Approach, which involves the following steps:

- student selects a particular word that he or she wants to learn
- teacher or tutor writes the word in blackboard-size cursive writing on a card and together the pronounce the word
- student finger-traces over the word, saying each syllable as it is traced
- this process is repeated until the learner feels capable of writing the word from memory
- when a word is mastered it is filed away in a card index box for later revision.

It can be argued that multisensory approaches using several channels of input may help a learner integrate, at a neurological level, what is seen with what is heard, whether it be a letter or a word. On the other hand, VAKT approaches may succeed where other methods have failed because they cause the learner to *focus attention* more intently on the learning task. Whatever the reason for its effectiveness, this teaching approach involving vision, hearing, articulation, and movement usually does result in improved assimilation and retention.

Evaluation studies of multisensory approaches to phonics and word recognition have indicated definite value for reading and spelling (e.g., Hughes, 2014; John, 2017). Hughes for example, concluded that 'The Orton-Gillingham method is a powerful language intervention for children and adults with delayed or non-existent reading skills due to language-based processing disorders or disabilities such as dyslexia' (p.7). Other reviews in settings from general education classrooms to clinical programmes suggest that the approach does result in improvement in word reading, decoding, and spelling.

For more information on multisensory teaching and learning visit: www.understood. org/en/school-learning/partnering-with-childs-school/instructional-strategies/multisensory-instruction-what-you-need-to-know

Games and apparatus

In the early stages of any intervention it is helpful to incorporate materials that hold a student's attention most effectively and provide additional opportunities for practising important skills. Games and word-building equipment such as plastic letters, magnet boards, and flashcards can be used as adjuncts to any literacy intervention. Games provide an excellent opportunity for learners to practise essential material that might otherwise be perceived as boring and dull. For example, games provide an enjoyable way of discovering and reinforcing letter-sound relationships and word recognition.

A game should always contribute to the objectives for the lesson—for example, by developing listening skills, strengthening phoneme awareness, reinforcing letter knowledge, and building vocabulary—rather than simply providing a distraction from 'real' learning. The use of games may also be seen as non-threatening, and thus serve a therapeutic purpose within a group or individual teaching situation.

Increasingly, digital technology has entered the literacy learning domain through motivating games and apps that help students learn and apply essential decoding, spelling and reading skills (Ronimus et al., 2019; Samur, 2019). Hand-held communication devices and e-learning apps have added considerably to the non-print media that can be incorporated into a literacy programme. The additional practice afforded by digital games is absolutely essential for children who learn at a slower rate or who are poorly motivated.

Examples of literacy games apps can be found at: www.ictgames.com/literacy.html

Digital technology and reading

Advances in information and communication technology have created many new and interesting ways for students with learning difficulties to engage in literacy activities for authentic purposes–for example, through sending and receiving emails, texting, surfing the Internet, using e-readers, accessing interactive reading websites, social networking, and creating blogs. Evidence supports the value of digital technology as a contemporary medium for language and literacy development (e.g., Hutchison & Woodward, 2014; Loh & Sun, 2019; Ozturk & Ohi, 2018; Wright et al., 2013). A common finding is that using digital technology can be a very valuable approach for enhancing reading skills, with improvements in achievement, engagement rates, and attitude.

In the UK, Vincent (2020) has reported on the value of using computer-assisted reading intervention (CARI) with primary school children, and Bippert (2019) has stated that secondary schools are turning increasingly to computer-assisted reading in an effort to provide more motivating and effective interventions for struggling adolescent readers. Whether used by one student alone, or by two students working together, the computer is an excellent tool for utilising and extending literacy skills in the classroom and beyond. A study by Walcott et al. (2014) found that computer-based reading activities can increase the on-task engagement of students with learning difficulties and also produce significant gains in reading skills. Programmes can focus on reading for meaning and vocabulary, but can also focus on spelling and word study for students requiring more assistance in these areas. Computers are infinitely patient, allow for self-pacing by the student, provide immediate feedback, and can be a means of differentiating and individualising a remedial programme.

The main strength of computer-based programmes is that they make use of well-established principles of effective instruction—clear presentation, easy steps, active student participation, scaffolding, corrective feedback, practice to mastery level, and a high success rate. Programmes often have an in-built monitoring system that can show at a glance a student's progress and error rate.

In the home situation, a computer can also aid literacy development because children can work alone or with parent support on early reading and writing skills. Parents who are adequately computer literate can help their children search for, read, and interpret information from the Internet for homework or personal interest.

The following chapter expands the discussion of literacy by considering methods for assisting the development of writing skills.

Online resources

- A useful summary of intervention methods and resources is available on the National Literacy Trust website: https://literacytrust.org.uk/resources/.
- The Dyslexia/SPELD Trust website: www.interventionsforliteracy.org.uk/.
- TES [UK]. (2018). Literacy intervention handbook: The how and what of literacy intervention. Details available at: www.tes.com/teaching-resource/literacy-intervention-handbook-sample-the-how-and-what-of-literacy-intervention-11663192.

Print resources

DeVries, B.A. (2019). *Literacy assessment and intervention for classroom teachers* (5th ed.). London & New York: Routledge.

Erickson, K.A., & Koppenhaver, D.A. (2020). *Comprehensive literacy for all: Teaching students with significant disabilities to read and write.* Baltimore, MD: Brookes.

Gipe, J.P., & Richards, J. (2019). *Multiple paths to literacy: Assessment and differentiated instruction for diverse learners, K-12* (9th ed). New York: Pearson.

Riley-Tillman, T., Burns, M.K., & Kilgus, S.P. (2020). *Evaluating educational interventions: Single-case design for measuring response to intervention* (2nd ed.). New York: Guilford Press.

Stahl, K.A.D., Flanigan, K., & McKenna, M.C. (2020). *Assessment for reading instruction* (4th ed.). New York: Guilford Press.

Chapter 11

Problems with writing

Achieving proficiency in writing is important for communication in all subjects within the curriculum. Traditionally, schools have recognised the need to encourage students to become efficient writers and daily activities are devoted to writing. However, recent studies have revealed that in many classrooms, the essential sub-skills required for composing, writing, and editing are not explicitly taught. Instead, teachers simply set writing assignments for their students and then correct the products later. These teachers often do assign stimulating and creative topics for students, but they do not actually teach students how to engage most effectively in the writing process. Their belief seems to be that students will become good writers if they simply engage in authentic writing every day and receive encouraging feedback.

During their initial professional training many of these teachers are not made sufficiently aware of the evidence-based practices that are known to build and improve students' writing skills (Brenner & McQuirk, 2019; Brindle et al., 2016; Hodges et al., 2019; Pelkey, 2018). Many teachers report that they lack expertise for helping the students who struggle most with the mechanical aspects of writing (handwriting, keyboarding, spelling, punctuation, and grammar) and who lack self-regulatory strategies for planning and organising their ideas for writing, composing grammatically correct sentences, proofreading, and then editing their work (Harrison & McManus, 2017). In this domain, Troia (2014, p.10) has written:

> Younger writers and those who struggle with writing will require greater explicitness, more practice, and enhanced scaffolding (e.g., repetitive modeling, graphic aids, checklists, incremental goals, expectations) than older writers and those who do not struggle with writing.

What do the processes of writing and composing involve?

Writing is one of the most complex skills that students must learn, and it is not surprising that some individuals have difficulty achieving proficiency. They may be able to read quite well, but reading and writing are separate processes and to some extent draw upon different areas of knowledge and skill and are controlled by different areas of the brain (James & Beringer, 2019). However, there is also overlap between reading and writing ability so that one skill set can support acquisition of the other. For example, automaticity in recognition of common words in reading is fairly closely linked with automaticity in writing those words easily and correctly; knowledge of phonics helps spelling as well as reading; vocabulary acquired from reading can be used to enrich one's writing; familiarity with grammar and sentence structure in books is one of the cueing systems that assists fluent reading, and is also an aid to writing.

The creation of written text involves two key areas of competence: (i) lower-order transcription skills such as handwriting or keyboarding, and spelling; and (ii) self-regulated planning for creating, sequencing, and expressing ideas through effectively composed sentences. The more automatic that lower-order skills become, the greater will be the cognitive capacity available to the writer for thinking, composing, and revising. Many of the problems that students with learning difficulties experience occur in the lower-order skills.

Since 2013, the revised National Curriculum in the UK has specified precisely the grammar and writing competencies that students at various ages are expected to achieve. These competencies then tend to become criteria for use within the mandated testing that accompanies the curriculum. A similar situation exists within the new Australian Curriculum and its national testing programme; and in the USA, the *Common Core State Standards* now specify what is expected in terms of writing competencies. These frameworks give teachers a clear idea of what most students should be achieving in writing each year, and this knowledge helps identify those who are having difficulties. It is important to recognise as early as possible any student who is experiencing problems so that additional instruction can be provided. A study of children in the UK found that at age 11 to 12 a high percentage of students could not meet the standard for speed of writing (25 words per minute) and at least 33 per cent could not meet the age-appropriate standard for spelling (Montgomery, 2008).

Learning difficulties that affect writing

The demands of written expression include generating ideas around a set topic, organising these ideas into a logical sequence, constructing effective sentences, using correct grammar and vocabulary, and writing in a style for a particular audience. These are extremely difficult competencies for some students to develop, because as well as needing the mechanical skills for writing they also draw heavily upon an individual's background experiences, general knowledge, depth of vocabulary, imagination, and sense of audience (Peterson, 2014). Students with learning difficulties often display the following weaknesses:

- poor ability to plan, execute and revise written work;
- a tendency to spend too little time thinking before beginning to write;
- difficulties formulating a goal for writing and generating relevant ideas;
- inability to decide upon an appropriate structure for writing on a given topic;
- slowness and inefficiency in executing the mechanical aspects of writing or typing;
- limited output in the available time.

A student who has problems writing will experience no satisfaction pursuing the task and will try to avoid writing whenever possible. Avoidance then reduces opportunities for practice, and lack of practice results in no improvement. The student has lost confidence and self-esteem in relation to writing and has developed a negative attitude accompanied by learned helplessness. The problem for the teacher is to motivate these students to want to write, and to provide them with enough support to ensure increased success. It is important to select approaches to teaching that can restore confidence and motivation, and make students feel more successful as writers. Fortunately, studies have clearly indicated that students with learning difficulties can be helped to improve in all areas of writing, and teaching approaches to achieve this improvement are discussed here (Datchuk & Kubina, 2013; Hansen & Wills, 2014; Peterson, 2014; Westwood, 2019).

Teaching approaches

Before considering the specific intervention approaches that can be used to assist struggling writers, it is relevant first to describe the two main approaches that should have been used at Tier 1. The traditional approach that has been used for many years is *skills-based,* with a focus on explicit teaching of sentence construction, grammar, paragraphing, punctuation, and spelling. In this skills-based approach, practice exercises are often used to help students master basic composition skills. The more recent approach is termed *process writing* (or *writing conference* approach) with a focus on generating ideas and experimenting freely with ways to express these ideas, first through rough drafts that are then revised and polished as a result of feedback and encouragement (Bayat, 2014; Hawkins, 2019; Williams, 2018). In the process approach, any teaching of grammar and style occurs informally, mainly through this feedback that students receive from teacher and peers, rather than from direct instruction and practice exercises.

In the 1980s and 1990s, as a feature of the prevailing whole-language approach, skills-based teaching fell completely out of favour in many schools. It was believed to be less motivating for students than allowing them to write about matters that they had chosen for themselves. There was also some doubt expressed that skills taught in traditional routine exercises ever transfer to students' free writing (Peterson & Portier, 2014). The accepted wisdom became that teachers must never teach isolated skills but instead should support students' efforts as they write freely for authentic purposes. More structured variants of the process approach (writing workshop, shared writing, and guided writing) are described later.

With the renewed attention now being given to improving students' standards in grammar and writing accuracy in Britain, Australia, and the US, some aspects of the skills-based explicit teaching approach are returning to classroom teaching.

General approaches at Tier 1

While whole-language approach at Tier 1 has been somewhat discredited as an adequate way to ensure that all students become literate, the various process approaches to writing still remain popular in many schools in the UK, USA, and Australia (Wyse, 2018). Evaluations have tended to yield effect sizes of around 0.32—which signifies some positive benefits but not a powerful effect (Graham & Perrin, 2007). No doubt, a process approach is a valuable method for advancing the skills of students who already possess the ability and aptitude for writing (Pacello, 2019), but there are many studies indicating that students with learning difficulties benefit more from a teacher-directed approach with adequate time devoted to practice and feedback (Clark & Neal, 2018; Graham et al., 2015; Harris et al., 2008; Liberty & Conderman, 2018; Nicholson & Dymock, 2018; Troia, 2014; Westwood, 2019). To be applicable for students who do not find writing easy, process approach really requires much more careful structuring and teacher direction. Three models of the process approach that can be more teacher-directed are *writers' workshop, shared writing,* and *guided writing.*

Writers' workshop

Writers' workshop is a Tier 1 whole-class approach where all students engage in writing activity at the same time with the support of classmates and teacher (Conroy et al., 2009). The underlying principle is 'writers working together', cooperating and providing feedback to one another. Group sharing and peer editing are essential elements in the sessions. Students in writing workshop are assisted through all stages of the writing process (prewriting, drafting, revising, and 'publishing') and their products can become part of the reading material available in the classroom. During the writing session the teacher confers with almost every student about his or her writing, providing advice, correction, and encouragement. This represents the necessary scaffolding whereby students gain increasing control over their own writing strategies. Differences in abilities among the students will determine the amount of time the teacher spends with each individual. The belief is that teachers' daily scaffolding in writers' workshop has a positive impact on students' writing skills, and over time promotes independence in writing (Brown, 2018).

Motivation during writing workshop comes mainly through the topics that children are offered. Choice of topic is usually (but not always) made by the writer rather than the teacher. At first, students begin work independently on their own writing, or they work in small groups with support available from the teacher. During this time, access to information technology, and word processing is usually appropriate (Kang, 2018; Thornton, 2013). Finally, children share their writings, and feedback and advice come from teacher and from peers.

The teaching of specific language skills during writing workshop takes place in three ways:

- individual students receive on-the-spot guidance and feedback during the session;
- a mini-lesson may be conducted occasionally for 5 to 10 minutes, covering for example a specific grammar or spelling rule, or use of adverbs and adjectives;
- principles of grammar, style, and spelling can also be a focus in whole-class discussion and feedback at the end of any session.

Shared writing

Shared writing emerges naturally within writing workshop or can be made part of any other lesson that involves students writing for an audience. Sharing your writing with others can be a valuable motivating force for students from early childhood onwards. By middle primary school, most children are capable of evaluating the quality of their own writing, but they still need guidance from teacher and peers on how best to revise and improve their work.

It is the responsibility of teachers to spend time modelling the critiquing process (giving positive and helpful advice as well as criticism) before expecting students to do this. They need to provide examples of giving descriptive praise, highlighting good points in a piece of writing, helping to shape new ideas, how to improve what is not clear, and how to polish the final product. *Peer critiquing* is often written about as if it is a simple strategy to employ in the classroom, but in reality, it needs to be done with great sensitivity because if implemented badly it may seem to draw public attention to certain students' weaknesses.

Guided writing and strategy training

Guided writing is a variant of the process approach, but involves much more direct input from the teacher, usually in the form of strategy training. The guided approach is thought to be more effective in fostering students' writing skills than unstructured use of the process method.

Guided writing is considered a useful approach from middle primary school years into secondary school (Calp, 2015; Gibson, 2008). The approach involves demonstrating specific writing strategies for different styles or genres, followed by guided practice and independent application by the students. A teacher might begin by demonstrating how to generate ideas for a given topic, how to create and structure an opening paragraph, and how to develop the remaining ideas in logical sequence. During strategy training, students are typically taught to use self-questioning and self-instruction to assist with the process of planning, evaluating, and improving a written assignment. Emphasis is placed on the metacognitive aspects of the writing process (self-monitoring, self-checking for clarity, self-correction). Students can also be given checklists to help them evaluate and revise their written work. For example, a checklist might contain the following items.

- Did you begin with an interesting sentence?
- Are your points easy to understand and presented in the best sequence?
- Did you give examples to help readers understand your points?
- Is your material interesting? How might you make it more interesting?
- Have you used paragraphs?
- Have you checked spelling and punctuation?

Many low-achieving students tend to write very little during times set aside for writing. This is part of the vicious circle which begins: 'I don't like writing so I don't write much, so I don't get much practice, so I don't improve...' Use of strategies such as 'LESSER helps me write MORE' can help reduce the problem of limited output. The strategy guides students' thinking and can result in a longer and more interesting assignment than they would otherwise produce.

L = List your ideas.
E = Examine your list.
S = Select your starting point.
S = Sentence one will tell us about this first idea.
E = Expand on this first idea with another related sentence.
R_3 = Read what you have written. Revise if necessary. Repeat for the next paragraph.

In a review of teachers' classroom practices, Cuevas (2016) found that exemplary teachers of writing frequently use modelling and research-supported strategies to improve adolescent writers' achievements. The students then begin to exhibit more sophisticated writing and greater confidence once they are taught effective strategies for planning and revising text (Datchuk et al., 2020; Nicholson & Dymock, 2018; Ray & Graham, 2019). Fletcher et al. (2018) suggest that teaching students to use self-regulatory strategies for writing can produce an effect size of at least 0.60 and can be as high as 1.17.

It is always necessary to maximise the possibility that a strategy will generalise beyond the training sessions into students' everyday writing. This may be supported by:

- continuing with instruction and practice until students have thoroughly internalised the strategy and can use it without prompting;
- frequently reminding students to consider where a particular strategy can be used.

Paired writing

In the same way that working with a partner can improve reading skills, having a partner for writing at Tier 1 is also beneficial (Storch, 2019). A study found that 5th and 6th Grade students who wrote with a peer were more motivated than students taught by usual classroom methods (De Smedt et al., 2019). Paired writing can be used routinely at Tier 1, or at Tier 2 for peer tutoring, cross-age tutoring, parent–child tutorial groupings, and in adult literacy classes.

When paired writing is used specifically for tutoring a struggling writer, the pair usually comprises a helper and a writer (Yeh, 2017). The helper's role initially is to stimulate ideas from the writer and to note these down. When sufficient ideas have been suggested, the helper and writer together review the notes and discuss the best sequence for presenting the ideas. A graphic organiser or concept map format could be used to indicate visibly how the ideas will be linked.

The writer then begins first draft writing, based on the notes and the graphic. In the case of very weak students, the helper may have to act as scribe while the tutee dictates material. The helper and writer then read aloud the draft that has been written. Working together, the pair edit the draft for clarity of meaning, sequence, spelling, and punctuation, with the writer taking the lead where possible. The writer then produces a final copy, and together the helper and writer evaluate the finished product. In recent years, word processors have provided additional ways of working collaboratively in this manner with a partner on written assignments (Guzmán et al., 2019; Smith, 2019).

Digital technology and writing

Students today have easy access to digital technology and most spend many hours a week using it to communicate (Dahlström, 2019; Kang, 2018; Kervin & Mantei, 2016). They can also use technology to search for information to enrich their projects and compositions when they are writing on particular topics for assignments. Saulsburry et al. (2015) have remarked that digital tools incorporated into writing sessions can help teachers motivate and engage students, particularly those who usually do everything they can to avoid writing. In this context, Corkett and Benevides (2016) have suggested that tablet technology has a valuable place in teaching and practising writing skills for students who have a learning difficulty. They found that digital writing sessions using an iPad with students in the 11.5 to 12.5 age range were effective in improving number of sentences written, number of ideas expressed, and spelling accuracy. Teachers have reported that the use of technology for writing also yields positive results for students with disabilities, and enables teachers to differentiate writing activities (Lim & Lee, 2019; Regan et al., 2019). Students come to digital writing with varying degrees of experience, so teachers may need to support those who lack proficiency (Martin & Lambert, 2015).

The most common form of technology that students use for assignment work in classrooms is word processing. There is now clear research evidence supporting the benefits of using word processors with learning-disabled students (e.g., Hetzroni & Shrieber, 2004; University of Washington, 2012). The use of a word processor is reported to yield a very positive effect size between 0.47 and 0.55 (Graham, 2008; Graham et al., 2012; Graham & Perrin, 2007). Undoubtedly, the arrival of word processors heralded a new opportunity for students of all levels of ability to enter the realm of writing and composing with more enthusiasm and enjoyment.

Using a word processor makes the task of writing less arduous and the writer receives immediate corrective feedback. Word processing seems to be of great benefit to students who do not usually write very much, and to those with the most severe spelling problems. Students with learning difficulties have been found to gain confidence in creating, editing, erasing, and publishing their own unique material through a medium that holds attention and is infinitely patient.

Tier 2 and Tier 3: paving the way for success

Students who exhibit difficulties in writing fall into one of two categories, but their instructional needs overlap. The first group comprises students who have learning difficulties of a cognitive or physical nature that impair their ability to write. The second group comprises reluctant and unmotivated students who can write, but do not like to do so.

In order to assist students with learning difficulties or disabilities, there is a need to structure every writing task carefully and provide appropriate support. They need help at two stages of the writing process: (i) planning what to write, and (ii) revising and polishing the final product. The teaching at each stage should embody basic principles of effective instruction —namely, demonstration by the teacher of the steps involved, followed by guided practice with feedback, and ultimately students engaging in independent practice and application.

Reluctant and unmotivated students have usually encountered negative or unrewarding experiences during the early stages of becoming writers, and may have acquired what has been termed *writing apprehension*. This state of anxiety now causes them to avoid the task of putting pen to paper or using a keyboard whenever possible. Their avoidance leads to habitually low levels of practice and productivity, so the teacher's challenge is to find ways of helping these students regain lost interest and re-build their confidence. An atmosphere that encourages students to experiment with their writing without fear of failure is a very necessary condition for struggling writers. In many cases, simply creating the supportive atmosphere is not enough, particularly with upper primary or secondary students with a history of bad experiences in writing. Much more than the ordinary amount of scaffolding and encouragement from the teacher will also be needed. Small booklets devoted to one topic or one story are usually better than exercise books for students who are reluctant writers. The opportunity to make a fresh start every week is far better than being faced with the accumulated evidence of past failures which accrue in a thick exercise book. For students of all ages, a loose-leaf folder with work samples and computer printouts is a useful replacement for the traditional exercise book.

Students with writing difficulties benefit from being given a framework they can use whenever they write. In later sections below, examples are provided of frameworks that teachers can provide to assist students in the early stages. They need specific guidance on how to begin their writing, how to develop an idea, and how to complete the task. Students with difficulties, and those lacking in confidence, benefit from:

- talking through the topic first, to think around the main theme, and generate a sequence of related ideas
- noting down some key vocabulary;
- drawing a graphic organiser to show how ideas will be linked.

The first important step in improving a student's writing skills is to allocate sufficient time for writing within every school day. When writing occurs daily, there is much greater like-lihood that skills, motivation, and confidence will all improve. Ideally, in a tutoring situation a student receiving extra assistance will choose his or her own topics for writing—if not, it is essential to assign an appropriately stimulating subject about which they have reasonable depth of knowledge and experience. The student must see a purpose in transferring ideas to paper or computer, and should perceive the task as worthwhile. In the early stages, it is important not to place undue stress on perfect accuracy in spelling or grammar since this can stifle the student's attempts to write freely. If the student is using a word processor, it is best not to stop to check spellings until the writing is complete, so that the student's full attention can be devoted to composing content and sequence.

The following sections describe various activities and frameworks that can be used with struggling writers.

The skeleton story

Getting started is the first obstacle faced by many students who find writing difficult. To address this problem, some teachers use writing frames (templates) and rubrics designed to scaffold the task of composing. One version is to provide a few stem sentences that must be completed using the student's own ideas and words. Students find it very much easier to complete a story when the demands for writing and sequencing are reduced in this way, and when a structure has been provided.

Example:

Something woke me in the middle of the night.
I heard.................................
I climbed out of the bed quietly and..............
To my surprise I saw...........................
At first I...
I was lucky because....................
In the end ....

Simple frameworks of this type can be used with an individual student in a tutorial session, or can be used as a group activity involving collaborative effort to complete a version of the story on the whiteboard or screen. Each student is then given a sheet with the same sentence beginnings, but he or she must write a different story. These stories are later shared in the group.

Patterned writing

For students with limited writing ability, a familiar story with repetitive and predictable sentence patterns can be used as a stimulus for writing a new variation on the same theme. The plot remains basically the same but the characters and the details are changed. For example, the children are familiar with the story of the 'Little Red Hen' so they write a similar story but involving a 'Big Grey Elephant' instead of a Little Red Hen. The Big Grey Elephant tries to get other animals to help him move a log from the path: 'Who will help me move the log?' 'Not I', said the rat. 'Not I', said the monkey, 'Not I', said the snake, and so forth.

Sentence combining

Activities involving the reconstruction of several simple sentences into a more interesting sentence have proved valuable for weaker writers. For example:

The giant was hungry.
The giant ate the meat pie.
The meat pie was huge.
The hungry giant ate the huge meat pie.

The main benefit from the experience of sentence combining is that the process can be revisited every time a student is asked to edit and improve a piece of his or her writing.

Story web

A story web is a form of graphic organiser that provides writers with a starting point for generating ideas for writing. The web is created by writing the main topic or title for the story in the centre of the paper (or whiteboard), then using spokes branching off from the main idea into different types of information—for example, the setting for the story, the characters involved, the type of action that takes place, and the outcome. In a group, students brainstorm for ideas that might go into the story, and these are added to the web.

- Prompts and cues can be used to stimulate students' thinking as the web is constructed.
- The class then reviews the ideas and decides upon an appropriate starting point for the story. Number 1 is written against that idea.
- How will the story develop? The children determine the order in which the other ideas will be used, and the appropriate numbers are written against each spoke.
- Some of the ideas may not be used at all and can be erased. Other ideas may need to be added at this stage, and numbered accordingly.
- The students now use the bank of ideas on the story web to start writing their own stories. Brief notes can be elaborated into sentences, and the sentences gradually

extended into paragraphs. By preparing the draft ideas and then discussing the best order in which to write them, the students have tackled two of the most difficult problems they face when composing – planning and sequencing.

Expanding an idea

Informative or narrative writing can be expanded beyond simple statement.

The teacher demonstrates the following procedure, incorporating ideas from the class. Students are then given guided practice and further modelling over a series of lessons, each time using a different theme.

- Begin by writing a short, declarative sentence.

  We have too many cars coming into our school parking area.

- Next, write two or three sentences that add information to and are connected with the first sentence. Leave a space between each statement.

  We have too many cars coming into our school parking area.

  The noise they make often disturbs our lessons.

  The cars sometimes travel fast and could knock someone down.

  What can we do about this problem?

- Now write more sentences in the spaces.

  We have too many cars coming into our school parking area.
  It is becoming very annoying.
  The noise they make often disturbs our lessons.
  The drivers sound their horns and rev the engines. Sometimes I can't even hear what our teacher is saying.
  The cars travel fast and could knock someone down. I saw a girl step out behind one car yesterday. She screamed when it reversed suddenly.
  What can we do about this problem?
  Perhaps there should be a sign saying 'NO CARS ALLOWED'. They might build some speed humps or set a speed limit.

- Edit the sentences into appropriate paragraphs and combine some short statements into longer, complex sentences. Use of a word processor makes these steps much faster and the process of editing and checking spelling easier.

Writing a summary

Students with learning difficulties often have problems when required to write a summary of something they have just read. Specific help is needed in this area and one or more of the following procedures can be helpful to such students. It can be used with an individual in a tutorial session (Tier 3) or with a group of students at Tier 2.

- After students have read the text together or independently, the teacher provides a set of 'true/false' statements based on information in the text. The statements are presented on a sheet in random order. Students must read each statement and place a tick against those that are true. They then decide the most logical sequence in which to arrange these true statements to form a logical summary when copied into an exercise book.
- The teacher provides some sentence starters in a sequence that will provide a framework for writing the summary. The student completes the unfinished sentences and in doing so writes the summary.
- For example:

  The first thing the travellers noticed when they arrived at the airport was …
  When they travelled by taxi to the city, they noticed …
  They begin to wonder if…
  In the end, they discovered that ….

- The teacher provides a summary with key words or phrases omitted. The students must provide the missing words. In the early stages, the words may be presented below the passage in random order, or clues may be given in terms of initial letters of word required. The student completes the cloze passage by supplying the missing words.
- Simple multiple-choice questions can be presented. The questions may deal with the main ideas from the text and with supporting detail. By selecting appropriate responses and writing these down, the student creates a brief summary.

All the suggestions above are designed to structure the task demands for writing, and at the same time motivate the reluctant student to complete the work successfully. In most cases, the use of a word processor will also add motivation and has an important element of control by the learner. Studies have indicated that interventions that target writing, particularly those involving direct instruction and self-regulated strategy development, do result in improvement in students' writing fluency (Datchuk et al., 2020).

The following chapter provides information on spelling and how to address the needs of students who have difficulty in mastering this skill.

Online resources

- A comprehensive description of process approach to writing can be found at: www.teachin genglish.org.uk/article/approaches-process-writing.
- Issues associated with difficulties in writing are discussed online by Dr Mel Levine at: www.pbs. org/wgbh/misunderstoodminds/writingdiffs.html.
- For information on a range of strategies for helping struggling writers see:
  - www.teachwriting.org/blog/2017/6/15/supporting-writers-at-all-levels.
  - www.teachwriting.org/blog/2017/6/14/12-strategies-to-support-struggling-writers-in-elementary.
  - www.teachwriting.org/blog/2017/3/18/5-strategies-to-build-confidence-in-young-writers.
  - www.readingandwritinghaven.com/14-ways-support-struggling-writers-build-confidence-increase-success/.

- Academic Therapy website has a very useful summary of the current computer apps to help students with writing difficulties online at: https://academictherapycenter.com/2014/05/apps-to-help-students-with-dysgraphia-and-writing-difficulties/.
- Overview of basic writing disabilities at: www.verywellfamily.com/what-are-basic-writing-disabilities-2162445.
- The National Institute of Neurological Disorders and Stroke has information about dysgraphia (a specific learning disability affecting writing): www.ninds.nih.gov/Disorders/All-Disorders/Dysgraphia-Information-Page.
- Troia, G., Evidence-based practices for writing instruction (Document No. IC-5). University of Florida website: http://ceedar.education.ufl.edu/tools/innovation-configuration/.

Print resources

Biays, J.S, & Wershoven, C. (2019). *Along these lines: Writing sentences and paragraphs* (7th ed.). New York: Pearson.

Fletcher, J.M., Lyon, G. R., Fuchs, L.S, & Barnes, M.A. (2018). *Learning disabilities: From identification to intervention* (2nd ed.). New York: Guilford.

Graham, J., & Kelly, A. (2013). *Writing under control* (3rd ed. ebook). London: Routledge.

Graham, S., MacArthur, C.A. & Fitzgerald, J. (Eds) (2018). *Best practices in writing instruction* (3rd ed.). New York: Guilford Press.

Nicholson, T., & Dymock, S. (2018). *Writing for impact: Teaching students to write with a plan and spell well.* Wellington: NZCER Press.

Chapter 12

Difficulties with spelling

Many students with learning difficulties find spelling a problem long after reading skills have improved. In part, this arises because the English language contains many words that are impossible to spell by a simple translation of sounds to letters—these words are usually described as 'irregular'. Students' difficulties can also be exacerbated when too little attention is devoted to the systematic teaching of spelling in the primary school, based on a misguided belief that spelling skill will be acquired incidentally if students simply engage in writing every day.

Teaching spelling ceased to feature prominently in the primary school curriculum for several decades from the 1970s, due mainly to the influence of whole-language approach to literacy. Teachers were encouraged to ignore spelling mistakes and accept 'invented' spellings in order not to focus too much attention on the mechanical aspects of writing at the expense of creativity and expression. This immersion approach was deemed to be a 'natural' way of acquiring spelling ability, and therefore regarded as preferable to any form of direct teaching. The reality was that the immersion approach proved totally inadequate for many children and they failed to become proficient spellers. Without explicit instruction, many students develop their own strategies for spelling difficult words, but usually these strategies are not reliable or effective and they create ongoing problems.

In recent years, systematic teaching of spelling has enjoyed something of a renaissance due to an increased awareness that accurate spelling is actually important, and children will not necessarily become adequate spellers if they are left to discover spelling principles for themselves (Connelly et al., 2019). Research evidence suggests that, although students do acquire some orthographic awareness through reading, when they are given explicit instruction in how to spell words they learn far more, particularly if the instruction improves their ability to analyse words into their component sounds (Conrad et al., 2019; Dymock, 2019; Neilson, 2019). The current view is that a systematic approach to spelling and word study is absolutely essential, and leads to measurable improvement in spelling ability. Current teaching approaches aim to help students become more independent and more capable of detecting and correcting spelling errors. Guidelines for national curriculum in the US, Britain and Australia now require that due attention be given to ensuring that all students can spell, and can use appropriate resources to obtain and check the spelling of complex words.

Best practices in spelling instruction

Research studies in recent years have confirmed that best practice in spelling involves teaching all students knowledge, skills, and strategies that are useful for tackling unfamiliar words required in authentic writing purposes (Cordewener et al., 2018; Graham & Santangelo, 2014; Puliatte & Ehri, 2018; Westwood, 2018b). In the early stages, this teaching should involve clear modelling by a teacher, imitation and practice by students, and corrective feedback from the teacher. Students also need to learn efficient methods for remembering irregular words, and for proofreading and self-correction.

There are specific principles that should guide a classroom approach to teaching spelling at Tier 1. These principles are:

- allocating adequate time for instruction and practice: recommended to be 15 minutes daily in the primary school years;
- arousing children's genuine interest in words and in producing accurate spelling;
- teaching a core vocabulary of words commonly used in writing;
- matching spelling activities to students' stage of development;
- teaching effective cognitive strategies for tackling words, proofreading, and self-correcting;
- making classroom self-help spelling resources readily available: dictionaries, common core word lists, topic-specific word lists, word walls, electronic spell checkers, computer access.

Developmental stages

It is important to recognise that acquisition of spelling ability has identifiable stages of development, and teaching must take these stages into account when selecting words and strategies to be taught to a particular age group of students. The stages have been described in the following way – although the exact name for each stage has differed among various researchers (e.g., Bissex, 1980; Scharer & Zutell, 2003).

Stage 1: Prephonetic. This stage represents the first tentative step towards invented spelling as a component of emergent writing. In the kindergarten years, children pretend to write words in imitation of the writing they have seen from others, often using a mix of capital and lower-case letters. There is no connection between these scribbles and real words, but studies have indicated that if developmentally appropriate feedback is provided to preschool children during this stage, they begin to pay closer attention to associations between oral and written language (Ouelette et al., 2013).

Stage 2: Phonetic. At this stage, children draw upon their increasing awareness of sounds within spoken words, and begin to gain some basic knowledge of letter-to-sound correspondences through incidental learning. The spellings that children invent at this stage are often very inaccurate but still quite recognisable, because they are based on phonic principles.

Towards the end of the phonetic stage, approximations move much nearer to regular letter-to-sound correspondences, as in 'sed' (said), 'becos' (because) or 'wotch' (watch). Sometimes, a phoneme may be equated incorrectly with a letter *name* rather than the sound, as in 'rsk' (ask), 'yl' (while), 'lfnt' (elephant). Some children still have difficulty identifying the second or third consonant in a letter-string, and may write 'stong' (strong) or 'bow' (blow); or they may fail to identify correctly a phoneme in a spoken word, and write incorrect letters, as in 'druck' (truck), 'jriv' (drive), 'sboon' (spoon), 'dewis' (juice). These inaccuracies are normal on the way to proficiency.

It should be noted that the majority of individuals with poor spelling have reached this phonetic stage but have not progressed beyond it. Their tendency is to be over-dependent on phonics and therefore write irregular words as if they have regular letter-to-sound correspondences. In order to move to the next stage, students need to be taught how to try different strategies—such as more carefully checking the visual image of the target word, or writing the word several times.

Stage 3: Transitional. At this stage there is clear evidence of a more sophisticated understanding of word structure, and more caution is applied when attempting unfamiliar words. Children become more aware of within-word letter strings and syllable junctures. Activities involving word analysis are useful for helping students recognise letter patterns within words (orthographic units) (Templeton et al., 2015). Common letter sequences such as *str-, pre-, -ough, -ious, -ea-, -ai-, -aw-, -ing* are used much more automatically and reliably. The process of building up orthographic images in memory (known as 'orthographic knowledge acquisition': Daigle et al., 2020) is also facilitated by study of word families with common letter sequences—for example, *gate, date, late, fate, mate.* Children who gain mastery over spelling at this stage also use words they know already in order to spell words they have never written before (spelling by analogy).

Stage 4: Independence. At this stage, children have gained mastery of quite complex grapho-phonic principles and also use visual memory more effectively when writing words. Flexible use is made of a wide range of spelling, proofreading, and self-correcting strategies. A growing awareness of the meaning of root words, prefixes, suffixes and derivations also signals increased control over spelling (Claravall, 2016; Wolter & Dilworth, 2014).

In general, spellings produced by children provide a window not only to their developmental stage but also to their current thought processes related to encoding written language. Examination of the written work produced by students with difficulties can reveal a great deal about their existing skills and their specific needs for instruction in spelling. This type of assessment should be the starting point for planning instruction.

Spelling as a complex behaviour

Spelling can be regarded as a very complex behaviour because it involves coordination of eye, ear, hand, brain, and speech (through the accurate pronunciation of words). The strategies used to teach spelling to all students should be based on the potential contribution of each of these five modalities. For many years, teachers regarded the correct spelling of words as a predominantly *visual* skill. If students were fortunate enough to receive any guidance at all in spelling, they were taught the 'look-say-cover-write-check' strategy, as discussed later. Much less importance was attached to careful listening (auditory processing) because it was argued that too many words in English are not written with perfect letter-to-sound translation. To counter this argument, it should be noted that more than 80 per cent of English words can be encoded 'as they sound' if attention is given not just to single letters but to *letter clusters* (e.g., *-ei-, -ie-, thr-, -ough, - tion, -ength*).

Auditory skills and phonic knowledge

The basic knowledge upon which successful spelling first develops depends upon grasping the concept that spoken words can be broken down into smaller units of sound (phonemes) and that these sounds can be represented by letters (Ehri, 2014). It is now accepted that carefully listening to words as they are pronounced enables young children to relate the sequence of phonemes they can hear to the single letters or groups of letters needed to represent those sounds in the written form (Sanchez et al., 2012). Later, at the transitional stage, children learn to encode using letter clusters rather than just single letters and they are able to spell much more efficiently (Murray, McIlwain et al., 2019). They will not always arrive at the perfect spelling of a tricky word, but they will come to a close approximation.

One group of students where the influence of auditory perception on spelling negatively affects their ability is those with significant hearing impairment (Bell et al., 2019; Bowers et al., 2016). Evidence suggests that for these students, reading still provides the main influence for developing orthographic awareness (Wass et al., 2019).

Visual skills

Of course, visual skills are also vitally important for learning and remembering the orthographic patterns of words. Proficient spellers make great use of visual images stored in memory when they check words they have written or typed to detect errors. For example, *brekfirst* should be recognised by the student as an incorrect visual image for the word *breakfast*—it doesn't 'look right'. The effective use of visual perception in learning to spell helps children build a memory bank of common letter clusters, and these images can be called upon whenever the student attempts to write an unfamiliar word. Over time, students develop orthographic awareness (Conrad et al., 2019), which means they recognise groups of letters that occur frequently within English words (e.g., *-ate* or *un-*)—and equally important, they realise that certain combinations of letters rarely or never occur in English (e.g., *vt, chk* or *tz*). Increasingly, this awareness guides them when selecting certain letter clusters and rejecting others when writing a tricky word.

Learning strategies that involve visual imagery, such as look-say-cover-write-check, are very effective for learning words with unpredictable letter-to-sound correspondences. It is necessary to examine the word very carefully, with every intention of trying to commit its configuration to memory. As this process of close scrutiny of words does not come naturally to children, it is important that they be given the necessary instruction and practice. By implication, this means devoting specific time for word study, over and above the help given to individual students as they write (Templeton et al., 2015). It is most unlikely that such an important skill as word analysis could be adequately developed through incidental learning alone.

Spelling by hand

In addition to combining visual and auditory skills, spelling is also a manual skill. The physical act of spelling of a word by writing or keyboarding involves muscle memory (or *kinaesthetic memory*). The ease with which a competent speller encodes a very familiar word in print supports this view. The frequent action of writing or keyboarding is one powerful way of establishing and maintaining the stock of word images and letter strings in long-term memory. Poorly executed handwriting and uncertain letter formation inhibit easy development of spelling at an automatic response level. It is essential that an easy style of writing be taught and practised thoroughly from the early years of schooling (James & Beringer, 2019). Most experts now recommend that cursive (joined) handwriting has benefits over manuscript style (in which each letter is written separately). According to Montgomery (2012) handwriting supports spelling, and the advantage of cursive style is that each written word consists of a continuous pattern with all elements flowing together. James and Beringer (2019) refer to evidence from brain research to argue that handwriting is still vitally important even in the digital age.

Spelling and the brain

The human brain plays the executive role in thinking about words, and in generating and checking plausible spelling alternatives. The learning of new words and the analysis of unfamiliar words are both brain-based (cognitive) activities. The brain coordinates various sources of perceptual information to help determine the spelling of a word. It is also the brain that makes the decision whether to apply auditory, visual, or some other strategy to encode the word. The ability to recall and apply spelling rules and strategies, or to recognise when a word is an exception to a rule, reflects a cognitive aspect of spelling. Working out the most probable way to spell an unfamiliar word may also require the writer to consider the meaning of the word, and the separate *morphemes* (small units of meaning such as prefixes, suffixes, plural endings) that make up the word (Bowers & Bowers, 2017).

Research has found that there are subtle brain differences between students with a specific learning disability that affects spelling, and those who are proficient spellers (Gebauer et al., 2012). While this information does not lead immediately to selection of a particular method of remediation for difficulties, it does support a view that individual differences in spelling performance may be inevitable.

Pronunciation

Accurate pronunciation of a word plays an important role in spelling (Papen et al., 2012). This issue is particularly relevant when teaching English as a second language, but it also applies to students from restricted language backgrounds, those using a strong regional dialect, and students with hearing impairment. In cases of serious spelling difficulty, it is always wise to check if the student is actually hearing and saying a target word correctly. For example, you are unlikely to spell *library* or *escape* correctly if you say '*libry*' and '*excape*'. In the early years, children benefit from guided experience in listening carefully to words, stretching words out and segmenting them into pronounceable sub-units.

Teaching spelling

The majority of students do not become good spellers simply by being immersed in reading and writing activities— specific time must be devoted to spelling instruction, particularly in the primary school years (Dymock, 2019). The starting point for enhancing spelling development is arousal of children's genuine interest in words; and this requires that teachers and tutors display personal enthusiasm for all forms of word study.

Effective instruction at Tier 1 does not set out to teach students how to spell each and every word they may need at some time in their writing. Students make most progress when they are explicitly taught strategies for working out how to learn new words and how to construct words by utilising the multiple linguistic influences that underpin English spelling. Students with spelling difficulties will always need more individualised attention, systematic error correction, more frequent practice, and sometimes even methods that involve multisensory input such as finger-tracing over a word. In the sections below, descriptions are provided for the main approaches that can be used, singly or in combination.

Applying a visual approach

A visual approach is most appropriate for the learning of irregular words. A visual approach requires students to memorise and retain the correct sequence of letters in long-term memory, rather than attending to sounds and syllables within the word. Research has suggested that children can improve their visual imagery for letter sequences, if given sufficient training (Roberts, 2012). One of the best-known methods is called 'look-say-cover-write-check', or simply 'copy-cover-compare' (Konrad & Joseph, 2014). This approach gives a student an independent system that can be applied at any time to the learning of corrections from free writing or for any words set for homework.

Look-say-cover-write-check involves the following steps:

- look very carefully at the target word;
- say the word clearly while looking closely at the left-to-right sequence of letters;
- cover the word so that it cannot be seen;
- write the word from immediate memory, pronouncing it quietly as you write;
- check your version of the word with the original—if it is not correct, go back through the steps again until you can produce the word accurately;
- for some students with severe problems, tracing over the word with a finger at steps 1 and 2 may help with attention to detail and retention of the letter sequence;
- check for recall a week later.

The simplest aid to make and use is the flashcard. The word is pronounced clearly and attention is drawn to any particular features in the printed word that may be difficult to recall later. The child is encouraged to make a 'mental picture' of the word and examine it. Some teachers say: 'Use your eyes like a camera. Take a picture of the word. Close your eyes and imagine you can still see the word.' With eyes closed, the child is then told to trace the word in the air. After a few seconds he or she writes the word from memory, articulating it clearly as it is written. The word is then checked against the flashcard. The rapid writing of the whole word using cursive style avoids the inefficient letter-by-letter copying habit that some students have developed.

Applying a phonological approach

Using the phonological approach for spelling should be an integral part of systematic phonics teaching for reading. In a comprehensive literacy programme, decoding and encoding processes are taught together; and writing and spelling are as much a focus of attention as reading. A phonological approach encourages students to attend carefully to sounds and syllables within words and to write the letters most likely to represent these sounds. The phonic knowledge necessary for effective spelling goes well beyond simply knowing each single letter. As indicated already, one also needs to use letter clusters (orthographic units) with vowels and consonants (e.g., -tion, -ail, pre-, ought) (Berninger et al., 2013). When students can function at this level, they are able to write correctly most of the 80 per cent of words they may need to use.

Applying a morphemic approach

Morphology is the study of word structure as it relates to meaning. A knowledge of morphological structure of words provides students with new insight on spelling patterns, because relating meaning to parts of words helps make spelling more predictable (Bowers & Bowers, 2017; Claravall, 2016). It has been found that when students understand how meaning influences the structure of a word, they have a better appreciation of the logic that governs English spelling (Apel et al., 2013; Wolter & Dilworth, 2014).

In a morphemic approach, students are taught to recognise and apply knowledge of sub-units of meaning within a word. The smallest unit of meaning is termed a 'morpheme' and the written equivalent of a morpheme is known as a 'morphograph'. For example, the word *throw* contains only one morpheme, but *throwing* contains two. The word *unhappiness* (un-happ[y]-ness) contains three morphemes—and this example also illustrates a common rule (changing y to i) when combining certain morphemes. These rules need to be taught and practised when using a morphemic approach (IDA, 2017). To facilitate study, students can be helped to compile 'word families' (e.g., *certain, uncertain, certainly, uncertainty, certainty, ascertain*). A dictionary is an easy resource to identify such words. Morphological awareness is one of the main topics addressed with students in typical Tier 1 'word study' sessions (Bowers & Bowers, 2017; Crosson & Moore, 2017; Nielsen, 2017) (see below).

The best-known commercial programme using a morphemic approach is *Spelling Through Morphographs* (Dixon & Englemann, 2006). The materials are appropriate for students from Year 4 upwards and can also be used with adults. In 140 lessons, the students learn all the key morphographs and the basic rules of how they can be combined in the spelling system. *Spelling Through Morphographs* has proved particularly valuable for students with learning difficulties. The same publishing house also produces *Mastery Spelling* for students in Grades 1 to 6. This programme includes visual, phonological, and morphologic learning strategies. An evaluation of *Spelling Mastery* by What Works Clearinghouse concluded that the programme can have positive effects for students with learning disabilities (Institute of Education Sciences, 2014).

Digital technology

Recently, there has been a noticeable increase in the use of technology to teach spelling, and this has proved very useful for students with learning difficulties (Ault et al. 2017; Elimelech & Aram, 2019). The concern expressed a few years ago that technology in the form of spell checkers would result in declining spelling standards has not turned out to be true. Rather than proving to be detrimental to spelling, technology has given us programs and apps that can be used for learning to spell and for deeper studying of words (Westwood, 2018b). Several computer programs designed to develop spelling skills using a visual approach are available, and studies have indicated that these can be quite effective (e.g., Kast et al., 2011). Any online search under 'spelling software' will yield details of a range of existing programs and apps.

When using digital technology to teach or practice spelling, teachers should ensure that the way in which words are presented on the screen causes a student to attend carefully to the left-to-right sequence of letters and requires the student to type the *complete word* from memory each time. Programs that focus too much attention on unscrambling jumbled words, spelling letter-by-letter, or inserting missing letters into spaces are far less effective.

Word study

Activities used in word study sessions are designed to help students analyze words more deeply by finding within-word letter patterns, identifying syllables and affixes, and attending to meaning. The actual processes involved in word study are described as: examining, manipulating, comparing, and categorising words, to reveal the logic within written language.

Findings from research support the belief that clear instruction in word analysis can successfully reveal connections between phonological, morphological, and orthographic features within words (Gray et al., 2018; IDA, 2017). It is believed that this type of word study helps all students achieve a better standard in spelling (Institute of Education Sciences, 2013), and is of particular help for students with language disorders, learning difficulties, and those learning English as a second language (Diaz, 2010; Wolter & Green, 2013). Putman (2017, p.24) has stated that 'based on what we know about the English spelling system, how children learn, and the brain, word study makes sense'.

One activity involving word study for all students (Tier 1) is *Word Sorting*. This approach represents an investigative and active way to help children discriminate among orthographic features within and across words. Comparing and contrasting words in this way helps older students (including adults) discover some basic spelling rules.

Students are provided with a set of cards containing the words to be studied and compared. The words might be *sock, black, back, truck, lock, dock, rack, luck, trick, track, block, lick, sack, stick, flock, flick, suck*. The students are asked, 'What is the same about some of these words?' The response might be that the words all end with /ck/. The words might now be categorised in other ways by sorting the cards into groups (for example, words ending in /ock/; words ending in /ack/). At a more advanced level, *Word Sorts* can involve words grouped according to the meaning–spelling connection, as discussed above under the morphemic approach—for example, *played, playfully, replay, player, playground, horseplay, playback*.

Spelling rules

Some experts advocate teaching spelling rules to students as a key part of the classroom spelling programme; but students with learning difficulties find most rules too obscure to be of help when they are faced with a particularly tricky word to spell. In many cases, rather than drilling complex rules, it is easier to help students spell the specific word they need for their immediate writing, but also to teach them effective strategies to use to learn that word for future use.

However, learning spelling rules may be of some value for older students and students of above average intelligence (Kempre et al., 2012). This is particularly the case if rules are incorporated into the morphemic approach described above. Intelligent students can often understand the rule and can apply it appropriately. Rules taught should be simple and have few exceptions (e.g. 'i' before 'e' except after 'c'—*receive*; words ending with 'e', drop the 'e' when adding an ending that begins with a vowel—*hope, hoping*; words ending in a single vowel must double the consonant before adding an ending that begins with a vowel—*stop, stopped, stopping*). At least one study has found that using a rules-based approach can be more effective than applying a look-say-cover-write-check strategy, in terms of transfer to other words (Dymock & Nicholson, 2017).

Dictation

The regular use of dictation has fallen out of favour in many schools, although it is suggested that dictation can develop listening skills and concentration, and at the same time gives spelling practice with words in context. Dictation still enjoys an accepted place in teaching English as a second or additional language.

When dictation is used for teaching rather than testing, the material at an appropriate level of difficulty should first be presented for students to study *before* it is dictated. In this way, there is an opportunity to clarify meaning of certain unfamiliar words and to point out any potentially difficult spellings. The passage is then dictated for students to write, and they are given a period of time to proofread and self-correct any words that they think are incorrect. The teacher checks the work and can observe two aspects of the student's performance. First, it is useful to look at the words the child has been able to self-correct (or at least knows to be wrong). Second, the teacher can record words that were in fact wrong but were not noticed by the student. If these are common words that should be known by the student, activities can be devised that will help the student master them.

Spelling lists

It is known that rote learning of words from a standard all-purpose list does not generally result in any transfer of spelling skill to everyday writing. The limitation of formal lists is that they usually fail to supply a particular word at the time when the student needs to use it for writing or proofreading. In addition, having one common word list for all students in the class ignores the fact that children are at different stages of spelling development and therefore have different learning needs. However, there is a place for judicious use of spelling lists if they are tailored to students' needs.

From the point of view of the weakest spellers, the most useful list will be one compiled according to everyday writing needs, and the words that are often incorrect in the student's writing. A copy of this list can be kept in the back of the exercise book or folder, and used when he or she is writing a rough draft or proofreading a final draft of a piece of work.

Other lists might contain words grouped by visual, phonemic, or morphemic similarity (word families). The value of lists comprising word families is that they represent yet another way of helping students establish awareness of commonly occurring orthographic units. This awareness enables a student to use a more rational approach to tackling an unfamiliar word—for example, by using *analogy* to move from the known to the unknown. The decision to use such lists with an individual student or group of students must be made in the light of their specific learning needs.

Word Walls represent one excellent method of ensuring that the words children need in their daily writing in any subject area are readily to hand. Words are written in blackboard-size writing on poster sheets on the classroom wall, so that children can locate and use them as necessary. Vocabulary is added regularly to the *Word Wall* as each new topic is introduced. This approach applies in secondary schools as well as primary schools. Students may not need to learn all the words on such a list, but they can refer to it when writing. It is often recommended in secondary schools as part of an 'across the curriculum' policy on literacy, that specialist subject teachers should provide their students with a list of core terms frequently used in that subject.

Developing strategic spellers

Students become truly independent in spelling when they can look at an unfamiliar word and select the most appropriate strategy for learning that word. For example, they need to be able to look at a word and decide for themselves whether it is phonemically irregular or regular. For an irregular word, they may need to apply the look-say-cover-write-check strategy, coupled perhaps with repeated writing of the word. If the word is phonemically regular, they recognise that they can spell it easily from its component sounds. When students can operate at this level, the shift is from rote learning to an emphasis on approaching words rationally.

This level of independence does not come easily; many students need to be taught how to learn and remember new spellings. Some students, if left to their own devices, fail to develop any systematic approach—or they may just look at the word and recite the spelling alphabetically—or they may copy letter-by-letter rather than smoothly writing the whole word—or they may use no particular strategy at all, believing that learning to spell the word is beyond them.

Where a student has no systematic approach, it is essential that he or she be taught one. Any serious attempt to help students with spelling difficulties must first involve observing how they set about learning any new group of words. Then, the teacher replaces the student's inefficient system of operating with a more effective way of mastering the correct spelling of a word. Cognitive and metacognitive approaches are designed to teach students self-regulatory strategies to use when learning new words or when checking spelling at the proofreading stage of writing (Westwood, 2014).

A typical strategy to teach to weaker spellers involves them asking themselves the following questions.

- What sounds can I hear in this word?
- Do I know any other words that sound like this word?
- Can I write this word correctly after a quick glance?
- How many syllables do I hear in this word?
- Do I have the right number of syllables in what I have written?
- Does this word look correct? I'll try it again.
- Does this look better?

Intervention strategies for Tier 2 and Tier 3

Several specific approaches have been developed to help struggling spellers. The paragraphs below describe some of the most useful that have survived the passage of time. Most of these intervention approaches involve intensive one-to-one instruction.

Simultaneous Oral Spelling

Simultaneous Oral Spelling (SOS) was first developed by Gillingham and Stillman in 1960, and it has been applied very successfully for remediation of spelling problems in individual tutorial settings. Note that the letter *name* is used, not its common sound. This makes the method particularly appropriate for older students or adults who may be embarrassed by 'sounding out' a word using phonics.

The SOS approach involves these steps:

- a target word is selected—perhaps a word that is a persistent spelling error;
- teacher or tutor pronounces the word clearly and checks that student can also pronounce it accurately;
- student then segments the word by saying each syllable e.g., *re-mem-ber* (or in the case of a single-syllable word, saying the onset and rime units (*s-un; b-et*));
- student then *names* the letters in the word in sequence, twice;
- without reference to the model, the student then writes the word *while naming each letter*;
- check against the original spelling—correct if necessary, and repeat,

Repeated writing

Writing a word several times is one way in which a kinaesthetic image of the word can be more firmly established in long-term memory. Only a few words (*no more than three*) should be practised in any one session. Repeated writing can easily be incorporated as the last step in the SOS strategy described above.

Repeated writing of a target word that the student is trying to master can be very helpful indeed if (i) the learner has every intention of trying to remedy an error and (ii) if he or she is attending fully to the task. However, if the student is thinking of other things or is distracted while carrying out the repeated writing the procedure is of little or no value. It simply becomes a mechanical performance that can be carried out without conscious effort, and the words are not remembered later.

Old Way/New Way method

Lyndon (1989) suggested that the reason for the difficulty many students have in 'unlearning' an incorrect spelling they have in memory is due to *proactive inhibition* (or proactive interference). This term refers to a situation where previously stored information interferes with one's ability to acquire a new correct response. What the individual already knows is protected from change. Lyndon's approach called 'Old Way/New Way' uses a student's error as the starting point for change. A memory of the old way of spelling of the word is used to activate later an awareness of the new (correct) way of spelling the word. Old Way/New Way has been described as a metacognitive strategy for achieving permanent error correction and habit unlearning (Baxter et al., 2004).

The following steps and procedures are used:

- student writes the word in the usual incorrect form;
- teacher and student agree to call this the 'old way' of spelling that word;
- teacher shows student a 'new way' (correct way) of spelling the word;
- attention is drawn to the similarities and differences between the old and the new forms: '*You used to write "biter", with only one "t". In the new way you spell it with "tt". Bitter.*'
- student writes word again in the old way;

- student writes word in the new way, and explains aloud the difference: '*Now I write it with two tts. Bitter.*'
- repeat five such writings of old way, new way and statement of differences;
- students may be asked to write five different sentences using the word in its 'new' form;
- revise the words taught after a week;
- if necessary, repeat this procedure every two weeks until the new response is firmly established in long-term memory.

Tutoring individual students

When planning an individualised programme in spelling, the following points should be kept in mind:

- first determine the developmental level at which the student is already functioning in spelling; analyse some samples of the students' written work and use appropriate spelling tests to discover existing skill level and areas of weakness; note any common errors that need to be remedied;
- set clear objectives for learning; discuss these with the student;
- in secondary schools, talk with the student's subject teachers to collect a list of subject or topic words frequently needed by the student in writing in their subject: for example, *ingredients, temperature, chisel, theory, science, hydrochloric, equation, gymnasium*;
- use this list for regular review and assessment;
- within each tutorial session, work on specific words misspelled in free writing lessons as well as on more general word lists or word families;
- when making a correction to a word, the student should rewrite the whole word, not merely erase the incorrect letters; where relevant, apply Old Way/New Way strategy and repeated writing;
- repetition and overlearning are important, so aim to achieve high levels of practice through a range of exercises, games, word puzzles, and computer tasks, to reinforce spelling of important words;
- daily attention will be needed for the least able spellers, with weekly revision and regular testing for maintenance;
- requiring a student to spell words aloud without writing them down and seeing them is of no value for weak spellers—although it is traditionally used in 'spelling bees';
- a neat, careful style of handwriting that can be executed swiftly and easily is an important factor associated with good spelling;
- smooth use of keyboard is also important for spelling (Feng et al., 2019).

In the next chapter, attention is turned to developing important numeracy skills. Often, students with learning difficulties find working with numbers and solving mathematical problems as tricky as learning literacy skills.

Online resources

- A paper titled Research-based tutoring of English spelling by Rosevita Warda is available online at: www.learnthat.org/pages/view/whitepaperenglishspelling.html.

- Ripple, M. 4 Spelling strategies you won't want to miss: https://blog.allaboutlearningpress.com/effective-spelling-strategies/.
- Top 8 spelling strategies: https://howtospell.co.uk/ESL–spelling-strategies.
- Teacher Network: How to teach spelling: www.theguardian.com/education/2013/may/20/spelling-classroom-teaching-resources.
- How should spelling be taught? http://dyslexiahelp.umich.edu/professionals/dyslexia-school/spelling/how-should-spelling-be-taught.
- Word Study: Learning word patterns. www.readingrockets.org/article/word-study-learning-word-patterns.

Print resources

Anonymous. (2020). *New KS2 English SAT Buster: Spelling Book 2*. Broughton-in-Furness, Cumbria: CGP Books.

Brown, A. (2018). *Understanding and teaching English spelling*. London & New York: Routledge.

Rudling, J. (2016). *Spelling strategies and secrets: The essential how to spell guide*. London: How to Spell Publishing.

Templeton, S.R., Bear, D.R., Invernizzi, M.A., Johnston, F.R., Flanigan, K., Townsend, D.R., Helman, L., & Hayes, L. (2015). *Vocabulary their way: Word study with middle and secondary students* (2nd ed.). Boston, MA: Pearson.

Waugh, D., Warner, C., & Waugh, R. (2019). *Teaching grammar, punctuation and spelling in primary schools*. London: Sage.

Chapter 13

Numeracy and basic mathematical skills

In this era of information and communication technology, the importance of numeracy has not decreased and continues to rank alongside literacy. In Australia, the Learning Sciences Institute (2016) suggests that when students leave school with a poor standard of numeracy this can have devastating social and economic consequences. Poor numeracy skills are known to affect a range of everyday competencies such as the ability to manage money, understand basic statistics and graphs in daily news reports, and comprehend details in medical reports, accounts, and invoices that one may receive. It is therefore acknowledged that in the current social, economic, scientific, and technological environment there is a need to ensure that students leave school and enter adult life with a good standard of numeracy.

In several countries around the world there has been growing concern that numeracy standards are falling below those required for the 21st century (Goss et al., 2016; Kuczera et al., 2016; OECD, 2016). To combat this situation, Kuczera et al. (2016) urge schools to provide much better teaching of numeracy at all year levels, and to provide effective early intervention for any students who are not progressing well. This chapter addresses the difficulties faced by too many students in becoming fully numerate, and presents some appropriate teaching methods to help overcome learning difficulties.

Contemporary perspectives on mathematics teaching

Reforms in mathematics education that began in many countries in the late 1980s encouraged schools to implement a *constructivist* approach—often referred to as activity-based or problem-based mathematics. Teachers were expected to create learning situations that provide opportunities for students to investigate mathematical concepts and discover number relationships for themselves, by engaging in real problem solving. This was deemed to be a more motivating and insightful way of learning, rather than receiving teacher-directed instruction in arithmetic skills. The constructivist approach places most emphasis on students developing deeper understanding of mathematical concepts while avoiding the rote-learning of poorly understood calculation procedures. It was said that too often in the past, students have been expected to remember algorithms, rules, and facts without grasping the underlying principles on which they are based. Currell (2018, p. 1) has written:

> During my schooling, math was a matter of following procedures and rules, and involved endless practice. I could follow and apply the steps as required, but understand little of it in a deeper, interconnected way.

Constructivism

Constructivist approaches have much to offer, but the notion that all students can learn mathematics entirely by immersion in problems has been challenged (e.g., Doabler et al., 2014; Westwood, 2011). Currently, there is concern that under a constructivist approach, the reduced attention given to practising basic arithmetic skills to the point of mastery means that too many students do not develop essential fluency and automaticity (Baker & Cuevas, 2018; Nelson et al., 2018). There is little doubt that students with learning difficulties make much better progress in mathematics, particularly in the early stages of learning, when they are directly taught and then given time to practise each skill (Doabler & Fien, 2013; Farkota, 2013; Witzel & Mize, 2018).

Teacher-led instruction

Critics have suggested that a constructivist approach makes unreasonable assumptions concerning children's ability to discover and remember mathematical relationships—and this is certainly not the way that mathematics is taught in places like Japan, Korea, China, Singapore, and Finland—where students currently rank highest in math achievement. In these countries, teachers use a much more teacher-controlled approach, that still involves active student participation but within a carefully structured programme and clearly defined expectations for standards of achievement. In these countries, the most effective teachers provide systematic instruction in mathematics in such a way that ensures understanding accompanies mastery of number skills and problem solving. The goal is always to construct meaning in mathematics, but not through the medium of unguided activity. The emerging perspective is that effective teaching and learning of mathematics requires a well-orchestrated combination of investigative activities and teacher-directed explicit instruction and practice (Doabler et al., 2014; Slavin et al., 2009a).

The value of groupwork

The use of a direct teaching approach at Tier 1 does not mean that teachers abandon the use of groupwork and collaborative learning in the classroom. Lessons within a well-balanced programme include some time spent in teacher-led whole-class activity and some time devoted to group activities. The groups are closely monitored and guided by the teacher to maintain a high success rate and strengthen students' motivation. Tasks involving students in discussion and sharing of ideas help them negotiate a better understanding of key concepts and processes that have already been more directly taught (Jacob & Jacob, 2018; James & Steimle, 2014). Groupwork also allows for some degree of differentiation of curriculum content according to students' ability levels and rate of learning.

Digital technology

Use can be made of online and computer-based activities as part of groupwork, paired assignments, or differentiated individualised learning in the mathematics lesson (Kaczorowski et al., 2019; Mutlu & Akgün, 2017; Serhan & Almeqdadi, 2020). For example, Outhwaite et al. (2019) have reported using an interactive math app for early years education, and they conclude that it can efficiently deliver high-quality math instruction and can raise basic math achievement in this age group. Similarly, using computer-based play to practise basic number processes is reported to yield good improvement in arithmetic operations in children aged 7 (Mohd-Syah et al., 2016). Mobile devices have also increased significantly the opportunities for engaging students in practice and revision work in numeracy at home. More will be said later on the broader role of technology in learning math.

Learning difficulties in mathematics

Students' level of achievement in numeracy is affected by many influences, including gender, socioeconomic family background, parents' level of education, and (most importantly) quality of instruction in school (OECD, 2013; Witzel & Mize, 2018). While many students find mathematics a difficult subject to study, it is suggested that some 7 per cent of students have very significant problems in learning even the most basic concepts and skills (Nelson & Powell, 2018). A few of these students may have a specific learning disability related to mathematics (*dyscalculia*), but most have simply encountered difficulty in the early stages and have lost confidence in their own ability. They quickly develop a poor attitude towards the subject, and this destroys their future motivation.

The major factors associated with learning difficulty in mathematics include:

- students falling behind and becoming discouraged;
- little or no differentiation of learning activities or assessment tasks to match students' diverse experiences and abilities;
- too little structuring of activity-based math, with students failing to learn anything;
- teacher's use of overly complex language when explaining mathematical relationships or when posing questions;
- students' weak reading skills contributing to difficulties in understanding math problems or printed explanations;
- too little teaching time devoted to ensuring that students achieve conceptual understanding.

Many difficulties can also be traced to poor teaching that has involved:

- abstract symbols being introduced too early in the absence of concrete materials and real-life examples;
- larger numbers involving complications of place-value being introduced before students have grasped simple relationships in numbers to twenty;
- too little time spent developing automaticity with number facts, leading to slowness and inaccuracy in calculations.

One of the negative affective outcomes from difficulty in learning mathematics is a high level of anxiety in situations where competency needs to be demonstrated (Pearn, 2014; Ramirez et al., 2018). The anxiety begins in the school years but remains into adult life, often preventing school-leavers from taking a career path that might involve dealing with math.

Math anxiety is now a well-recognised phenomenon and has attracted much research interest. High anxiety is not only emotionally draining but also seriously impedes learning processes in the brain (Buckley, 2013; Buckley & Reid, 2013). Students who display this anxiety usually require therapeutic counselling as well as intensive math intervention at Tier 3. The main challenge for teachers is to present the subject in such a way that students begin to succeed and enjoy the work, rather than fail (Pappano, 2014). One way of stimulating interest of students with learning difficulties is to avoid making textbook and whiteboard exercises the only materials used in lessons. Greater use should be made of authentic topics and materials from outside the classroom (e.g., sports results in the television news, data in newspaper reports, poll results, holiday planning, and costings from online advertisements, air fares, etc.) (NCETM, 2014).

Assisting students with learning difficulties

It is important that students with learning difficulties in mathematics should be identified early and given appropriate support. The most important components in intervention at Tier 3 include:

- providing individualised help that is matched to the student's current level of understanding;
- giving additional practice opportunities to achieve mastery of basic facts and procedures;
- sequencing curriculum material carefully and controlling difficulty level;
- providing extended time to complete assignments and to work on problems;
- encouraging the use of concrete or graphic materials where necessary and helpful;
- reading word-problems aloud to the student to avoid any reading difficulty;
- permitting use of a calculator;
- using cue cards to display the steps to take in carrying out a specific process;
- facilitating individual support by using a classroom assistant or by adopting peer tutoring.

Several early intervention programmes exist that focus on fundamental skills of counting, numeral recognition, grouping, solving simple addition and subtraction problems, and understanding place value. A report issued by the Australian Council for Educational Research (ACER, 2013) reviewed almost a dozen such programmes and recommended that a specific intervention should only be adopted if the content aligns reasonably well with learning objectives in the mainstream mathematics curriculum for that age group, and has credible evidence of effectiveness. Examples of useful programmes include:

- *Mathematics Recovery* (Wright, 2003): Involves 30 minutes a day of individualised assessment-based instruction for low-achieving children aged 6 to 7 years.
- *QuickSmart Numeracy* (Bellert, 2009): Targets students in the middle-school years and is effective in building up fluency and confidence in basic arithmetic and in strategy use.
- *Numeracy Recovery* (Dowker, 2005): Targets 6- to 7-year-old children and involves 30 minutes instruction per week over a period of approximately 30 weeks.
- *GRIN (Getting Ready in Numeracy)* (Kalogeropoulos et al., 2020): This small group or individual tutoring program involves 15- to 25-minute sessions delivered at least three times per week. The purpose is to prepare primary and secondary school students who are weak at math for the upcoming mathematics lessons in their main classroom. The classroom math teacher communicates details of the content of future digital lessons in advance to the tutor.

What should be taught?

In recent years, content of mathematics courses in the UK and Australia has generally been delineated in guidelines that accompany national curricula (ACARA, 2014b; DfE [UK], 2014c). Similarly, in the USA the *Common Core State Standards* also describes the mathematical skills and concepts that must be mastered, from kindergarten through to high school (CCSS, 2014). In the three countries, it is agreed that all students need to develop problem-solving skills, but that to achieve this goal it is important also at Tier 1 that they acquire fluency in mental arithmetic and written calculation through the use of effective evidence-based methods. It is acknowledged that to achieve this outcome, adjustments and differentiation often need to be made to the learning activities, resource materials, and objectives for students with learning difficulties; and that for some students additional teaching and re-teaching will be required at Tier 2 and Tier 3.

Traditionally, students with learning difficulties were placed in the lowest-ability group and given a modified version of the mainstream math curriculum. Sometimes (particularly in special schools and secondary special classes) an alternative math curriculum would be developed with a focus on teaching survival math—such as managing money, giving change, paying bills, and simple linear measurement, together with practice in basic addition, subtraction, multiplication, and division. It was thought that a functional approach geared to everyday life was more likely to enhance students' motivation and engagement, and would also increase the likelihood that skills taught would generalise beyond the school setting (Dawes, 2014). More recently, with the advent of inclusive education policies, it is generally agreed that as far as possible all students should be helped to engage with the mainstream Tier 1 mathematics curriculum. It is argued that students with special needs are entitled to engage in interesting, relevant, and inclusive mathematics, rather than a watered-down version. For this reason, it is now believed that content in mathematics courses in mainstream schools should be reduced as little as possible for lower-ability students in order to maintain sufficient challenge.

A diagnostic approach

There are three levels at which diagnostic work in mathematics can be conducted—concrete, semi-concrete, and abstract. During diagnostic work with a student, the teacher may move up or down within this continuum from concrete to abstract in an attempt to discover the level at which the student can succeed with each concept or process. At the *concrete level* the student may be able to solve a problem or complete a process correctly if allowed to use counters. At the *semi-concrete level,* pictorial representation of objects, together with symbols or tally marks will provide sufficient visual information to ensure success. At the *abstract level,* a student can work mentally with numerals, signs and symbols.

The first step in intervention at Tiers 2 and 3 should be to ascertain what the student can already do in each area of the appropriate math curriculum. The next step is to locate any gaps in knowledge and skills, and determine precisely what he or she needs to be taught next. The teacher is really finding answers to the questions: 'What can the student do independently in mathematics?' and 'What can he or she do if given a little help and guidance (scaffolding)?' It is also essential to gain an impression of the student's level of confidence (or anxiety).

The first question can be answered by conducting some informal testing and examining the student's workbooks to determine the level at which he or she is functioning. A student's errors tend to reveal much about their current knowledge and skills, and can help identify faulty procedural knowledge, gaps in understanding, and misconceptions. Appropriate follow-up testing can then be used. For this purpose, teachers usually construct their own informal 'mathematical skills inventory' containing items covering key concepts, knowledge, and skills presented in earlier years, together with essential material from the current curriculum. Observing a student working through the items can indicate what the student can do, what he or she is not sure about, and how confident he or she is in tackling math problems.

Assessment should not be confined to the four arithmetic processes but should also include age-appropriate word problems to be solved. Observing how a student goes about solving a problem can reveal much about his or her flexibility in thinking, underlying knowledge, and number skills proficiency. When a student explains or demonstrates how he or she tackles a problem, the teacher can identify the exact point of confusion and can intervene from there.

Teachers usually check the following capabilities when appraising problem solving. Can the student:

- detect what is called for in a problem;
- identify relevant information;
- select and perform correct procedure;
- estimate an approximate answer;
- compute the solution;
- check the answer, and if necessary self-correct.

By referring to any items the student fails to solve in a test or during deskwork, the teacher should consider:

- *Why* did the student get this item wrong?
- Can he or she carry out the process if allowed to count on fingers, or use a number-line or calculator?
- Can the student work through an example step by step, explaining aloud each action. At what point does the student misunderstand, or forget the next step?

Teaching at concrete and semi-concrete levels

Having used a diagnostic approach to discover what a student can already do, and having planned an intervention, it is important to consider age-appropriate methods and activities for Tiers 2 and 3. The following pages identify some issues to consider.

Real and structural materials

When working with young or intellectually disabled children it is essential at first to use real objects to illustrate quantitative relationships. However, in Tier 2 and Tier 3 remedial teaching contexts, real objects can be supplemented by materials such as counters, picture cards, Multibase Arithmetic Blocks (MAB), Cuisenaire Rods, or Unifix. These can be used to illustrate concepts such as conservation of number, grouping and re-grouping, place value, multiplication, division, and so forth. Blocks can also be used to represent visually the quantities referred to within a word problem (e.g., 6 cars and 3 trucks; 14 girls and 4 boys). This is particularly important for students with learning difficulties, as it helps them store *visual representations* of number relationships in memory. It must be recognised however that a student must not rely for too long on having blocks or counters, but must progress to the next stage of processing number relationships mentally.

Counting

Counting is the most fundamental of all early number skills and underpins most of the basic number concepts and processes required in early learning (Gibbs et al., 2018). Nguyen et al. (2016) have found that counting strategies in preschoolers are highly predictive of their later mathematics achievement; so, counting must be recognised as a very important foundation for numeracy development. This essential skill includes rote counting (reciting the number names in correct order), counting on fingers, accurate counting of small groups using one-to-one correspondence, and more advanced counting strategies such as 'counting on' from a given number, counting back, and counting by 2s, 5s, and 10s. In the beginning stages, physically counting items in a set helps the youngest children reinforce the important concept of number conservation—the understanding that no matter how items in a group are rearranged, the number of items does not change unless you put more in or take some out.

If a young or severely disabled child has not acquired accurate counting of real objects, the skill must be taught by direct instruction (Greer & Erickson, 2019). The problem is often that these students can rote count but fail to make a correct one-to-one correspondence between the spoken number word and each object touched in a sequence. Teachers should take every opportunity during any school day to have preschool children count with one-to-one correspondence— for example, when walking up steps, when counting out books, when counting children into groups, and so forth. Counting activities using pictorial material and animations can now be presented also on a computer screen, to supplement any hands-on concrete counting activities (Mutlu & Akgün, 2019).

Recognition and writing of numerals

Alongside counting, the ability to recognise instantly the numerals from 1 to 10 (and later from 11 to 20, etc.) is an important step in increasing a preschool child's exact number system. It is helpful that numerals are very frequently on display in preschool children's educational television programmes and picture books, with the cardinal value of number symbols related to a wide variety of objects.

Activities that can help to establish numeral recognition include:

- numeral-to-group matching games—for example, the numeral 11 on a card to be matched with 11 birds, 11 kites, 11 cars, 11 dots, 11 tally marks;

- lotto cards with a selection of number symbols (1 to 10; 1 to 20; or 25 to 50, etc.) — when the teacher says a number, the child covers the numeral on the lotto card; and at the end of the game, must read each number aloud to the teacher;
- the same lotto cards can be used for basic addition and subtraction facts, the numerals on the cards now representing correct answers to some simple oral question from the teacher ('5 add 4 = …' 'The number 1 less than 8 is …');
- numeral cards can also be devised for students to sort and arrange in correct sequence from one to ten, one to twenty, etc;
- basic items from Unifix can also be helpful at this stage (e.g., inset pattern boards, number indicators, and number line one-to-twenty).

At this stage, correct writing of numerals should also be taught as part of normal handwriting instruction. Correct formation of numerals should be established thoroughly, to reduce the incidence of reversals of certain figures like 3, 5, 9 in written recording. A tendency to reverse a figure or place value needs to be remedied before it becomes stored in muscle memory as an incorrectly motor habit.

Number facts

Number facts are those associations that can instantly be retrieved from memory (e.g., $5 + 2 = 7$; $3 \times 2 = 6$; up to $9 + 9$ and 9×9). These facts are always involved within sub-routines carried out in all calculations, and for this reason they need to be recalled with a high degree of automaticity. Being able to recall number facts easily is important because it makes calculation simpler and faster. Knowing number facts is partly a matter of learning through repetition (constant exposure and practice) and partly a matter of grasping a rule and developing insight (e.g., that zero added to any number does not change it: $3 + 0 = 3$, $13 + 0 = 13$, etc.; or if $7 + 3 = 10$, then $7 + 4$ must be 'one more than ten', etc.). Number facts only become automatic after a great deal of practice. Many students with learning disabilities have difficulty recalling number facts and tables, so they require extra attention devoted to this key area.

Using a number line

A number-line or number track is a linear representation of numbers placed in correct visual sequence. This line is a very useful aid for supporting students' counting skills and for making clear processes of simple addition (counting on from a given number) and subtraction (counting back) (Woods et al., 2018). The number-line can also be used to teach 'interval counting' in twos, fives, and tens.

Many students discover the value of a number-line for themselves without formal instruction; and even older students will often be seen using calibrations on a ruler to count forward or back as an aid to mental calculation. In primary school, teachers can use a number-line to demonstrate basic operations such as multiplication and division, or as an aid to problem solving. Unifix has a 1-to-100 number track divided into 10-unit sections. In kindergarten, one would use only the section for 1 to 10 or 1- to 20. In primary school, the sections from 20 to 100 can be added and children can place blocks in the track to model operations such as $22 + 13$, $45 + 17$, 21×3, $26 \div 4$, etc.

Bar modelling

One approach that has proved very useful for representing number relationships visually is *Bar Modelling* (also referred to as the *Singapore Math Model Method*). This approach spans the concrete-pictorial-abstract (CPA) stages and teaches students a strategy they can use for problems involving addition, subtraction, multiplication and division. Students are taught to 'draw' (represent) quantities stated within a word problem to help them visualise the number relationships and then decide what action to take.

Example:

Mrs Wilkinson made 11 pancakes on Sunday. Only a few children liked them, so she made only 8 on Monday and 3 on Tuesday. How many pancakes had she made altogether?

11 + 8 + 3 = 22 pancakes

How many more pancakes were made on Sunday than on Tuesday?

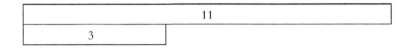

On Monday, how many children could have 2 pancakes each?

| 2 | 2 | 2 | 2 |

8 ÷ 2 = 4 children

The Bar Model strategy is an important component within the Singapore Math Method®, now adopted in the UK. The approach has been particularly effective for students with learning difficulties, who benefit most when a math problem is made visible (Preston, 2016; Sharp & Shih-Dennis, 2017). For more details see https://jimmy maths.com/singapore-math-model-method/

Teaching computation skills

Computation skills are those used in applying routine procedures involved in addition, subtraction, multiplication, and division. Once young students are ready to learn conventional ways of recording number operations, they must be taught how to encode vertical and horizontal forms of computation. For example, a student should be able to watch as 'a ten rod and two extra ones' (12) are added to a set already containing 'a ten rod and three extra ones' (13) and then write the operation as:

12 + 13 = 25

or

$$
\begin{array}{r}
12 \\
+\ 13 \\
\hline
25
\end{array}
$$

When children are first learning a new algorithm, it is usual practice to teach them self-instructions for carrying out each step in a particular calculation. An example is provided below for a subtraction item (HTU) using the *decomposition method*.

$$
\begin{array}{r}
5 \quad \overset{7}{8}\ \overset{11}{1} \\
-\ 1 \quad 3 \quad 9 \\
\hline
4 \quad 4 \quad 2
\end{array}
$$

The student would be taught to verbalise the steps in some way similar to the wording below. Once mastered, the procedure becomes automatic through practice and this self-cueing is phased out.

The child says:

'Start with the units. I can't take 9 from 1, so I must borrow a ten. Cross out the 8 tens and write 7 tens.

Write the borrowed ten next to the 1 to make 11.

Now I can take 9 from 11 and write 2 in the answer space.

Under the 10's column: 7 take away 3, leaves 4 tens.

In the 100's column: 5 take away 1, leaves 4. Write 4 in the answer space.

My answer is 442.'

A support teacher, tutor, or parent who attempts to help a student in this area of school work should liaise with the class teacher in order to find out the precise verbal scripts that are used in teaching the four arithmetic processes, so that exactly the same words and directions are used in the remedial programme to avoid confusion.

With the advent of the constructivist approach, teaching these verbal scripts fell into disrepute. It is argued that mindlessly following a memorised script may represent nothing more than rote learning; and it is also felt by some experts that scripts inhibit the mathematical thinking of more-able students and may prevent them from devising insightful methods of calculation. However, without such verbal cues in the early stages, lower-ability students are likely to remain totally confused and frustrated.

Calculators

The most common form of technology in the mathematics classroom is, of course, the calculator. This handheld device has proved to be a boon for many students, allowing them to complete more work and spend more time on problem solving (Yang & Lin, 2015). Calculators are of particular value for students of high ability, enabling them to tackle some very complex and challenging problems and to explore mathematical ideas more deeply (Kissane, 2017).

Calculators have an important role that is far more than simply acting as a tool to avoid tedious calculations by hand. For students with special needs, a calculator provides a means of temporarily bypassing computation weaknesses. In math tutoring at Tier 2 and

Tier 3, calculators can certainly be used to add variety to lessons and help develop important skills for everyday use.

In the Australian Curriculum, guidelines state that from Year 3 onwards students should be able to use a calculator to check the solution and reasonableness of an answer. By Year 7 they should be able to investigate problems with digital technologies; and beyond Year 7 calculators are recommended to support graphical, computational, and statistical aspects in mathematics lessons. Guidelines within the revised National Curriculum in the UK suggest that calculators should only be a regular tool in later stages of Key Stage 2 (age approximately 10 years). In the primary school years, children still need to develop sound and reliable skills in mental and written calculation without relying on a calculator. The Department for Education in England has stated:

> Calculators should not be used as a substitute for good written and mental arithmetic. They should therefore only be introduced near the end of Key Stage 2 to support pupils' conceptual understanding and exploration of more complex number problems, if written and mental arithmetic are secure. In both primary and secondary schools, teachers should use their judgement about when ICT tools should be used.
>
> (DfE, 2013b)

An interesting discussion on calculator use was posted online in 2019 on the NCETM website at: www.ncetm.org.uk/resources/53171

Developing problem-solving skills and strategies

The whole purpose of learning mathematics is to acquire knowledge, skills, and strategies that enable an individual to solve problems they may encounter during school time, working life, at home and during leisure. From the learner's perspective, solving a real-life problem involves much more than simply applying a pre-taught algorithm. Non-routine problems need to be analysed carefully, and procedures selected must be suitable for purpose. Instructing students in problem solving is more difficult than teaching them basic arithmetic processes. However, there is evidence that all students can be helped to become more proficient at solving math problems if adequate time is devoted to this important aspect of mathematics.

Mathematical problem solving is particularly challenging for children with learning difficulties because it often involves close reading of a word problem, interpreting and integrating information, selecting an appropriate computation process, performing the calculation, and checking the result obtained. These students commonly display confusion and anxiety when faced with complex mathematical problems in printed form (Passolunghi et al., 2019). They may begin by having difficulty reading the words or comprehending the exact meaning of specific terms. Next, they do not really understand what they are being asked to find out, and this uncertainty compounds their difficulty in selecting a process to use. Their constant lack of success with math problems leads to loss of confidence, and undermines self-esteem and motivation.

Most students with these difficulties need to be directly taught a range of effective problem-solving strategies (Krawec, 2014; Lussier et al., 2014). The aim is to show them how to process the information in a problem thoughtfully and sequentially—and without feeling helpless. They need to be able to sift the relevant from the irrelevant information and impose some degree of structure on the problem. It is generally accepted now that there are teachable steps through which an individual must pass when solving mathematical problems. These steps can be summarised as:

- interpretation of the problem;
- identification of processes and steps needed;
- translation of the information into an appropriate algorithm or algorithms;
- careful calculation;
- checking of the result;
- self-correction when necessary.

While working through a problem, a student needs to think:

- what needs to be worked out here? (identify the problem)
- can I picture this problem in my mind? Can I draw it? (visualisation)
- how will I do this? (select a process or strategy)
- perform relevant calculations
- is this working out OK? (self-monitoring)
- check if my final solution is correct (reflection, reasoning, evaluation)
- do I need to correct any error and try again? (self-correction)

The sequence for teaching problem solving to students with learning difficulties begins with direct teaching, followed by guided practice, and ending with independent control. Once students have been taught a particular strategy, they must have many opportunities to apply the strategy themselves under teacher guidance and with corrective feedback. Finally, they must be able to use the strategy independently and generalise its use to other problem contexts.

An example

A problem-solving strategy might use a particular mnemonic to aid recall of the procedure. For example, in the mnemonic 'RAVE CCC' the word RAVE can be used to identify the first four possible steps to take:

R = Read the problem carefully.
A = Attend to words that may suggest the process required (*share, altogether, less than, how many*).
V = Visualise the problem, and perhaps make a sketch, diagram or table.
E = Estimate the possible answer.

The letters CCC suggest what to do next:

C = Choose the numbers to use.
C = Calculate the answer.
C = Check the answer against your estimate.

Additional teaching points to consider when improving the problem-solving abilities of students with learning difficulties include:

- pre-teaching any difficult vocabulary associated with a specific word problem, so that comprehension is enhanced;
- providing cues (such as directional arrows) in the early stages to indicate where to begin calculations and in which direction to proceed;
- deliberately linking math problems to the students' life experiences;
- providing more examples than usual, to establish and strengthen the application of a particular strategy;
- giving students experience in setting their own problems for others to solve;
- stressing the value of self-checking and self-correction;
- using appropriate computer-aided instruction (CAI).

Students with specific talents in mathematics

Students who possess extremely high aptitude for mathematics can be regarded as having 'special educational needs'—in that they require a curriculum that is far deeper and more demanding than that usually offered in the mainstream. It is all too easy for these students to become bored and frustrated in math lessons where the material is pitched at the average standard and the pace of progress is too slow. Some form of differentiation that provides greater intellectual challenge and enrichment is absolutely essential in meeting the needs of talented mathematicians. Such differentiation is achieved by modifying curriculum content, creating non-routine problems, and using a variety of higher-level resource materials (including computer software). Investigative projects that require talented students to use initiative, creativity, and mathematical reasoning, must become the norm. Some schools have also found it valuable to offer extra-curricular activities with a focus on mathematics, and to find mentors who can work with gifted students to advance their mathematical reasoning and skills.

As a contrast to students with high aptitude for mathematics, there are a few gifted students who may achieve highly in most school subjects but exhibit a specific learning disability in the area of mathematics (*dyscalculia*) (Ribeiro et al., 2017). These students usually require Tier 3 intensive support, and are known to learn best when teachers use explicit instruction, with lesson content broken down into achievable steps, and instructional scaffolding is provided (Witzel & Mize, 2018). They may also need personal therapeutic counselling if their disability in mathematics is causing them worry or anxiety. There are now many computer programs and apps for mobile devices that can be used by students with dyscalculia to help practice number facts and basic computation processes.

The remaining two chapters provide additional information on teaching methods that produce the most effective outcomes, and on how teaching methods, learning materials, and assessment can be adapted for students with learning difficulties and disabilities.

Online resources

- The Common Core State Standards for mathematics in the US can be found at: www.corestandards.org/Math/Practice/.
- The guidelines for mathematics in the revised National Curriculum in England can be found at: www.gov.uk/government/publications/national-curriculum-in-england-mathematics-programmes-of-study/national-curriculum-in-england-mathematics-programmes-of-study.

- Mathematics in the Australian Curriculum can be located at: www.australiancurriculum.edu.au/f-10-curriculum/mathematics/?layout=1.
- General teaching advice can be found in the online at: https://dera.ioe.ac.uk/13798/1/mathematics.pdf.
- Important considerations when adapting the mathematics curriculum for students with special needs are discussed in an online document from the Board of Studies in New South Wales at: https://educationstandards.nsw.edu.au/wps/portal/nesa/k-10/learning-areas/mathematics/mathematics-k-10/introduction/students-with-special-education-need.
- A full explanation of the Bar Model method can be found online at: www.hmhco.com/~/media/sites/home/education/global/pdf/white-papers/mathematics/elementary/math-in-focus/mif_model_drawing_lr.pdf?la=en.

Print resources

Bay-Williams, J., & Kling, G. (2019). *Math fact fluency: 60+ games and assessment tools to support learning and retention.* Alexandria, VA: Association for Supervision and Curriculum Development.

Goos, M., Geiger, V., Dole, S., & Forgasz, H. (2019). *Numeracy across the curriculum: Research-based strategies for enhancing teaching and learning.* Sydney: Allen & Unwin.

Hattie, J., Fisher, D., & Frey, N. (2016). *Visible learning for mathematics Grades K-12: What works best to optimize student learning.* Thousand Oaks, CA: Sage.

Mattock, P. (2019). *Visible maths: Using representations and structure to enhance mathematics teaching in schools.* Bancyfelin, Carmarthen: Crown House Publishing.

Westwood, P. (2019). Becoming numerate: Enduring theories, recent research and current issues. *Australian Journal of Learning Difficulties,* 24(1), 21–46.

Chapter 14

Teaching methods

In recent years, pre-service teacher education courses in the USA, Britain, New Zealand, and Australia have tended to advocate methods that are almost entirely based on a *constructivist theory* of learning—meaning that students must construct meaning and understanding for themselves, and that lessons must be student-centred rather than teacher-directed. The role of the teacher is to be a 'creator of opportunities' for students to learn, and to be a facilitator rather than an instructor (Hughes et al., 2017; Wolfe, 2019). At the same time, there has been a tendency to suggest to trainee teachers that traditional teacher-led instruction is 'old fashioned' and unsound, and should be avoided.

While constructivist, student-centred methods such as discovery learning and activity-based approach are popular, there is often very little research evidence available to prove their efficacy. Indeed, the research evidence that is available strongly supports direct teaching as the most effective way of raising achievement standards and reducing failure rates (e.g., Hattie, 2003; Hattie & Yates, 2014; Kruit et al., 2018; Muijs & Reynolds, 2017). Direct teaching appears to be the most powerful method for introducing new knowledge or skills, particularly in literacy and numeracy domains, and particularly for addressing the needs of students with learning difficulties and disabilities (Anderson, 2019; Satsangi et al., 2019a; Spooner et al., 2019). It has been suggested that teacher-directed learning for all students in the early stages is the best preparation for efficient self-directed learning later (Tan, 2018).

This chapter describes Tier 1 approaches ranging from those that are regarded as 'teacher led' (or *instructive*) to those that are clearly more 'learner oriented' (or *constructive*). The strengths of each method are summarised, with reference to achieving particular types of learning objectives and their suitability for teaching students with learning difficulties or disabilities.

Selecting Tier 1 teaching methods

There is no single method that is superior to all other methods for all teaching purposes. One particular method cannot possibly be appropriate for all types of learning or for all ages and abilities of students. Methods must be selected according to their suitability for a given purpose with a specific age group. A teacher's decision to select an approach for use at a particular time must depend upon the nature of the lesson content to be taught, the learning objectives, and the salient characteristics of the students in the group. Selection of approach should also be based on hard evidence that the method has been proved by research to be the most effective. Unfortunately, the latter criterion is too rarely applied, and teachers tend simply to use an approach with which they feel comfortable and have most experience. When an inappropriate teaching approach is used, learning difficulties are exacerbated (Agarwal & Bain, 2019; Farkota, 2005). An example of this is the use of student-centred immersion methods for teaching the beginning stages of reading, writing, and mathematics, regardless of the fact that research has shown conclusively that children make significantly better progress in these skills when directly taught (Smith, Poling & Worth, 2018). Much more needs to be done in our universities to ensure that trainee teachers are taught how to use explicit instruction for the early stages of teaching basic skills (Scarparolo & Hammond, 2018).

Teacher-led approaches

It is relevant to begin by exploring Tier 1 methods that are teacher-directed and structured. The effectiveness of these approaches has been strongly supported by research evidence.

Explicit instruction

Explicit instruction is a method for presenting new information clearly and directly to learners in a form they can access and understand (Agarwal & Bain, 2019; Braun et al., 2017). The approach involves teachers informing, demonstrating, explaining, and narrating, but may also involve showing students an instructional video or setting students to work through a computer program that presents new information in a clear and systematic manner. Explicit instruction is not simply a passive 'transmission' approach that attempts to fill up 'empty' students with information; good explicit instruction involves a great deal of interaction between teacher and students—particularly when teachers use questioning effectively. The approach can be greatly enhanced by appropriate use of visual and technological support, such as interactive whiteboards, graphic organisers, on-screen PowerPoint material, pictures, models, illustrated textbooks, and web-based resources. This form of teaching can be used across the curriculum when introducing any new topic to a class, when clarifying a concept, when providing important information, when setting out the steps in a new procedure or process, and when consolidating or reviewing content at the end of a lesson or series of lessons. Braun et al. (2017) have described explicit instruction as a model for teaching that utilises thorough and carefully planned lessons in which the teacher clearly outlines learning goals and implements structured lessons with the aim of student mastery of sequential learning objectives. Explicit instruction has proved to be of particular importance for students with learning difficulties and disabilities, and those learning English as a second language (Colovic-Markovic, 2019; Ennis & Losinski, 2019; Muijs & Reynolds, 2017).

No teacher would ever use explicit instruction as his or her *only* approach—but the ability to teach curriculum content and skills explicitly *when necessary* should be part of a teacher's classroom expertise (Hammond & Moore, 2018). The most essential skill for a teacher to possess for explicit instruction is the ability to explain things simply and clearly. This skill depends partly on the teacher's ability to view a new topic from the perspective of a student learning it for the first time, partly on the ability to organise information into sequential, teachable, and learnable units, and partly on the ability to express ideas in plain language that can be understood by learners of that age and ability

(Hollo & Wehby, 2017). It is also vital that the teacher knows how to motivate and involve the students actively within the lesson, and can establish a good working relationship with the students.

Explicit instruction was once the most commonly used approach in classrooms around the world for teaching almost all subject matter, but in many countries, dropped out of favour with the coming of constructivist learning theories that stress student-centred activity methods. It is pertinent to note that the countries still using forms of explicit teaching as a main approach for academic subjects (e.g., China, Korea and Japan) are also the countries that report the highest student achievement levels. It is fair to assume that this relationship is not a coincidence.

The dichotomy between teacher-led and student-centred methods is actually artificial, because it is rare that explicit instruction would occupy a whole lesson. The lesson may commence with explicit instruction and explanation, but then change quickly to student activity, with the teacher adopting a more supportive and facilitative role. The teacher also makes effective use of instructional media to gain and hold students' attention (Hennessy & Warwick, 2010). In the course of a single lesson a teacher may switch several times between teacher-directed input and student-guided and independent activity. In the final stage of the lesson there is then a return to teacher direction in order to consolidate learning and check for understanding.

Although explicit instruction at Tier 1 has proved to be of great value to all students, it is important to consider the following cautionary points:

- when used with large mixed-ability classes, teacher-led lessons do not easily take account of individual differences among learners—such as their prior knowledge and skills, language background, literacy level, attention span, or motivation;
- if used too frequently without adequate active participation by students, teacher-led lessons can lead to some students becoming disengaged;
- explicit instruction does not mean passive lecturing: almost any lesson at any age level requires active participation from the students.

Interactive whole-class teaching

Interactive whole-class teaching embodies many of the elements of explicit instruction but ensures very high levels of active participation and responses from the students. The lesson operates through a two-way process in which the teacher explains, then asks questions and challenges students' thinking, and the students offer their own suggestions, explain their thinking, express their opinions, and ask questions of the teacher and each other (Sherry, 2019). The activities the teacher designs for use within a lesson are intended to encourage this type of dialogue.

Teaching strategies often incorporated into interactive whole-class teaching include *unison responding* (answering together) (Tincani & Twyman, 2016) and the use of *response cards* (Owiny et al., 2018). Unison responding simply involves all (or several) students answering a question or repeating information together, rather than the traditional method of asking them to raise a hand and then calling upon one student. When response cards are used, the teacher provides all students in the class with a set of blank cards at the beginning of the session. At certain times during the lesson the teacher asks the students a particular question and every student immediately writes his or her response on the card and holds it up for the teacher to check. Both unison responding and response cards ensure a high rate of active participation by all students, and have been shown to produce positive learning outcomes (Owiny et al., 2018; Tincani & Twyman, 2016).

In Britain, interactive whole-class teaching is advocated as an approach for improving literacy and numeracy standards in primary schools, and is regarded as much more productive than individual programming or unstructured group work. It is claimed that effective use of interactive whole-class teaching helps to close the learning gap that usually appears between higher-achievers and lower-achievers when 'work at your own pace' methods are used.

Some points to consider concerning interactive whole-class teaching include:

- the teacher needs to be skilled in drawing all students into discussion, otherwise some students will not participate actively in the lesson;
- some teachers, particularly those who believe strongly in informal methods, appear to find this fast-paced, interactive approach difficult to implement and sustain;
- if the pace of the lesson is too brisk, students with learning difficulties tend to fall behind and opt out.

Direct teaching

Direct teaching is the general term applied to all forms of teacher-led instruction, (including explicit instruction) that attempt to take students through the curriculum in a reasonably structured and systematic manner (Davis, 2018). Direct teaching is characterised by precise learning objectives, clear demonstrations and explanations, modelling by the teacher, guided practice, corrective feedback, and independent practice by the students. Learning is usually assessed at very regular intervals, and re-teaching provided if necessary. Direct teaching can be thought of as the complete opposite of 'immersion methods' that simply expose students to learning situations with the minimum of guidance.

The most formal and structured version of direct teaching is Direct Instruction (DI), with the capitalised name, for teaching reading, spelling, and arithmetic. It can be used as a Tier 1 approach with young students (particularly socio-economically disadvantaged children) but is more commonly associated with Tier 2 small-group intervention.

DI is associated most closely with the work of Engelmann and others at the University of Oregon (e.g., Adams & Engelmann, 1996; Engelmann, 1999). The commercial material associated with DI usually comprises student workbooks and a scripted manual of pre-planned lessons for the teacher —to be delivered verbatim to small groups of students at Tier 2. In a typical DI lesson, approximately 6 to 8 children are seated in a semi-circle facing the teacher. The teacher gains and holds their attention and then follows the teaching steps clearly set out in the script. This ensures that all steps and questions in the planned teaching sequence are followed. Unison responding by the whole group is used as a strategy for maximising participation. This form of DI has been very well researched over many years, with a diverse range of students with special needs and disadvantages (e.g., Adams & Engelmann, 1996; Head et al., 2018; Thompson et al., 2019). Direct instruction of this type has proved very effective indeed in raising achievement levels in basic academic skills in students with learning difficulties and those with intellectual disability.

Since DI is highly effective, one would expect to find the method being widely used for teaching the foundation stages of basic literacy and numeracy; but this is not the case. While DI has enjoyed some popularity in special education settings, it has had limited impact in mainstream schools, where primary and early childhood teachers prefer to use immersion methods that encourage children to learn at their own rate and in their own way. These teachers react very negatively towards DI, claiming that it is too highly structured, too rapidly paced, and allows no creativity on the part of teachers. It is also clear that most teacher education institutions in the past thirty years have tended to omit coverage of DI in their methodology courses, instead devoting their full attention to methods that are child-centred and guided by constructivist learning theory.

The following points need to be considered when deciding to use DI:

- published DI programmes must be implemented exactly as the designer has pre-scribed; it is not appropriate to pick and choose certain parts to be used and to omit others;
- the fact that DI must be implemented on a daily basis, using small group instruction rather than a whole-class teaching, can cause problems in scheduling and staffing.

Teaching approaches based on constructivist principles

In contrast to teacher-led instruction, the approaches described below endeavour to place learning in the hands of the students. Descriptions are provided of discovery learning, project-based learning, resource-based learning, inquiry-based and issues-based learning, and situated learning.

Discovery learning

Discovery learning (DL) draws upon constructivist theory that believes students construct knowledge about a topic or concept best through their own engagement with materials and by accessing whatever human, technological, and other resources they require. All variations of DL place emphasis on students being active investigators, rather than passive recipients of information delivered to them by a teacher, textbook or computer programme.

Discovery learning has been in use in schools and universities for many generations, and its popularity ebbs and flows according to the prevailing beliefs about the nature of learning (Bakker, 2018). DL has spawned several offshoots such as *inquiry-based learning, problem-based approach* and *guided discovery*. The guided discovery approach recognises that some degree of input from a teacher can enhance the discovery process (Großmann & Wilde, 2019).

In unstructured discovery situations, learners are given very little direction from the teacher and must decide for themselves the appropriate way to investigate a given topic or problem. This unstructured approach is often used in secondary school science and mathematics and sometimes for topics in social studies. The outcome is not always good, particularly for students with poor literacy skills and difficulties with inductive reasoning (Hattie & Yates, 2014). In order to participate successfully in open discovery activities, learners must have adequate inductive reasoning ability to recognise principles or cause-effect relationships emerging from their observations. Jacobsen et al. (2009) reviewed research on the effectiveness of discovery learning and concluded that some students can develop serious misconceptions and become very confused and frustrated in unstructured discovery activities.

Guided discovery has a much tighter structure, and teachers have found that learning is more successful when skills required in the investigative process are explicitly taught and the students have the prerequisite understandings. The teacher sets clear objectives, provides initial explanation to help students begin the task efficiently, and may offer suggestions for a step-by-step procedure to find the target information or to solve the problem. The approach is also known as *guided inquiry* when it combines a fair degree of teacher direction (Torrington, 2013).

The major benefits of DL include:

- learners are actively involved in the process of learning and the topics studied are often intrinsically motivating;
- activities used in authentic discovery contexts are usually more meaningful than classroom exercises and textbook study;
- it is claimed (but is by no means certain) that learners are more likely to remember facts and concepts if they discover them;
- DL builds on learners' prior knowledge and experience;
- DL encourages independence in learning because learners acquire new investigative skills that can be applied in many other contexts;
- DL can also foster positive groupworking skills.

The following points must be considered when using DL:

- the approach can be very time-consuming, often taking much longer for concepts to be 'discovered' and understood than would occur with direct teaching;
- DL relies on learners having adequate literacy, numeracy and independent study skills;
- students may learn little of value from discovery activities if they lack adequate prior knowledge for interpreting their discoveries accurately;
- 'activity' does not necessarily equate with 'learning' – learners may appear to be actively involved but may still not understand or recognise underlying concepts, rules, or principles;
- children with learning problems often have difficulty forming opinions, making predictions and drawing conclusions based on evidence;
- poor outcomes occur when teachers are not good at creating and managing discovery learning environments;

Project-based learning

The project approach has been used in primary and secondary schools for many years. It lends itself easily to curriculum areas such as social studies, environmental education, geography, history, civics, science, mathematics, and the languages, enabling students to apply and extend their knowledge.

Project work can help students integrate ideas and information from different subjects. It has also been found that the collaborative activities that are typically involved in classroom project work can enhance the working relationship between students and their teachers (Pieratt, 2011). All teacher education programmes should equip trainee teachers with the knowledge and skills necessary to design and use project-based learning effectively in their subject areas (Grossman et al., 2019).

Information technology can be fully utilised in project work, resulting in students learning both ICT skills and specific content knowledge simultaneously (Tong et al., 2020). The extended timeframe usually provided for project work allows students to plan carefully, revise, and reflect more deeply upon their learning. Currently, it is suggested that the notion of a '5E model' should underpin project-based learning. The five Es being engagement, exploration, explanation, elaboration, and evaluation (Rodriguez et al., 2019).

Quint and Condliffe (2018) have observed that there is a paucity of research studies that have evaluated the real effects of project-based learning, and that the conclusion they reached was it is a 'promising but not proven' approach. Some studies have found positive impacts associated with the use of projects in science and social studies classes, and some schools have pointed to positive effects on students' engagement, motivation, and development of self-efficacy.

There are many potential benefits from project work:

- it is an inclusive approach in that all learners can participate to the best of their ability;
- projects promote meaningful learning and can connect new information to students' past experience and prior knowledge;
- the generic learning processes involved in gathering data can transfer easily to other topics and situations;
- students become better at self-direction;
- undertaking a project encourages decision-making and allows for student choice;
- in addition to acquiring facts, learners use higher-order thinking and planning abilities;
- preparing the project helps students apply basic reading, writing, and ICT skills;
- assessment can be performance based;
- if undertaken with a partner or in a group, project work can increase cooperative skills.

Important points to consider when using project-based learning include:

- some students lack adequate independent study skills for researching, collating, and interpreting information, and will need to be supported;
- when working on projects, some students may give the outward impression of productive involvement, but may in fact be learning and contributing very little;
- when projects involve the production of posters, models, charts, recordings, photographs, and written reports for display, there is a danger that these are actually 'window dressing' that hides a fairly shallow investigation and poor overall understanding of the topic;
- when different aspects of a topic are given to different group members to research, there is a likelihood that individual members never really grasp a deep overall understanding of the whole topic.

Resource-based learning

Resource-based learning (RBL) is also underpinned by constructivist learning principles and is closely associated with project work and guided discovery. RBL can be used across the curriculum, but is mainly applied in social studies, history, geography, science, and environmental studies. Resource-based learning is an approach that can be used in differentiated programs, where the resources are carefully matched or adapted to students' different levels of ability and special needs.

The main aim of RBL is to foster students' autonomy in learning by providing opportunities to work individually or collaboratively while utilising appropriate resources such as books, community publications, photographs, reports, recordings, and online information, to investigate authentic topics. Students obtain information they must then interpret and collate before organising their findings into an appropriate form for presentation. The use of authentic resources and tools in a meaningful context makes the approach interesting and motivating for a wide ability range (Herrington et al., 2014).

Typically, in RBL situations the teacher introduces a topic or problem to be investigated through the use of a variety of relevant resources. The teacher and students together clarify the nature the task and set goals for inquiry. In some cases, it may be necessary to pre-teach researching skills such as online searches, locating information, extracting relevant data, summarising, locating websites, and taking notes. The students then work individually or in groups to carry out the necessary investigation over a series of lessons.

Advantages claimed for RBL include:

- the use of print, electronic media, and other authentic resources motivates students and encourages self-directed learning;
- students learn from their own active interpretation and collation of information;
- students' study skills are strengthened and extended in ways that may easily generalise to other learning contexts
- RBL topics can stimulate higher-order thinking, problem solving, reasoning, and critical evaluation;
- RBL can increase students' academic engagement time.

Points to consider when using RBL:

- RBL requires a resource-rich learning environment, including easy access to reference books and digital media;
- effective engagement in RBL depends on students having adequate literacy and numeracy skills, and also demands motivation, initiative and self-management;
- care must be taken to guard against students simply using a copy-and-paste approach to recording and collating information without fully understanding the material;
- students with learning difficulties may need to be placed with a supportive partner or group in order to participate successfully.

Problem-based, inquiry-based and issues-based learning

These approaches are varieties of discovery learning. Their use is widely recommended in many official guidelines for school curricula, and they are considered particularly useful in programmes for gifted students (Hua et al., 2014). Currently, problem-based learning (PBL) is still not widely used as a main approach in primary and lower secondary schools, but has become very popular in senior school and in higher education. PBL is now seen as the method of choice in training programmes for many professions (e.g., medicine, law, sciences, engineering) (Euefueno, 2019; Korpi et al., 2019).

In problem- and issues-based learning, students are presented with a real-life situation or issue that requires investigation and a decision leading to action. With older learners, the problems are often intentionally 'messy' (ill-defined) in the sense that not all of the information required for solution is provided in the problem, and there is no clear path or procedure to follow. It is believed that through tackling the issue students will acquire new skills and insights (Alayont, 2014; Ali, 2019).

Problem-based, inquiry-based and issues-based approaches at Tier 1 are often difficult for students with special needs, and there is a danger that they can become marginalised in group activities. When this occurs, they eventually opt out of making much effort. It is suggested that instead of presenting them with problems that are totally unstructured, a teacher should provide guidance through what is termed *learner-centred scaffolding* (LCS). According to studies by Kim et al. (2019), use of such scaffolding over time plays an important role in ultimately improving students' self-directed learning.

The advantages of these approaches are considered to be:

- learning objectives are authentic and can link school learning with the real world;
- the process of tackling problems and identifying, locating, and using appropriate resources can be motivating for learners;
- participating in the approaches involves active construction of new knowledge, and usually requires the integration of information and skills from different disciplines;
- knowledge obtained is likely to be retained and can be transferred to other situations;
- the method encourages self-direction in learning and prepares students to think critically and analytically;
- investigating problems or issues usually requires teamwork and can thus enhance communication and collaborative skills.

Issues to consider when applying problem-based, inquiry-based, and issues-based learning include:

- the problem or issue to be studied must be of genuine interest and significance to the students;
- the school needs to have the appropriate resources to support and facilitate students' investigations;
- the students need to have adequate prior knowledge to make sense of the topic or content of the problem;
- the students must possess the prerequisite independent study skills to engage successfully with the problem or issue, or they need to have adequate support provided through direction and input from the teacher;
- students with learning difficulties will usually require much scaffolding to achieve successful outcomes.

Situated learning

Situated learning is an attempt to combat criticism that much of the teaching that goes on in schools is artificial because it is not presented in a real-life context, and often learners do not recognise the social and functional value of what they are taught. Whenever possible, teachers should make use of authentic tasks and real-life contexts for teaching information, skills, and strategies. This is referred to as *situated learning* (D'Souza & Clare, 2018), and places students in a physical and social setting that is real (or close to real) where the knowledge and skills will be applied later in real life. Examples might be an airport, bus station, workshop, supermarket, or kitchen (Northern Illinois University, 2014). Within that setting, a range of instructional methods may be used, including direct teaching, practice with feedback, problem solving, and enquiry. This type of reality-based teaching and learning has long been a feature in special schools for students with intellectual disability.

The advantages of situated learning include:

- situated learning represents a motivating and participatory approach to learning;
- opportunities are provided for learning and practising in real or simulated contexts where the skills can be acquired for immediate use;
- experts or mentors are available to provide learners with support; instructional scaffolding and direct coaching are provided as necessary;
- students are more likely to become confident and independent thinkers;
- learning is likely to generalise more easily to new contexts;
- collaboration among learners can be encouraged.

Issues to consider when providing situated learning in school contexts include:

- the task of arranging and maintaining real-life learning situations (often off campus) adds considerably to teachers' workload and planning;
- technical expertise is often required for developing or assembling situated resources;
- some teachers are not confident in teaching in unusual settings and without clear lesson structures;
- class size can be a major obstacle to organising work off campus.

Computer-based instruction (CBI) and computer-aided learning (CAL)

There are at least a dozen different terms currently in circulation related to the use of computers for educational purposes. In most cases the differences in meaning are almost negligible. For the purposes of this chapter the preferred terms are *computer-based instruction* (CBI) and *computer-aided learning* (CAL). The use of CBI and CAL in the classroom has increased very rapidly in the past decade, with positive effects reported for students' academic achievement and for increased motivation, engagement, and self-esteem (Armstrong, 2014; Karich et al., 2014; Stultz, 2017; Turner, 2019).

Computer-based instruction is the broad term applied to all forms of instruction where a computer is used to present curriculum content. Usually the student responds to material displayed on screen and followed up with embedded questions or problems. The computer programme often monitors the learning that is taking place as the student works through the material, and may provide corrective feedback and re-teaching of key points. CBI can be used as a starting point for studying a new topic independently, or later for extension and application work once a topic has been introduced by other methods such as explicit teaching and class discussion.

CBI embodies the basic principles of any form of effective instruction—namely, clear presentation of information, careful sequencing of steps, embedded practice, feedback, and applications (Hattie & Yates, 2014). These programmes normally contain on-screen text, graphics, sound, and video, and are very effective in gaining and holding students' attention and participation. CBI programmes often provide direct links to other web-based resources and can greatly increase students' access to information.

Computer-aided learning is the term usually applied to the planned integration of computer materials to supplement or reinforce other forms of teaching. Often one-to-one programmes are designed to provide additional practice exercises or new problems, or may present additional examples to enrich the content taught during face-to-face lessons. Immediate corrective feedback to the learner is always a strong feature of CAI, and usually the programme does not move ahead until the student has mastered current content. According to Hattie and Yates (2014) use of a computer to supplement traditional teaching produces stronger results than using computer-based instruction alone as a total alternative.

CAL has proved useful for students with learning difficulties and disabilities, and they frequently display a positive attitude towards using a computer. Students with learning difficulties usually require more time and direction than others in the early stages in order to develop confidence and competence in basic computer skills (Mutlu & Akgün, 2019; Smith et al., 2013). In the case of students with behaviour problems or with ADHD, working at a computer can significantly improve on-task engagement and productivity.

CBI and CAL have both played an important role in the current trend to move away from traditional models of teaching to a more technology-based and independent learning approach. This is most clearly evident in the notion of the 'flipped classroom' (Douch, 2014; Maycock, 2019). 'Flipped' in this context means a reversal of the conventional sequence where a teacher first presents new information through a formal lesson, and then students work on related class exercises and homework. In the flipped classroom, new curriculum topics are not introduced first by the teacher, but instead the students first study the topic by themselves via a computer programme and online resources. Back in the classroom, the students then use the knowledge they have gained to engage in work that requires application, discussion, and expansion of what they know. The teacher monitors in-class work, sets follow-up activities, and acts as tutor when students require help or direction. The teacher's role is to consolidate and expand upon concepts and skills the students have acquired independently, regularly assess their progress, and provide appropriate feedback. The approach has been suggested as particularly appropriate for academically gifted learners (Siegle, 2014) and is currently more widely used in tertiary education than in primary or secondary schools.

CBI and CAI have the following benefits:

- mode of presentation ensures that learners make active, self-initiated responses and are in charge of the learning situation;
- software can be matched to students' ability level and rate of learning, and is therefore one valuable way of differentiating instruction;

- learners usually gain immediate knowledge of results after every response they make, so reinforcement and corrective feedback can be provided efficiently;
- students move towards greater independence and self-regulation in learning;
- CBI and CAL provide a private method of making errors and self-correcting;
- learners can engage in extra practice and overlearning to master basic skills;
- most (but not all) students enjoy working at a computer more than using textbooks and print resources;
- students can extend their computer competencies, now regarded as essential life skills;
- teaching subjects such as science, social studies, mathematics, environmental education and the arts can be enhanced by documentary or simulation programs, and by giving access to Internet resources.

Issues to consider in relation to CBI or CAL:

- students with literacy problems may have difficulty comprehending text displayed on the screen;
- some students lack prerequisite computer skills;
- technical failures occur, resulting in lost time and frustration;
- a few students actually prefer group interactions with peers and teacher, rather than using technology.

E-learning

The term e-learning covers all forms of digital-age online and web-based teaching and learning that occur through the electronic medium of information and communication technology (ICT). A narrow definition is that e-learning is carried out at home using computers and Internet; but more broadly, e-learning can be integrated into any school programme and delivered not only through conventional computers (PCs) but also via online web-based learning resources and by using a range of hand-held devices (Cole, Swartz & Shelley, 2020; Murray, Luo et al., 2019). These and many other forms of technology are enriching the quality of educational programmes, and can greatly enhance students' motivation and participation.

The availability of online learning has proved to be a boon for students who are unable to attend school for reasons as diverse as severe disability, illness, or simply living in a remote region (distance education). Tam et al. (2018, p.447) have written:

> Educators and school administrators are interested in the myriad possibilities offered by new technologies to enrich teaching materials and to provide ubiquitous learning environments to enhance students' learning.

E-learning is being incorporated increasingly into the education of students with special needs (Abed, 2018; Mølster & Nes, 2018; Smith et al., 2013). Combining e-learning and CAL with other forms of teaching has proved to be an effective approach with students with a variety of special needs. Naturally, aspects of e-learning can be problematic for students with hearing or vision impairment, and Lee and Oh (2017) have suggested that to improve accessibility of e-materials for these students it is usually necessary to provide additional in-built supports in the form of online guidance and assistance. Chatzara et al. (2016) refer to this as 'cognitive support' for students with special needs using e-learning. Commenting on the effective design of e-learning materials, Radovan and Perdih (2016, p.167) have suggested: 'If the materials are designed appropriately and allow for adaptation to individual needs, they can enable all types of learners, including those with dyslexia, to gain easier access to higher-quality educational content.'

Effective use of e-learning and technology relies entirely on a teacher's pedagogical judgement and skills to determine how, when, and where to integrate it effectively into the curriculum (Hattie & Yates, 2014). The term *blended teaching* is often used now to describe the mixing of face-to-face instruction with the use of computer-aided learning and web-based resources (Seage & Türegün, 2020; Zhang & Zhu, 2020). Pre-and in-service professional training for teachers needs to provide more guidance in how best to utilise e-learning and other technologies as an integral part of a differentiated approach in inclusive classrooms (Adavbiele, 2017).

The final chapter provides information and suggestions for adapting or modifying some of the methods described here, to make them more inclusive of a wider range of students. The main theme of Chapter 15 is differentiation of methods, materials, and curriculum content.

Online resources

- An overview of teacher-led and student-centred methods can be found at: https://teach.com/what/teachers-know/teaching-methods/.
- A list of evidence-based teaching strategies can be found at: https://teaching.utk.edu/evidence-based-teaching-strategies/.
- A paper discussing interactive whole-class teaching can be found online at: www.leeds.ac.uk/educol/documents/00003267.htm.
- A useful essay on explicit instruction can be found at: https://mrgmpls.wordpress.com/2019/05/19/scaffolding-the-curriculum-renaissance-with-explicit-instruction/.
- Information on problem-based learning can be found at: www.studygs.net/pbl.htm.
- Comments on the effectiveness of Direct Instruction (DI) can be located at: www.jefflindsay.com/EducData.shtml.
- A helpful explanation of CBI and CAL can be located online at: www.studynet2.herts.ac.uk/ptl/common/LTDU.nsf/Teaching+Documents/04739C2AEC9B471B8025729F00330361/$FILE/whatiscal.pdf.
- An overview of the advantages and disadvantages of E-learning can be found at: www.academia.edu/4052785/Advantages_and_Disadvantages_of_e_Learning.

Print resources

Bates, B. (2019). *Learning theories simplified: and how to apply them to teaching* (2nd ed.). Thousand Oaks, CA: Sage.

Borich, G.D. (2017). *Effective teaching methods: Research-based practice* (e-text). New York: Pearson.

Burden, J., & Byrd, D.M. (2018) *Methods for effective teaching* (8th ed.). Boston, MA: Pearson.

Muijs, D., & Reynolds, D. (2017). *Effective teaching: Evidence and practice* (4th ed.). Thousand Oaks, CA: Sage.

Petty, G. (2018). *How to teach even better: An evidence-based approach.* Oxford: Oxford University Press.

Roblyer, M.D., & Hughes, J.E. (2019). *Integrating educational technology into teaching* (8th ed.). New York: Pearson.

Chapter 15

Differentiating the curriculum and adapting instruction

The advent of the inclusive schooling movement in the 1990s brought with it the urgent need to adapt aspects of Tier 1 teaching so that students with special learning needs or disabilities could participate successfully in the mainstream curriculum. The term *differentiation* is now used to describe these adjustments. In simple terms, differentiated instruction can be regarded as the fine-tuning of classroom teaching procedures and learning activities to address important differences evident among learners.

Adaptations and differentiation

Meeting students' special educational needs successfully in the mainstream usually requires that subject matter, learning activities, teaching procedures, resource materials, methods of assessment, and patterns of classroom organisation must *at times* be adapted or modified. It is claimed that for many students it is often differentiation during whole-class teaching at Tier 1 that makes the difference between success and failure (Dosch & Zidon, 2014; Turner & Solis, 2017). There will still be some students with special needs who may require additional teaching or tutoring beyond that given through differentiation at Tier 1 (Mays, 2020).

In the UK, curriculum guidelines and the *Special Educational Needs and Disability Code of Practice* have endorsed a differentiated approach as a necessary component for inclusive education to give almost all learners access to the National Curriculum (DfE, 2013a; DfE/DOH, 2015). The guidelines also state that teachers have an obligation to plan lessons to include successful participation by students who are low-attainers or who come from disadvantaged backgrounds—thus indicating that a differentiated approach does not simply target students with disabilities but includes students with other special needs. Some students will require consolidation of what they have been taught while others, such as gifted learners, will need to deepen their understanding. Randall (2016) suggests that differentiation should be seen as the way to maximise the potential of all students.

Similarly, the Australian Curriculum Assessment and Reporting Authority (ACARA, 2016b) offers specific guidance on how the Australian Curriculum (described as a 'curriculum for all') can accommodate the learning needs of students with disabilities and learning difficulties, gifted and talented students, and students with English as an additional language or dialect (EAL/D). In the USA, the expectation is also that teaching methods and curriculum will be differentiated to ensure that as many as possible students can achieve the required level in the *Common Core State Standards* (Tomlinson & Imbeau, 2014).

In this chapter, generic principles and practices for differentiation are discussed, with suggestions for adapting curriculum content, student resources, teaching approaches and assessment procedures. Some problems associated with differentiation are also highlighted. Differentiation is described as a 'complex philosophy of teaching and learning' (Dack, 2019) and the complexity must not be underrated.

The approach is not without its critics, most of whom see it as too readily accepting (and therefore perpetuating) a gap in achievement between high achievers and those who struggle with learning (Gustafsson, 2018; Stripp, 2015; Taylor, 2017). Their argument is that we should be attempting instead to close this gap by using highly effective Tier 1 methods that ensure all students cover exactly the same curriculum in the same way. The small amount of evaluation research that has been carried out suggests that differentiated teaching may only have a slightly positive effect on students' overall achievement—there are rarely any dramatic improvements (Pablico, 2016).

Key principle: keep it simple

Sustaining a differentiated approach in inclusive classes invariably places very heavy demands on teachers' time, knowledge, ingenuity, and organisational skills. It is no simple task to teach and manage a class in which many different activities and levels of work are occurring simultaneously, and while individual students are requiring different amounts of guidance and direct support (Erden, 2020; Parsons & Vaughn, 2013). So, from the beginning it is essential to stress the *simplicity principle*: adaptations and modifications should not be made unless absolutely unavoidable. Whenever possible, a student with special needs should be helped to use mainstream learning materials and participate in regular learning activities.

Differentiation does not mean that every single lesson and every topic taught must be planned and presented through content and activities adjusted to each individual in the class—to attempt to do this is totally unrealistic and largely unnecessary. Adaptations to curriculum are most effective and most easily sustained when they are simple, easy to implement, and based on typical assignments and learning activities. Differentiation should be less about drastically changing the content of the curriculum for some individuals and more about providing *alternative pathways* and *additional support* to achieve common outcomes in a particular curriculum topic (Knackendoffel et al., 2017).

Starting points for differentiation

An appropriate place to begin planning differentiated instruction is by identifying essential core information, concepts, or skills associated with the curriculum topic to be taught. All students in the class will be expected to master this core content to the best of their individual abilities. Differentiating the topic then becomes a process of creating different ways that students with difficulties can achieve this goal through engaging in a variety of coherent experiences matched to their abilities. As a general rule, all students in the group will learn best if provided with a variety and combination of activities and pathways.

Planning needs to include consideration of strategies for delivering additional help to certain students during the lesson (e.g., via peer assistance, a learning-support assistant, from the teacher, or from digital resources). It is also important to consider how students will be grouped, and how the available time will be used most effectively. When planning differentiated objectives for a lesson it is helpful to keep in mind the three stem statements:

- All students will ...
- Some students will ...
- A few students may ...

In other words, *all students* will be expected to master the essential core knowledge and skills, but possibly through engaging in different learning activities. *Some students* will achieve more than this core; and *a few students* may achieve one or two higher-order objectives through extension and enrichment activities.

Typical adjustments that can be made include the following examples. Many of these adaptations and accommodations are explained in more detail later:

- providing alternative teaching materials for some curriculum topics (e.g., simplified reading material with more illustrations, graded worksheets, concrete materials and visual aids for math, Braille texts, captioned videos, computer apps that match a student's ability level);
- using more direct and explicit teaching when necessary, more modelling by the teacher of skills and cognitive strategies, more frequent guided practice, and more personalised support and re-teaching for some students;
- scaffolding students' learning through more prompting, guidance, feedback, and correction;
- varying time allocation for classroom tasks to take account of students' differing learning rates;
- providing alternative ways for students to demonstrate their learning (e.g., oral rather than written assignments and tests; assistive technology; augmentative and alternative communication systems);
- improving access to learning activities and resources (e.g., seating arrangements; wider aisles for wheelchair access; modified furniture; assistive technology);
- organising flexible groupings of students and facilitating more peer assistance and peer tutoring;
- making any necessary accommodations for certain students during tests and examinations (e.g., allowing an adult to read questions aloud and then write the student's responses; giving more time to complete a test; presenting the test via computer rather than paper-and-pencil; larger writing on the whiteboard);
- utilising additional support personnel such as classroom assistants (paraprofessionals), parents, volunteer helpers to work with groups or individuals;
- adjusting the timetable to accommodate out-of-classroom therapy sessions for students with a physical disability or speech disorder, or for accommodating a behaviour modification programme for a student with a conduct disorder.

It can be seen that manageable differentiation and adaptations are usually associated with adjustments to learning activities, instructional materials, and student support strategies.

Adapting curriculum content and learning activities

Differentiation of curriculum usually means that for some students, content to be studied may be increased or decreased in terms of quantity, depth, and complexity, while still ensuring that core concepts and skills are covered (Westwood, 2016). Differentiation is most easily implemented where it does not involve drastic changes to curriculum content.

In many countries, modifications to curriculum are guided by an *individual education plan* (IEP). The IEP should specify precisely any modifications to curriculum that are necessary, and may also suggest alternative activities and provision of additional services. In the UK, much the same function is embodied in the *Education, Health and Care Plan (EHCP)*, although the plan covers more than just education (Council for Disabled Children, 2017).

Modifying curriculum content usually implies that students with learning difficulties will cover activities or exercises that are a little easier to accomplish, and perhaps involve smaller steps in learning or with more repetition. In the case of gifted students, the reverse would be true – lesson content would be made more challenging and students would cover content in greater depth, often through independent computer-based and online studies.

Learning activities represent the main way in which learners engage actively with curriculum content and can be completed via different methods (e.g., responding to a computer program, tackling a textbook exercise, watching a video) (MCA, 2019). It is important that activities and tasks set for students with special needs are not simply 'busy work' that is less demanding and less interesting. One approach to differentiating activities and tasks is termed *tiered assignments*, with work on a topic provided at three or four levels of challenge. Students are first allocated tasks at a level that matches their own ability and rate of learning; they can then progress to higher levels over time. Hodgson (2013) presents some excellent examples of tiered reading comprehension and writing activities around the theme of 'motor-cycles'. These examples have the great advantage of using a format that does not immediately label the worksheets (in the eyes of the peer group) as being for a specific ability level. Students do not like to be given simplified materials because this marks them out as different, and undermines their status in the peer group. Adolescents in particular are acutely sensitive to peer-group reactions and deeply resent being overtly treated as if they are lacking in ability. Teachers can use various ways of grouping students within the class to allow for different tiered activities to take place, under differing amounts of teacher direction. At various times, the classroom can be set up to support individualised projects or for cooperative groupwork, and use may be made of learning centres, computer-aided instruction, or resource-based learning (Heick, 2018).

Obviously, greater adjustments to the curriculum are always required for students with moderate to severe intellectual disability. In such cases it will be necessary to modify significantly the mainstream curriculum content and activities to match more closely the students' cognitive level, priority needs, and rate of learning. Often there is a greater necessity to help these students acquire essential everyday living skills and greater autonomy, rather than studying traditional subject matter (Rochford, 2016) (see Chapter 2).

Several potential problems exist when modifying the curriculum and the associated activities; for example, reducing the complexity and demands of tasks, and setting easier objectives for some students, may sound like very good advice, but watering down the curriculum in this way can have the long-term effect of increasing the achievement and knowledge gap between students with learning difficulties and other students (Westwood, 2018a). By reducing the demands placed on students of lower ability we may be exaggerating the effect of individual differences and perpetuating inequalities among students. The ideal to be aimed for is that all students experience basically the same curriculum a far as possible, but receive varying amounts and types of additional support to ensure success.

Homework assignments

Differentiated homework assignments are an important way of meeting the needs of gifted and able students as well as those of students with difficulties (Vatterott, 2018). Some students may be given homework that involves additional practice at the same level of difficulty while others may have extension tasks involving more challenging applications, critical thinking, and reflection. It is often helpful to discuss with students the exact purpose of a homework assignment so that they can appreciate its relevance for their overall progression.

Adapting instructional materials

Instructional materials and learning resources represent another area where modifications can be made to improve access to the curriculum. A variety of texts and materials at various levels of complexity and readability should be available for students to use. The resources within a lesson (worksheets, exercises, whiteboard notes, computer software, captioned videos) will need to be carefully selected to match a student's ability level, and additional equipment may need to be provided for some students (e.g., assistive technology; a calculator with audio output for a student with impaired vision; a modified keyboard; a touch screen).

Listed below are suggestions for preparing instructional materials for students with poor literacy skills. Often these simple adjustments enable a student to access text without the need for further assistance.

When preparing print materials (worksheets, assignment cards, study notes, independent learning contracts) a teacher may:

- pre-teach recognition and meaning of key terms and important new vocabulary;
- simplify the language by using short sentences and substituting simple words for difficult terms;
- modify sentence construction to facilitate comprehension–active voice is easier to process than passive voice: *The teacher reads the story*, rather than *A story was read by the teacher*.
- make printed instructions or questions clear and simple;
- present information in small blocks of text rather than as dense paragraphs;
- use bullet points and lists rather than dense paragraphs;
- improve legibility of print and layout; if necessary enlarge the size of print;
- highlight important information by using underlining or printing the words in bold type or colour;
- provide clear illustrations or diagrams where possible;

- give cues or prompts where written responses are required from the students—for example, provide the initial letter of the answer, or use dashes to show the number of words required in the answer.

Differentiating products from lessons

Often the output from a lesson will be tangible products such as written work, graphics, or models; but sometimes the product is another form of evidence of learning, such as an oral report, a performance, a presentation to the group, participation in discussion, or the answering of oral questions (NSW DEC, 2015). Digital technology has increased the range of options that students can utilise when presenting their work.

Differentiating the products of learning may mean that:

- each student is not expected to produce exactly the same amount or quality of work as every other student;
- a student may be asked to produce work in a different format—for example, an audio recording, a drawing or poster, scrapbook, a multiple-choice exercise—rather than a formal essay;
- individual students may negotiate what they will produce and how they will produce it in order to provide evidence of their learning in a particular topic.

Teachers should devise product assignments at varying degrees of difficulty to match students' readiness and ability. Students should be encouraged to use varied types of resources and materials in preparing their products.

The potential danger in setting out from the start to accept less work from some students or of an inferior quality is that this strategy represents a lowering of expectations that can result in a self-fulfilling prophecy— a student produces less and less, and the teacher in turn expects less and less of them. A different perspective suggests that teachers need to help students achieve more by working on the same product as other students *but with more support*. Differentiation of product should never be seen as offering certain students a soft option; and it should never lead to a student consistently managing to avoid tasks he or she does not like to complete.

Adapting teaching strategies

When teaching procedures and processes are differentiated some of the following strategies may be used:

- making great use of explicit and direct forms of instruction when introducing new topics, and when re-teaching certain groups at Tier 2;
- re-teaching information to some students using simpler language and more examples;
- asking questions at different levels of difficulty, targeting different individuals;
- monitoring the work of some students much more closely throughout the lesson;
- using effective tactics to gain and maintain the interest of poorly motivated or distractible students;
- giving corrective feedback and descriptive praise, with more detail or less detail according to the students' needs;

- giving more assistance or less assistance to individual students according to need;
- providing extra practice for some students, often via differentiated homework assignments;
- setting extension work for the most-able students, requiring independent study, investigation, and application;
- using tiered activities on the same topic, with different degrees of challenge;
- establishing learning centres (or interest centres) in the classroom to encourage students to explore topics independently that are of particular interest to them.

General areas in which teachers can adapt their teaching approach include varying the pace of instruction, and the use of additional support to individuals. The rate at which new information is presented and activities carried out during lessons can be varied. The speed at which students are required to complete tasks, answer questions, and produce outputs can be adjusted to individual needs. The nature of learning tasks set for students will be matched to their learning rate and abilities, with some tasks taking longer to complete than others. Teachers can vary the amount of direct help given to individuals during a lesson. This represents the most commonly adopted differentiation strategy and is relatively easy for teachers to employ in a mixed-ability class. They may also encourage greater peer assistance and collaboration among students, and may use the services of a classroom assistant or volunteer helper to give extra individual assistance to students.

There is evidence to suggest that teachers are much better at using modifications to teaching processes than they are at modifying curriculum content (Chan et al., 2002). They appear to find teaching modifications more 'natural' and easier to accomplish within their personal teaching approach. For example, skilled teachers already provide additional help and re-teaching to students when necessary, and use prompting and guidance. They also differentiate the level of their questioning, and they make greater use of targeted praise, encouragement, and rewards during lessons. These are all strategies that can be applied while the teacher is still following a common curriculum with the whole class—and for this reason they are regarded as the most feasible adaptations for teachers to make.

Adapting assessment

Assessment refers to any process used to determine how much learning, and what quality of learning, has occurred for each student in the class. Assessment thus provides an indication of how effective a particular episode of teaching has been. Outcomes from assessment highlight anything that may need to be taught again to all students, revised, or given additional practice time for some students.

Differentiation of assessment procedures may often be necessary for any students with a disability because these students may have problems demonstrating what they know or can do. Their difficulties are magnified when an assessment method requires them to use literacy, numeracy, or motor skills at a level they have not yet achieved. Modifications to assessment processes are therefore necessary to enable equal access for students with special needs. Typical modifications include:

- simplifying the instructions for tests and for questions embedded within assessment tasks;
- shortening tests and tasks;

- allowing longer time for some students to complete the work;
- allowing a student with special needs to have some assistance in completing the test (e.g., questions read aloud to the student; student dictating answers to a scribe);
- enabling the student to present the work in a different format (e.g., notes rather than an essay; oral answers; a computer printout).

Classroom tests are one of the ways in which teachers routinely assess progress of their students. These teacher-made tests may require modification to their format for students with special needs. Modification to formats may involve:

- enlarging the print;
- leaving more space for the student to write an answer;
- using different types of questions (e.g., short answer, multiple-choice, sentence completion, gapped paragraphs, matching items format);
- rewriting instructions in simple language and highlighting key points;
- keeping directions brief and simple;
- providing prompts such as *Begin the problem here. Answer in one sentence only.*

Modifications to test administration procedures include:

- using oral questioning and accepting oral answering;
- using a scribe to write down a student's answers;
- giving short rest breaks during the test without penalty;
- allowing extra time to complete the test;
- avoiding penalties for poor spelling or handwriting;
- allowing a student to use a laptop to undertake the test;
- giving credit for drawings if these will help to indicate that the student knows the concept or information;
- administering the test in a quiet environment other than the classroom to reduce distractions for some students (e.g., social worker's office, withdrawal room).

In the UK, the *Rochford Review* (Rochford, 2016) provided valuable guidelines for carrying out assessment with students who have severe disabilities and for whom a mainstream subject-based curriculum is inappropriate. The *Review* suggests that assessment for these students should focus on acquisition of daily living skills and development of the attributes that enable them to engage in learning—attention, responsiveness, curiosity, persistence, initiation, and investigation. These attributes are seen as prerequisites for possibly progressing later to a more subject-specific curriculum.

Accommodations for students with disabilities

The specific needs of students with disabilities are usually identified within their individual education plan, and the IEP should be seen as the main source of advice for the types of differentiation and adaptation needed. The term *accommodation* usually conveys the notion of making adjustments or allowances to ensure that students with disabilities can participate fully or partially in the mainstream curriculum. This accommodation for most students with special needs is achieved (as described above) by varying the type of activities or the method of instruction, providing additional human and technical support, modifying the ways in which the student can respond, or adapting the classroom environment.

Many students with disabilities will also need additional support and assistive technology such as modified keyboard, computer with a visual display and touch screen or with voice synthesiser, audio books with text-to-speech features, simple predictive spelling apps, Braillers for blind students, enlarged text on computer screen for a student with partial sight, radio-frequency hearing aids for students with impaired hearing. Less sophisticated aids might include basic communication boards for students without speech (Redford, 2019). It is beyond the scope of this book to discuss assistive technology in great detail, but some basic information was provided in Chapter 4. Satsangi et al. (2019b) have remarked that the use of assistive technology has grown over the past four decades, and in inclusive settings, this technology now plays a vital role in providing access to academic content for students with disabilities.

Universal Design for Learning

In recent years, much has been written about the notion of Universal Design for Learning (UDL) as a model for providing differentiated pathways to studying a common curriculum. The assumption behind UDL is that it should be possible to prepare and present information and skills to students in multiple ways that match their aptitudes and enable them to express themselves and demonstrate their learning. In principle, UDL caters for the needs of all students, ranging from those with difficulties through to those with gifts and talents, and from school age students to adults. Under this principle, it should be possible for students of differing abilities in any classroom or in any online learning situation to have equal access to the curriculum and to achieve the planned learning objectives by taking different pathways tailored to their abilities and needs (Murawski & Scott, 2019; Rogers-Shaw et al., 2018).

The three essential features of UDL that must be incorporated when designing curricula are: (i) *multiple means of representation* (e.g. print medium, Braille, video, audio, ICT, concrete materials, diagrams, simulations); (ii) *multiple means of engagement* (looking, listening, hands on, participating, discussing, individual, group, independent, collaborative, interacting, peer tutoring); and (iii) *multiple means of expression* (e.g. oral, written, photographic illustration, art, creative performance) (Gargiulo & Metcalf, 2017). It is suggested that digital formats and e-learning tend to be flexible enough to incorporate many of these features in ways that can adapt to individual differences among learners. Digital technology can utilise many variations in modes of presentation, engagement, and response, thus relieving the teacher of the massive burden of designing multiple pathways in advance. UDL obviously has much in common with differentiated instruction, in the sense that barriers to learning are reduced by offering multiple pathways to achievement.

Unfortunately, up to this time UDL is largely an unfulfilled ideal and remains a practice more written about than implemented. There is a need for more research to indicate whether UDL initiatives can improve learning outcomes for a wide ability range, and importantly, whether the average teacher can sustain the model on a daily basis (Capp, 2017).

Many teachers are now experimenting with ways of addressing individual differences, for example by making more effective use of technology, multi-media kits, peer tutoring, flexible grouping and tiered assignments. Similarly, designers of e-learning software are becoming increasingly skilled at producing multi-level motivating and interactive programs.

It has been said that inclusive schooling requires all teachers to be able to adapt instruction according to the diverse needs and aptitudes of their students and the nature of the topic at hand (Segedin et al., 2019). It is hoped that the chapters in this book have given teachers additional understandings and skills necessary to achieve this level of professional expertise.

Online resources

- 'It's differentiation Jim, but not as we know it!' at: www.hertsforlearning.co.uk/blog/its-differ entiation-jim-not-we-know-it.
- Westwood, P. (2016). Teaching methods: Differentiated instruction. Teacher magazine [online], 11 April, 2016. Available at: www.teachermagazine.com.au/articles/teaching-methods-differentiated-instruction.
- Common Core State Standards: Where does differentiation fit? Webinar with Carol Ann Tomlinson and Sherida Britt. On line at: www.ascd.org/professional-development/webinars/tomlinson-and-britt-webinar.aspx.
- A selection of differentiation strategies available at: www.prodigygame.com/blog/differentiated-instruction-strategies-examples-download/.
- Adapting materials for mixed-ability classes: www.teachingenglish.org.uk/article/adapting-materials-mixed-ability-classes.
- Differentiated-textbook-instruction: www.teachervision.com/teaching-strategies/differentiated-textbook-instruction.
- Differentiation of student products: www.lessonplanet.com/article/gifted-and-talented-education/differentiation-of-student-products.

Print resources

Brulles, D., & Brown, K.L. (2018). *A teacher's guide to flexible grouping and collaborative learning: Form, manage, assess, and differentiate in groups.* Golden Valley, MN: Free Spirit Publishing.

Cowley, S. (2018). *The ultimate guide to differentiation.* London: Bloomsbury Education.

Doubet, K., & Hockett, J. (2018). *Differentiation in the elementary grades: Strategies to engage and equip all learners.* Alexandria, VA: ASCD.

Murawski, W.W., & Scott, K.L. (Eds). (2019). *What really works with Universal Design for Learning.* Thousand Oaks, CA: Corwin.

Tomlinson, C. (2017). *How to differentiate instruction in academically diverse classrooms* (3rd ed.). Alexandria, VA: ASCD.

Westwood, P. (2018) *Inclusive and adaptive teaching: Meeting the challenge of diversity in the classroom* (2nd ed.). London: Routledge.

References

AAIDD (American Association on Intellectual and Developmental Disabilities). (2019). *Self-determination. Position statement.* Retrieved from: https://aaidd.org/news-policy/policy/position-statements/self-determination.

Abed, M.G. (2018). Teachers' perspectives surrounding ICT use amongst SEN students in the mainstream educational setting. *World Journal of Education,* 8(1), 6–16.

Abu, N.K., Akkanat, Ç., & Gökdere, M. (2017). Teachers' views about the education of gifted students in regular classrooms. *Turkish Journal of Giftedness and Education,* 7(2), 87–109.

ACARA (Australian Curriculum Assessment and Reporting Authority). (2013). *Student diversity and the Australian Curriculum.* Sydney: ACARA.

ACARA (Australian Curriculum Assessment and Reporting Authority). (2014a). *Review of the Australian Curriculum.* Sydney: ACARA.

ACARA (Australian Curriculum Assessment and Reporting Authority). (2014b). *Australian Curriculum: Mathematics.* Sydney: ACARA.

ACARA (Australian Curriculum Assessment and Reporting Authority). (2016a). *Students with disability.* Retrieved from https://acara.edu.au/curriculum/student-diversity/students-with-disability.

ACARA (Australian Curriculum Assessment and Reporting Authority). (2016b). *Student diversity and the Australian Curriculum.* Retrieved from: https://acara.edu.au/curriculum/student-diversity.

ACARA (Australian Curriculum Assessment and Reporting Authority). (2019). *School students with disability.* Retrieved from: www.acara.edu.au/reporting/national-report-on-schooling-in-australia-data-portal/school-students-with-disability.

ACER (Australian Council for Educational Research). (2013). *Literacy and numeracy intervention in the early years: A report to the NSW Ministerial Advisory Group on Literacy and Numeracy.* Melbourne: ACER.

Adams, G.L., & Engelmann, S. (1996). *Research on Direct Instruction: 25 years beyond DISTAR.* Seattle, WA: Educational Achievement Systems.

Adamson, R.M., McKenna, J.W., & Mitchell, B. (2019). Supporting all students: Creating a tiered continuum of behavior support at the classroom level to enhance schoolwide multi-tiered systems of support. *Preventing School Failure,* 63(1), 62–67.

Adani, A., Eskay, M., & Onu, V. (2012). Effects of self-instruction strategy on the achievement in algebra of students with learning difficulty in mathematics. *US-China Education Review,* A12, 1006–1021.

Adavbiele, J.A. (2017). Challenges to e-learning in public secondary schools in Edo State in the 21st century. *International Journal of Education and Practice,* 5(7), 110–117.

Agarwal, P.K. & Bain, P.M. (2019). *Powerful teaching: Unleash the science of learning.* San Francisco, CA: Jossey-Bass-Wiley.

Ain, G.I. (2018). What is the appropriate curriculum for students with disabilities? Standards-based curriculum versus functional curriculum for students with disabilities. Online Submission: ERIC Database. Document ED593728.

Al Otaiba, S., Baker, K., Lan, P., Allor, J., Rivas, B., Yovanoff, P., & Kamata, A. (2019). Elementary teacher's knowledge of Response to Intervention implementation: A preliminary factor analysis. *Annals of Dyslexia*, 69(1), 34–53.

Alasim, K.N. (2018). Participation and interaction of deaf and hard-of-hearing students in inclusion classroom. *International Journal of Special Education*, 33(2), 493–506.

Alayont, F. (2014). Using problem-based pre-class activities to prepare students for in-class learning. *Primus*, 24(2), 138–148.

Alberto, P.A. & Troutman, A.C. (2013). *Applied behavior analysis for teachers* (9th ed.). Upper Saddle River, NJ: Pearson-Merrill.

Ali, S.S. (2019). Problem-based learning: A student-centered approach. *English Language Teaching*, 12(5), 73–78.

Allman, T., Wolters Boser, S., & Murphy, E.M. (2019). Including students who are deaf or hard of hearing: Principles for creating accessible instruction. *Preventing School Failure*, 63(2), 105–112.

Al-Salahat, M.M. (2016). Using video modeling in teaching a simple meal preparation skill for pupils of down syndrome. *Journal of Education and Practice*, 7(9), 82–90.

Alter, C. & Vlasak, E. (2014). Back to school meets Positive Behavioural Interventions and Supports (PBIS). *The Exceptional Parent*, Mayissue (not paginated).

Altintas, E. & Özdemir, A.S. (2015). The effect of differentiation approach on creativity of gifted students: Cognitive and affective factors. *Educational Research and Reviews*, 10(8), 1191–1201.

Anderson, K.L. (2019). Explicit instruction for word solving: Scaffolding developing readers' use of code-based and meaning-based strategies. *Preventing School Failure*, 63(2), 175–183.

Andres, H.P. (2019). Active teaching to manage course difficulty and learning motivation. *Journal of Further and Higher Education*, 43(2), 220–235.

AngloInfo. (2019). *Special needs education in Australia*. Retrieved from: www.angloinfo.com/how-to/australia/family/schooling-education/special-needs.

APA (American Psychiatric Association). (2013). *Diagnostic and statistical manual of mental disorders (DSM-5)*. Arlington, VA: American Psychiatric Association.

Apel, K., Brimo, D., Diehm, E., & Apel, L. (2013). Morphological awareness intervention with kindergartners and first- and second-grade students from low socioeconomic status homes: A feasibility study. *Language, Speech and Hearing Services in Schools*, 44(2), 161–173.

Arendale, D.R. (Ed.). (2018). *2018 EOA Best Practices Clearinghouse Directory* (4th ed.). Minneapolis, MN: Educational Opportunity Association and University of Minnesota.

Argyropoulos, V., Paveli, A., & Nikolaraizi, M. (2019). The role of DAISY digital talking books in the education of individuals with blindness: A pilot study. *Education and Information Technologies*, 24(1), 693–709.

Arias, V.B., Arias, B., Burns, G.L., & Servera, M. (2019). Invariance of parent ratings of attention deficit hyperactivity disorder symptoms for children with and without intellectual disability. *Journal of Applied Research in Intellectual Disabilities*, 32(2), 288–299.

Armstrong, A. (2014). Technology in the classroom: It's not a matter of 'if,' but when and how. *The Education Digest*, 79(5), 39–43.

Assouline, S.G., Nicpon, M.F., & Whiteman, C. (2010). Cognitive and psychosocial characteristics of gifted students with written language disability. *Gifted Child Quarterly*, 54(2), 102–115.

Astle, D.E., Bathelt, J., & Holmes, J. (2019). Remapping the cognitive and neural profiles of children who struggle at school. *Developmental Science*, 22(1), e12747.

Atkinson-Jones, K., & Hewitt, O. (2019). Do group interventions help people with autism spectrum disorder to develop better relationships with others? A critical review of the literature. *British Journal of Learning Disabilities*, 47(2), 77–90.

Ault, M., Baggerman, M.A., & Horn, C.K. (2017). Effects of an app incorporating systematic instruction to teach spelling to students with developmental delays. *Journal of Special Education Technology*, 32(3), 123–137.

Austin, C.R., Vaughn, S., & McClelland, A.M. (2017). Intensive reading interventions for inadequate responders in Grades K–3: A synthesis. *Learning Disability Quarterly*, 40(4), 191–210.

Azano, A. (2013). The CLEAR Curriculum Model. In C.M. Callahan & H.L. Hertberg-Davis (Eds). *Foundations of gifted education* (pp. 301–314). New York: Routledge.

Baker, A.T. & Cuevas, J. (2018). The importance of automaticity development in mathematics. *Georgia Educational Researcher*, 14(2), 13–23.

Baker, S.K., Santiago, R.T., Masser, J., Nelson, N.J., & Turtura, J. (2018). *The alphabetic principle: From phonological awareness to reading words.* Eugene, OR: National Center on Improving Literacy, University of Oregon.

Bakker, A. (2018). Discovery learning: Zombie, phoenix, or elephant? *Instructional Science: An International Journal of the Learning Sciences*, 46(1), 169–183.

Barlow-Brown, F., Barker, C., & Harris, M. (2019). Size and modality effects in braille learning: implications for the blind child from pre-reading sighted children. *British Journal of Educational Psychology*, 89(1), 165–176.

Barth, A., Roberts, G., Vaughn, S., Fletcher, J., & Stuebing, K. (2013). Effects of a response-based, tiered framework for intervening with struggling readers in middle school. *Reading Research Quarterly*, 48(3), 237–254.

Bates, C.C., D'Agostino, J.V., Gambrell, L., & Xu, M. (2016). Reading Recovery: Exploring the effects on first-graders' reading motivation and achievement. *Journal of Education for Students Placed at Risk*, 21(1), 47–59.

Baxter, P., Lyndon, H., Dole, S., & Battistutta, D. (2004). Less pain, more gain: Rapid skill development using "old way new way." *Journal of Vocational Education and Training*, 56(1), 21–50.

Bayat, N. (2014). The effect of the process writing approach on writing success and anxiety. *Educational Sciences: Theory and Practice*, 14(3), 1133–1141.

Bayless, S.D., Jenson, J.M., Richmond, M.K., Pampel, F.C., Cook, M., & Calhoun, M. (2018). Effects of an afterschool early literacy intervention on the reading skills of children in public housing communities. *Child & Youth Care Forum*, 47(4), 537–561.

Beal, C.R. & Rosenblum, L.P. (2018). Evaluation of the effectiveness of a tablet computer application (app) in helping students with visual impairments solve mathematics problems. *Journal of Visual Impairment & Blindness*, 112(1), 5–19.

Beal-Alvarez, J.S. & Huston, S.G. (2014). Emerging evidence for instructional practice: Repeated viewings of sign language models. *Communication Disorders Quarterly*, 35(2), 93–102.

Beane, A.L. (2008). *Protect your child from bullying.* San Francisco, CA: Jossey-Bass.

Beauchamp, F., Bourke-Taylor, H., & Brown, T. (2018). Therapists' perspectives: Supporting children to use switches and technology for accessing their environment, leisure, and communication. *Journal of Occupational Therapy, Schools & Early Intervention*, 11(2), 133–147.

Bell, N., Angwin, A.J., Wilson, W.J., & Arnott, W.L. (2019). Spelling in children with cochlear implants: Evidence of underlying processing differences. *Journal of Deaf Studies and Deaf Education*, 24(2), 161–172.

Bellert, A. (2009). Narrowing the gap: A report on the *QuickSmart* mathematics intervention. *Australian Journal of Learning Difficulties*, 14(2), 171–183.

Bennett-Rappell, H. & Northcote, M. (2016). Underachieving gifted students: Two case studies. *Issues in Educational Research*, 26(3), 407–430.

Berninger, V.W., Lee, Y-L., Abbott, R.D., & Breznitz, Z. (2013). Teaching children with dyslexia to spell in a reading-writers' workshop. *Annals of Dyslexia*, 63(1), 1–24.

Betts, G. (1985). *The Autonomous Learner Model for the gifted and talented.* Greeley, CO: ALPS Publishing.

Betts, G. & Kercher, J.K. (2009). The autonomous learner model for the gifted and talented. In J. Renzulli (Ed.), *Systems and models for developing programs for the gifted and talented* (2nd ed., pp. 49–100). Waco, TX: Prufrock Press.

Betts, G.T., Carey, R.J., & Kapushion, B.M. (2016). *Autonomous Learner Model resource book*. Waco, TX: Prufrock Press.

Bhat, C.S. (2018). Proactive cyberbullying and sexting prevention in Australia and USA. *Journal of Psychologists and Counsellors in Schools*, 28(1), 120–130.

Bippert, K. (2019). Perceptions of technology, curriculum, and reading strategies in one middle school intervention program. *RMLE Online: Research in Middle Level Education*, 42(3), 1–22.

Bissex, G. (1980). *GYNS AT WRK: A child learns to write and read*. Cambridge, MA: Harvard University Press.

Black, A. (2019). Future secondary schools for diversity: Where are we now and were could we be? *Review of Education*, 7(1), 36–38.

Blankenship, A.P. & Canto, A.I. (2018). Traumatic brain injuries and special education services in the schools. *Exceptionality*, 26(4), 218–229.

Blik, H., Harskamp, E.G., van Leeuwen, S., & Hoekstra, R. (2017). Video instruction with explanation to another person for intellectually disabled students. *Journal of Computer Assisted Learning*, 33(6), 606–620.

Bolt, T.D., Hansen, B.D., Caldarella, P., Young, K.R., Williams, L., & Wills, H.P. (2019). Varying opportunities to respond to improve behavior of elementary students with developmental disabilities. *International Electronic Journal of Elementary Education*, 11(4), 327–334.

Bosnjak, A., Boyle, C., & Chodkiewicz, A.R. (2017). An intervention to retrain attributions using CBT: A pilot study. *Educational and Developmental Psychologist*, 34(1), 19–30.

Bouck, E.C. & Cosby, M.D. (2019). Response to Intervention in high school mathematics: One school's implementation. *Preventing School Failure*, 63(1), 32–42.

Bowers, J.S. & Bowers, P.N. (2017). Beyond phonics: The case for teaching children the logic of the English spelling system. *Educational Psychologist*, 52(2), 124–141.

Bowers, L.M., Dostal, H., McCarthy, J.H., Schwarz, I., & Wolbers, K. (2016). An analysis of deaf students' spelling skills during a year-long instructional writing approach. *Communication Disorders Quarterly*, 37(3), 160–170.

Bradley, R.L. & Noell, G.H. (2018). The effectiveness of supplemental phonics instruction employing constant time delay instruction for struggling readers. *Psychology in the Schools*, 55(7), 880–892.

Bradshaw, C.P. (2013). Preventing bullying through Positive Behavioral Interventions and Supports (PBIS): A multitiered approach to prevention and integration. *Theory into Practice*, 52(4), 288–295.

Braun, G., Austin, C., & Ledbetter-Cho, K. (2017). *Intensive intervention practice guide: Explicit instruction in reading comprehension for students with autism spectrum disorder*. Washington, DC: Office of Special Education Programs, US Department of Education.

Brenner, D. & McQuirk, A. (2019). A snapshot of writing in elementary teacher preparation programs. *New Educator*, 15(1), 18–29.

Brindle, M., Graham, S., Harris, K.R., & Hebert, M. (2016). Third and fourth grade teacher's classroom practices in writing: A national survey. *Reading and Writing: An Interdisciplinary Journal*, 29(5), 929–954.

Brock, M.E., Dueker, S.A., & Barczak, M.A. (2018). Brief report: Improving social outcomes for students with autism at recess through peer-mediated pivotal response training. *Journal of Autism and Developmental Disorders*, 48(6), 2224–2230.

Broomhead, K.E. (2019). Acceptance or rejection? The social experiences of children with special educational needs and disabilities within a mainstream primary school. *Education 3–13*, 47(8), 877–888.

Brown, K.M. (2018). *Scaffolding and Lucy Calkins writers' workshop: A case study in first grade*. ProQuest LLC, DEd. Dissertation, Capella University. ERIC document number ED588005.

Buckingham, J., Beaman-Wheldall, R., & Wheldall, K. (2012). A randomised control trial of a MultiLit small group intervention for older low-progress readers. *Effective Education*, 4(1), 1–26.

Buckley, S. (2013). Deconstructing maths anxiety: Helping students to develop a positive attitude towards learning maths. *ACER Occasional Essay*, pp. 1–3: issued July 2013.

Buckley, S. & Reid, K. (2013). *Learning and fearing mathematics: Insights from psychology and neuroscience*. Paper delivered at ACER Conference'How the Brain Learns: What lessons are there for teaching?'Melbourne, 4–6 August 2013.

Burrell, M., Horsley, J., & Moeed, A. (2017). Identification of, and academic provision for high-ability science students: What does the literature say? *European Journal of Science and Mathematics Education*, 5(2), 110–118.

Bustamante, A.S., Hindman, A.H., Champagne, C.R., & Wasik, B.A (2018). Circle Time revisited: How do preschool classrooms use this part of the day? *Elementary School Journal*, 118(4), 610–631.

Calp, M. (2015). The comparison of fourth grade students' essays based on free and guided writing technique in terms of the quality of written expression. *Educational Research and Reviews*, 10(4), 444–452.

Capp, M.J. (2017). The effectiveness of Universal Design for Learning: A meta-analysis of literature between 2013 and 2016. *International Journal of Inclusive Education*, 21(8), 791–807.

Carter, E.W., Brock, M.E., & Trainor, A.A. (2014). Transition assessment and planning for youth with severe intellectual and developmental disabilities. *Journal of Special Education*, 47(4). 245–255.

Casanova, E.L. & Casanova, M.F. (2018). *Defining autism: A guide to brain, biology, and behavior*. London: Jessica Kingsley.

Catts, H.W. & Kamhi, A.G. (2017). Prologue: Reading comprehension is not a single ability. *Language, Speech, and Hearing Services in Schools*, 48(2), 73–76.

CCSS (Common Core State Standards Initiative: US). (2014b). *Core Standards for Mathematical Practice*. Retrieved from: www.corestandards.org/Math/Practice/.

CDC (Centers for Disease Control and Prevention: US). (2019). *School connectedness*. Retrieved from: www.cdc.gov/healthyyouth/protective/school_connectedness.htm.

CEC (Council for Exceptional Children [US]). (2019). *CEC professional standards*. Retrieved from: www.cec.sped.org/Standards.

Cerveny, L.D. (2016). *Evaluation of the effectiveness of a preference-based teaching approach with children with developmental disabilities*. Psychology Master's Thesis, State University of New York. Retrieved from: http://digitalcommons.brockport.edu/psh_theses/13.

Çetin, H. & Çetin, I. (2018). Views of middle school students about Class Dojo education technology. *Acta Didactica Napocensia*, 11(3–4),89–96.

Chan, C., Chang, M.L., Westwood, P.S., & Yuen, M.T. (2002). Teaching adaptively: How easy is 'differentiation' in practice? A perspective from Hong Kong. *Asian-Pacific Educational Researcher* 11(1), 27–58.

Chan, H.C. & Wong, D.S.W. (2019). Traditional school bullying and cyberbullying perpetration: Examining the psychosocial characteristics of Hong Kong male and female adolescents. *Youth & Society*, 51(1), 3–29.

Chang, B. & Kang, H. (2016). Challenges facing group work online. *Distance Education*, 37(1), 73–88.

Chatzara, K., Karagiannidis, C., & Stamatis, D. (2016). Cognitive support embedded in self-regulated e-learning systems for students with special learning needs. *Education and Information Technologies*, 21(2), 283–299.

Childress, T. (2015). For all students everywhere: Technology means independence in a beautiful digital world. *Odyssey: New Directions in Deaf Education*, 16, 56–59.

Chodkiewicz, A.R. & Boyle, C. (2016). Promoting positive learning in Australian students aged 10- to 12-years-old using attribution retraining and cognitive behavioral therapy: A pilot study. *School Psychology International*, 37(5), 519–535.

Chow, J.C. & Wehby, J.H. (2019). Profiles of problem behavior in children with varying language ability. *Journal of Emotional and Behavioral Disorders*, 27(2), 110–118.

Chua, B.Y.E. & Poon, K.K. (2018). Studying the implementation of PECS in a naturalistic special education school setting. *Educational & Child Psychology*, Special issue (September), 60–75.

Claravall, E.B. (2016). Integrating morphological knowledge in literacy instruction: Framework and principles to guide special education teachers. *Teaching Exceptional Children*, 48(4), 195–203.

Clark, S.K. & Neal, J. (2018). Teaching second-grade students to write sequential text. *Journal of Educational Research*, 111(6), 764–772.

Clarke, A. (2016). Why public and school libraries should stock decodable books. *Learning Difficulties Australia Bulletin*, 48(1), 18–19.

Clarke, A. (2018). Why are children not getting the systematic explicit phonics they need? *Learning Difficulties Australia Bulletin*, 50(3), 7.

Cole, M.T., Swartz, L.B., & Shelley, D.J. (2020). Threaded discussion: The role it plays in e-learning. *International Journal of Information and Communication Technology Education*, 16(1), 16–29.

Coleman, L.J. & Cross, T.L. (2014). Is being gifted a social handicap? *Journal for the Education of the Gifted*, 37(1), 5–17.

Colmar, S. (2014). A parent-based book reading intervention for disadvantaged children with language difficulties. *Child Language Teaching and Therapy*, 30(1), 79–90.

Colovic-Markovic, J. (2019). 'The class changed the way I read': The effects of explicit instruction of academic formulas on ESL writers. *Applied Language Learning*, 29(1–2),17–51.

Connell, N.M., Schell-Busey, N.M., & Hernandez, R. (2019). Experiences versus perceptions: Do students agree that they have been bullied? *Youth & Society*, 51(3), 394–416.

Connelly, V., O'Rourke, L., & Sumner, E. (2019). How being a poor speller can seriously limit your talent as a writer. *Learning Difficulties Australia Bulletin*, 51(1), 17–21.

Conrad, N.J., Kennedy, K., Saoud, W., Scallion, L., & Hanusiak, L. (2019). Establishing word representations through reading and spelling: Comparing degree of orthographic learning. *Journal of Research in Reading*, 42(1), 162–177.

Conroy, M., Marchand, T. & Webster, M. (2009). *Motivating primary students to write using Writers' Workshop*. Action Research Project for MA Degree, Saint Xavier University, Chicago, IL.

Cook, P., Rodes, D.R., & Lipsitz, K.L. (2017). The Reading Wars and Reading Recovery: What educators, families, and taxpayers should know. *Learning Disabilities: A Multidisciplinary Journal*, 22(2), 12–23.

Cooney, P., Tunney, C., & O'Reilly, G. (2018). A systematic review of the evidence regarding cognitive therapy skills that assist cognitive behavioural therapy in adults who have an intellectual disability. *Journal of Applied Research in Intellectual Disabilities*, 31(1), 23–42.

Cordewener, K.A., Hasselman, F., Verhoeven, L., & Bosman, A.M. (2018). The role of instruction for spelling performance and spelling consciousness. *Journal of Experimental Education*, 86(2), 135–153.

Corkett, J.K. & Benevides, T. (2016). iPad versus handwriting: Pilot study exploring the writing abilities of students with learning disabilities. *Journal of International Special Needs Education*, 19(1), 15–24.

Council for Disabled Children [UK]. (2017). *Education, health and care plans: Examples of good practice*. Retrieved from: https://councilfordisabledchildren.org.uk/help-resources/resources/education-health-and-care-plans-examples-good-practice.

Cranmer, S. (2020). Disabled children's evolving digital use practices to support formal learning: A missed opportunity for inclusion. *British Journal of Educational Technology*, 51(2), 315–330.

Crawford, M. (2018). Acceleration for gifted girls facilitated by multiplicity and flexibility of provision and practices. *Australasian Journal of Gifted Education*, 27(2), 28–39.

Crosson, A.C. & Moore, D. (2017). When to take up roots: The effects of morphology instruction for middle school and high school English learners. *Reading Psychology*, 38(3), 262–288.

Cuevas, K.S. (2016). *Teaching writing: Exemplary teachers describe their instruction*. ProQuest LLC, PhD Dissertation, University of Nevada, Reno. ERIC document number ED582950.

Curran, H. (2019). 'The SEND Code of Practice has given me clout': A phenomenological study illustrating how SENCos managed the introduction of the SEND reforms. *British Journal of Special Education*, 46(1), 76–93.

Currell, J. (2018). *Understanding relational and instrumental mathematics*. Retrieved from: https://mathsnoproblem.com/understanding-relational-and-instrumental-mathematics/.

Da Fonte, M. A. & Capizzi, A.M. (2015). A module-based approach: Training paraeducators on evidence-based practices. *Physical Disabilities: Education and Related Services*, 34(1), 31–54.

Dack, H. (2019). Understanding teacher candidate misconceptions and concerns about differentiated instruction. *Teacher Educator*, 54(1), 22–45.

D'Agostino, J.V. & Harmey, S.J. (2016). An international meta-analysis of Reading Recovery. *Journal of Education for Students Placed at Risk*, 21(1), 29–46.

Dahlström, H. (2019). Digital writing tools from the student perspective: Access, affordances, and agency. *Education and Information Technologies*, 24(2), 1563–1581.

Daigle, D., Berthiaume, R., Costerg, A., Plisson, A., Ruberto, N., & Varin, J. (2020). Do all roads really lead to Rome? The case of spelling acquisition. *Reading and Writing: An Interdisciplinary Journal*, 33(2), 313–328.

Datchuk, S.M. & Kubina, R.M. (2013). A review of teaching sentence-level writing skills to students with writing difficulties and learning disabilities. *Remedial and Special Education*, 34(3), 180–192.

Datchuk, S.M., Wagner, K., & Hier, B. (2020). Level and trend of writing sequences: A review and meta-analysis of writing interventions for students with disabilities. *Exceptional Children*, 86(2), 174–192.

Davis, A. (2018). Evidence-based approaches to education: Direct Instruction, anyone? *Management in Education*, 32(3), 135–138.

Dawes, M. (2014). *Improving low-attaining pupils' calculation ability during KS3*. London: National Center for Excellence in Mathematics Teaching.

De Smedt, F., Graham, S., & Van Keer, H. (2019). The bright and dark side of writing motivation: Effects of explicit instruction and peer assistance. *Journal of Educational Research*, 112(2), 152–167.

Debenham, L. (2018). *Non-verbal learning disabilities*. Retrieved from: www.aboutlearningdisabilities.co.uk/nonverbal-learning-disabilities.html.

Delisle, J.R. (2006). *Parenting gifted kids*, Waco, TX: Prufrock Press.

Dennis, M. (2012). *Attention in spina bifida: Findings from the SANDI Project*. Paper delivered at the Second World Congress on Spina Bifida Research and Care, Las Vegas, 11–14 March 2012.

DES (Department of Education and Science: UK). (1978). *Special Educational Needs: Report of the Committee of Enquiry into the Education of Handicapped Children and Young People (The Warnock Report)*. London: HMSO.

DfE (Department for Education, UK). (2012). *Year 1 Phonics screening check: Technical Report*. London: Standards and Testing Agency.

DfE (Department for Education: UK). (2013a). *Including all learners*. Retrieved from: http://webarchive.nationalarchives.gov.uk/20130903160926/http://www.education.gov.uk/schools/teachingandlearning/curriculum/b00199686/inclusion/needs.

DfE (Department for Education: UK). (2013b). *Mathematics programmes of study: Key stages 1 and 2 in the National Curriculum in England*. London: Department for Education.

DfE (Department for Education). (2013c) *Children with Special Needs 2013: Statistical Analysis*. London: Department for Education.

DfE (Department for Education: UK) (2014a). *The National Curriculum in England: Framework document*. Retrieved from: https://assets.publishing.service.gov.uk/government/uploads/system/uploads/attachment_data/file/381344/Master_final_national_curriculum_28_Nov.pdf.

DfE (Department for Education: UK). (2014b). *Cyberbullying: Advice for headteachers and school staff*. Retrieved from: https://assets.publishing.service.gov.uk/government/uploads/system/uploads/attachment_data/file/374850/Cyberbullying_Advice_for_Headteachers_and_School_Staff_121114.pdf.

DfE (Department for Education: UK). (2014c) *Statutory guidance for National Curriculum in England: Mathematics programmes of study*. Retrieved from: www.gov.uk/government/publications/national-curriculum-in-england-mathematics-programmes-of-study/national-curriculum-in-england-mathematics-programmes-of-study.

DfE/DoH (Department for Education and Department of Health). (2015). *Special educational needs and disabilities code of practice: 0 to 25 years*. https://assets.publishing.service.gov.uk/government/uploads/system/uploads/attachment_data/file/398815/SEND_Code_of_Practice_January_2015.pdf.

DfE (Department for Education: UK). (2016). *Special educational needs and disability: Managing the September 2014 changes to the system*. London: Department for Education.

DfE (Department for Education: UK). (2018). *Special educational needs in England: January 2018*. Retrieved from: https://assets.publishing.service.gov.uk/government/uploads/system/uploads/attachment_data/file/633031/SFR37_2017_Main_Text.pdf.

Diaz, I. (2010). *The effect of morphological instruction in improving spelling, vocabulary, and reading comprehension of high school English language learners*. ProQuest LLC: PhD Dissertation, TUI University. ERIC document number ED514872.

Dillon, M.B., Radley, K.C., Tingstrom, D.H., Dart, E.H., & Barry, C.T. (2019). The effects of tootling via ClassDojo on student behavior in elementary classrooms. *School Psychology Review*, 48(1), 18–30.

Dix, P. (2017). Quoted in R. Vukovic (Ed.). Behaviour management: 'Focus on the 95%'. *Teacher* magazine [online], 31 May(not paginated).

Dixon, R. & Englemann, S. (2006). *Spelling through morphographs*. Desoto, TX: SRA-McGraw Hill.

Doabler, C. & Fien, H. (2013). Explicit mathematics instruction: What teachers can do for teaching students with mathematics difficulties. *Intervention in School and Clinic*, 48(5), 276–285.

Doabler, C., Nelson, N., Kosty, D., Fien, H., Baker, S., Smolkowski, K., & Clarke, B. (2014). Examining teachers' use of evidence-based practices during core mathematics instruction. *Assessment for Effective Intervention*, 39(2), 99–111.

Dominica, S. (2019). *Teaching students with orthopedic impairment*. Retrieved from: www.brighthubeducation.com/special-ed-inclusion-strategies/71197-having-a-child-with-an-orthopedic-impairment-in-the-class/.

Donne, V., Hansen, M.A., & Zigmond, N. (2019). Statewide alternate reading assessment of students who are deaf/hard of hearing with additional disabilities. *Communication Disorders Quarterly*, 40(2), 67–76.

Dorn, B. (2019). The changing role of teachers of students who are deaf or hard of hearing: Consultation as an increasing part of the job. *Journal of Educational and Psychological Consultation*, 29(2), 237–254.

Dosch, M. & Zidon, M. (2014). 'The course fit us': Differentiated instruction in the college classroom. *International Journal of Teaching and Learning in Higher Education*, 26(3), 343–357.

Douch, A. (2014). Teaching methods: Flipped learning. *Teacher* magazine [online]. July issue (not paginated). Melbourne: Australian Council for Educational Research.

Dowker, A. (2005). Early identification and intervention for students with mathematics difficulties. *Journal of Learning Disabilities*, 38(4), 324–332.

D'Souza, D.A.C. & Clare, A.C. (2018). Effect of situated learning model on critical problem-solving skills among higher secondary pupils. *Journal on School Educational Technology*, 14(1), 27–34.

Ducic, B., Gligorovic, M., & Kaljaca, S. (2018). Relation between working memory and self-regulation capacities and the level of social skills acquisition in people with moderate intellectual disability. *Journal of Applied Research in Intellectual Disabilities*, 31(2), 296–307.

Duke, N.K. & Mesmer, H.A.E. (2019). Phonics faux pas: Avoiding instructional missteps in teaching letter-sound relationships. *American Educator*, 42(4), 12–16.

Dymock, S. (2019). Yes, spelling should be taught. *Learning Difficulties Australia Bulletin*, 51(1), 31–35.

Dymock, S. & Nicholson, T. (2017). To what extent does children's spelling improve as a result of learning words with the look, say, cover, write, check, fix strategy compared with phonological spelling strategies? *Australian Journal of Learning Difficulties*, 22(2), 171–187.

Dymond, S.K. & Orelove, P. (2001). What constitutes effective curriculum for students with severe disabilities? *Exceptionality*, 9(3), 109–122.

EEF (Education Endowment Foundation). (2019). *Metacognition and self-regulation*. Retrieved from: https://educationendowmentfoundation.org.uk/evidence-summaries/teaching-learning-toolkit/meta-cognition-and-self-regulation/.

Egeberg, H. & McConney, A. (2018). What do students believe about effective classroom management? A mixed-methods investigation in Western Australian high schools. *The Australian Educational Researcher*, 45(2), 195–216.

Ehri, L.C. (2014). Orthographic mapping in the acquisition of sight word reading, spelling memory, and vocabulary learning. *Scientific Studies of Reading*, 18(1), 5–21.

Elder, L. (2018). *What is Discrete Trial Training?* Retrieved from: www.autismspeaks.org/expert-opinion/what-discrete-trial-training.

Elimelech, A. & Aram, D. (2019). A digital early spelling game: The role of auditory and visual support. *AERA Open*, 5(2), 1–11.

Engelmann, S. (1999). The benefits of direct instruction: Affirmative action for at-risk students. *Educational Leadership*, 57(1), 77–79.

Ennis, R.P. & Jolivette, K. (2014). Existing research and future directions for self-regulated strategy development with students with and at risk for emotional and behavioral disorders. *Journal of Special Education*, 48(1), 32–45.

Ennis, R.P. & Losinski, M. (2019). Interventions to improve fraction skills for students with disabilities: A meta-analysis. *Exceptional Children*, 85(3), 367–386.

Erden, H. (2020). Teaching and learning in multi-graded classrooms: Is it sustainable? *International Journal of Curriculum and Instruction*, 12: 359–378.

Estrapala, S., Rila, A., & Bruhn, A.L. (2018). Don't quit cold turkey: Systematic fading to promote sustained behavioral change. *Teaching Exceptional Children*, 51(1), 54–61.

Euefueno, W.D. (2019). Project/problem-based learning in STEM: Impacts on student learning. *Technology and Engineering Teacher*, 78(8), 8–12.

Everhart, R.S., Miller, S., Leibach, G.G., Dahl, A.L., & Koinis-Mitchell, D. (2018). Caregiver asthma in urban families: Implications for school absenteeism. *Journal of School Nursing*, 34(2), 108–113.

Fallon, L.M. & Kurtz, K.D. (2019). Coaching teachers to implement the Good Behavior Game: A direct training approach. *Teaching Exceptional Children*, 51(4), 296–304.

Farkota, R. (2005). Basic math problems: The brutal reality! *Learning Difficulties Australia Bulletin*, 37(3), 10–11.

Farkota, R. (2013). *Evidence-based learning in the classroom: Direct instruction at work*. Workshop on direct instruction held at Treacy Conference Centre, Melbourne, 23 March, 2013.

Fast, D. & Wild, T. (2018). Teaching science through inquiry-based field experiences using orientation and mobility. *Journal of Science Education for Students with Disabilities*, 21(1), 29–39.

Fava, L. & Strauss, K. (2010). Multi-sensory rooms: Comparing effects of the Snoezelen and the stimulus preference environment on the behavior of adults with profound mental retardation. *Research in Developmental Disabilities: A Multidisciplinary Journal*, 31(1), 160–171.

Feldhusen, J.F. & Kolloff, M.B. (1988). A Three-Stage Model for gifted education, *Gifted Child Today Magazine*, 11(1), 14–20.

Feng, L., Lindner, A., Ji, X.R., & Malatesha J.R. (2019). The roles of handwriting and keyboarding in writing: A meta-analytic review. *Reading and Writing: An Interdisciplinary Journal*, 32(1), 33–63.

Filippello, P., Harrington, N., Costa, S., Buzzai, C., Sorrenti, L. (2018). Perceived parental psychological control and school learned helplessness: The role of frustration intolerance as a mediator factor. *School Psychology International*, 39(4), 360–377.

Fletcher, J.M., Lyon, G. R., Fuchs, L.S, & Barnes, M.A. (2018). *Learning disabilities: From identification to intervention* (2nd ed.). New York: Guilford.

Foley, E.A., Dozier, C.L., & Lessor, A.L. (2019). Comparison of components of the Good Behavior Game in a preschool classroom. *Journal of Applied Behavior Analysis*, 52(1), 84–104.

Forslund, F.K. & Hammar-Chiriac, E. (2018). Student collaboration in group work: Inclusion as participation. *International Journal of Disability, Development and Education*, 65(2), 183–198.

Foster, L., McDuffie-Landrum, K., Oh, S., & Azano, A. (2011). *The CLEAR Curriculum: An integration of three gifted models*. Retrieved from: http://nrcgtuva.org/presentations/CEC2011.pdf.

Fournier, G. (2018). Locus of Control. *Psych Central*. Retrieved from: https://psychcentral.com/encyclopedia/locus-of-control/.

Friedman C., Rizzolo, M.C., & Spassiani, N.A. (2019). Self-management of health by people with intellectual and developmental disabilities. *Journal of Applied Research in Intellectual Disabilities*, 32(3), 600–609.

Gaesser, A.H. (2018). Befriending anxiety to reach potential: Strategies to empower our gifted youth. *Gifted Child Today*, 41(4), 186–195.

Gage, N.A., Rose, C.A., & Kramer, D.A. (2019). When prevention is not enough: Students' perception of bullying and School-Wide Positive Behavior Interventions and Supports. *Behavioral Disorders*, 45(1), 29–40.

Gaintza, Z., Ozerinjauregi, N., & Arostegui, I. (2018). Educational inclusion of students with rare diseases: Schooling students with spina bifida. *British Journal of Learning Disabilities*, 46(4), 250–257.

Gargiulo, R.M. & Metcalf, D. (2017). *Teaching in today's inclusive classrooms: A Universal Design for Learning approach* (3rd ed.). Belmont, CA: Cengage.

Garvik, M., Idsoe, T., & Bru, E. (2014). Effectiveness study of a CBT-based adolescent coping with depression course. *Emotional and Behavioural Difficulties*, 19(2), 195–209.

Garwood, J.D., Varghese, C., & Vernon-Feagans, L. (2017). Internalizing behaviors and hyperactivity/inattention: Consequences for young struggling readers, and especially boys. *Journal of Early Intervention*, 39(3), 218–235.

Gebauer, D., Enzinger, C., Kronbichler, M., Schurz, M., Reishofer, G., Koschutnig, K., Kargl, R., Purgstaller, C., Fazekas, F., & Fink, A. (2012). Distinct patterns of brain function in children with isolated spelling impairment: New insights. *Neuropsychologia*, 50(7), 1353–1361.

Gerow, S., Davis, T., Radhakrishnan, S., Gregori, E., & Rivera, G. (2018). Functional Communication Training: The strength of evidence across disabilities. *Exceptional Children*, 85(1), 86–103.

Gerzel-Short, L. (2018). 'We conquered this together': Tier 2 collaboration with families. *School Community Journal*, 28(2), 85–112.

Ghanouni, P., Jarus, T., Zwicker, J.G., Lucyshyn, J., Mow, K., & Ledingham, A. (2019). Social Stories for children with autism spectrum disorder: Validating the content of a virtual reality program. *Journal of Autism and Developmental Disorders*, 49(2), 660–668.

Gibbs, A.S., Hinton, V.M., & Flores, M.M. (2018). A case study using CRA to teach students with disabilities to count using flexible numbers: Applying skip counting to multiplication. *Preventing School Failure*, 62(1), 49–57.

Gibson, S.A. (2008). Guided writing lessons: Second-grade students' development of strategic behavior. *Reading Horizons*, 48(2), 111–132.

Gilbert, F. (2018). Riding the reciprocal teaching bus: A teacher's reflections on nurturing collaborative learning in a school culture obsessed by results. *Changing English: Studies in Culture and Education*, 25(2), 146–162.

Gill, K. & Thompson-Hodgetts, S. (2018). Self-regulation in fetal alcohol spectrum disorder: A concept analysis. *Journal of Occupational Therapy, Schools & Early Intervention*, 11(3), 329–345.

Gill, K., Thompson-Hodgetts, S., & Rasmussen, C. (2018). A critical review of research on the Alert Program®. *Journal of Occupational Therapy, Schools & Early Intervention*, 11(2), 212–228.

Gillingham, A. & Stillman, B.W. (1956). *Remedial training for students with specific disability in reading, spelling, and penmanship.* Cambridge, MA: Educators Publishing Service.

Goodall, C. (2018). Mainstream is not for all: The educational experiences of autistic young people. *Disability & Society*, 33(10), 1661–1665.

Goodman-Scott, E., Carlisle, R., Clark, M., & Burgess, M. (2017). A powerful tool: A phenomenological study of school counselors' experiences with social stories. *Professional School Counseling*, 20(1), 25–35.

Gorard, S., Siddiqui, N., & See, B.H. (2015). *Fresh Start: Evaluation report and executive summary.* London: Education Endowment Foundation.

Goss, P., Sonnemann, J., Chisholm, C., Nelson, L. (2016). Widening gaps: What NAPLAN tells us about student progress, Grattan Institute. Retrieved from: https://grattan.edu.au/wp-con tent/uploads/2016/03/937-Widening-gaps.pdf.

GOV.UK. (2013). *Children with special needs (SEN).* Retrieved from: www.gov.uk/children-with-special-educational-needs/overview.

GOV.UK. (2014a). *Improving the quality of teaching and leadership.* Retrieved from: www.gov.uk/government/policies/improving-the-quality-of-teaching-and-leadership/activity.

GOV.UK. (2014b). *Disability facts and figures.* Retrieved from: www.gov.uk/government/publica tions/disability-facts-and-figures/disability-facts-and-figures.

GOV.UK. (2015). *Children with special educational needs and disabilities.* Retrieved from: www.gov. uk/children-with-special-educational-needs/extra-SEN-help.

Graham, L., Bellert, A., Thomas, J., & Pegg, J. (2007). 'QuickSmart': A basic academic skills intervention for middle school students with learning difficulties. *Journal of Learning Disabilities*, 40(5), 410–419.

Graham, S. (2008). *The power of word processing for the student writer.* Wisconsin Rapids, WI: Renaissance Learning.

Graham, S. & Perrin, D. (2007). *Writing Next: Effective strategies to improve writing of adolescents in middle and high school.* Washington, DC: Alliance for Excellence in Education.

Graham, S. & Santangelo, T. (2014). Does spelling instruction make students better spellers, readers, and writers? A meta-analytic review. *Reading and Writing: An Interdisciplinary Journal*, 27(9), 1703–1743.

Graham, S., Harris, K.R., & Santangelo, T. (2015). Research-based writing practices and the common core: Meta-analysis and meta-synthesis. *The Elementary School Journal*, 115(4), 498–522.

Graham, S., McKeown, D., Kiuhare, S., & Harris, K.R. (2012). A meta-analysis of writing instruction for students in the elementary grades. *Journal of Educational Psychology*, 104(4), 879–896.

Grattan, G. & Demchak, M.A. (2014). Stimulus Preference Assessments. *Nevada Dual Sensory Impairment Project Newsletter*, 23(1), 1–4.

Gray, C. (2015). *The new social story book.* Arlington, TX: Future Horizons.

Gray, S.H., Ehri, L.C., & Locke, J.L. (2018). Morpho-phonemic analysis boosts word reading for adult struggling readers. *Reading and Writing: An Interdisciplinary Journal*, 31(1), 75–98.

Greer, C.W. & Erickson, K.A. (2019). Teaching students with significant cognitive disabilities to count: Routine for achieving early counting. *Teaching Exceptional Children*, 51(5), 382–389.

Grenier, M., & Yeaton, P. (2019). Social thinking skills and cooperative learning for students with autism. *Journal of Physical Education, Recreation & Dance*, 90(3), 18–21.

Griffin, M.M., Fisher, M.H, Lane, L.A., & Morin, L. (2019). In their own words: Perceptions and experiences of bullying among individuals with intellectual and developmental disabilities. *Intellectual and Developmental Disabilities*, 57(1), 66–74.

Groff, P. (2015). Decodable words versus predictable text. *Learning Difficulties Australia Bulletin*, 47(3), 9–10.

Gronostaj, A., Werner, E., Bochow, E., & Vock, M. (2016). How to learn things at school you don't already know: Experiences of gifted grade-skippers in Germany. *Gifted Child Quarterly*, 60(1), 31–46.

Grossman, P., Dean, C.G., Kavanagh, S.S., & Herrmann, Z. (2019). Preparing teachers for project-based teaching. *Phi Delta Kappan*, 100(7), 43–48.

Großmann, N. & Wilde, M. (2019). Experimentation in biology lessons: Guided discovery through incremental scaffolds. *International Journal of Science Education*, 41(6), 759–781.

Gustafsson, J. (2018). Differentiation through individualization: An ethnographic investigation of how one Swedish school creates inequality. *Ethnography and Education*, 13(1), 52–68.

Guzmán G., Derly Y., Moreno C., & Johana, A. (2019). The use of Plotagon to enhance the English writing skill in secondary school students. *PROFILE: Issues in Teachers' Professional Development*, 21(1), 139–153.

Haggerty, N.K., Black, R.S., & Smith, G.J. (2005). Increasing self-managed coping skills through social stories and apron storytelling, *Teaching Exceptional Children*, 37(4), 40–47.

Hallahan, D.P., Kauffman, J.M., & Pullen, P.C. (2019). *Exceptional Learners: An Introduction to Special Education* (14th ed.). Upper Saddle River, NJ: Pearson.

Hamblet, E.C. (2014). Nine strategies to improve transition planning for students with disabilities. *Teaching Exceptional Children*, 46(3), 53–63.

Hammerschmidt-Snidarich, S.M., Maki, K.E., & Adams, S.R. (2019). Evaluating the effects of repeated reading and continuous reading using a standardized dosage of words read. *Psychology in the Schools*, 56(5), 635–651.

Hammond, L. & Moore, W.M. (2018). Teachers taking up explicit instruction: The impact of a professional development and directive instructional coaching model. *Australian Journal of Teacher Education*, 43(7), 110–133.

Hampshire, P.K. & Hourcade, J.J. (2014). Teaching play skills to children with autism using visually structured tasks. *Teaching Exceptional Children*, 46(3), 26–32.

Hansen, B.D. & Wills, H.P. (2014). The effects of goal setting, contingent reward, and instruction on writing skills. *Journal of Applied Behavior Analysis*, 47(1), 171–175.

Harris, K.R., Graham, S., Mason, L., & Friedlander, B. (2008). *Powerful writing strategies for all students*. Baltimore, MD: Brookes.

Harris, L.G. (2014). *Social-emotional development in children with hearing loss*. Theses and Dissertations: Communication Sciences and Disorders, 4. https://uknowledge.uky.edu/commdisorders_etds/4.

Harrison, G.L. & McManus, K.L. (2017). Clinical reasoning in the assessment and intervention planning for writing disorder. *Canadian Journal of School Psychology*, 32(1), 73–86.

HASA (Hearing and Speech Agency). (2019). *Language-based learning disabilities*. Retrieved from: https://hasa.org/topics/language-based-learning-disabilities/.

Hassan, N.M., Landorf, K.B., Shields, N., & Munteanu, S.E. (2019). Effectiveness of interventions to increase physical activity in individuals with intellectual disabilities: A systematic review of randomised controlled trials. *Journal of Intellectual Disability Research*, 63(2), 168–191.

Hathcock, S.J. (2018). Interdisciplinary science through the Parallel Curriculum Model: Lessons from the sea. *Gifted Child Today*, 41(1), 28–40.

Hattie, J. (2003). *Visible learning*. Abingdon, Oxon: Routledge.

Hattie, J. (2012). *Visible learning for teachers*. London: Routledge.

Hattie, J. & Yates, G.C.R. (2014). *Visible learning and the science of how we learn*. London: Routledge.

Hawkins, L.K. (2019). Writing conference purpose and how it positions primary-grade children as authoritative agents or passive observers. *Reading Horizons*, 58(1), 22–47.

Haynes-Stewart, T.L., Clifton, R.A., Daniels, L.M., Perry, R.P., Chipperfield, J.G., & Ruthig, J.C. (2011). Attributional retraining: Reducing the likelihood of failure. *Social Psychology of Education: An International Journal*, 14(1), 75–92.

Head, C.N., Flores, M.M., Shippen, M.E. (2018). Effects of Direct Instruction on reading comprehension for individuals with autism or developmental disabilities. *Education and Training in Autism and Developmental Disabilities*, 53(2), 176–191.

Hébert, T.P. & Smith, K.J. (2018). Social and emotional development of gifted students. *Gifted Child Today*, 41(4), 176–176.

Heick, T. (2018). *The ultimate list: 50 strategies for differentiated instruction*. Retrieved from: www.tea chthought.com/pedagogy/50-strategies-for-differentiated-instruction/.

Hellawell, B. (2019). An ethical audit of the SEND CoP 2015: Professional partnership working and the division of ethical labour. *Journal of Research in Special Educational Needs*, 19(1), 15–26.

Heller, K.W. & Bigge, J.L. (2010). Augmentative and alternative communication. In S.J. Best, K.W. Heller, & J.L. Bigge (Eds) *Teaching individuals with physical or multiple disabilities* (6th ed.). Upper Saddle River, NJ: Pearson-Merrill.

Hennessy, S. & Warwick, P. (2010). Editorial: Research into teaching with whole class Interactive technologies. *Technology, Pedagogy and Education*, 19(2), 127–131.

Henshon, S.E. (2018). Toward a visionary future: An interview with Sally Reis. *Roeper Review*, 40(4), 215–221.

Herrington, J., Parker, J. & Boase-Jelinek, D. (2014). Connected authentic learning: Reflection and intentional learning. *Australian Journal of Education*, 58(1), 23–35.

Hertberg-Davis, H. (2009). Myth 7: Differentiation in the regular classroom is equivalent to gifted programs and is sufficient. *Gifted Child Quarterly*, 53(4), 251–253.

Hetzroni, O.E. & Shrieber, B. (2004). Word processing as an assistive technology tool for enhancing academic outcomes of students with writing disabilities in the general classroom. *Journal of Learning Disabilities*, 37(2), 143–154.

Hewett, D. (Ed.). (2018). *Intensive interaction handbook* (2nd ed.). London: SAGE.

Hinduja, S. & Patchin, J.W. (2019). Connecting adolescent suicide to the severity of bullying and cyberbullying. *Journal of School Violence*, 18(3), 333–346.

Hines, M.E., Catalana, S.M., & Anderson, B.N. (2019). When learning sinks in: Using the Incubation Model of Teaching to guide students through the creative thinking process. *Gifted Child Today*, 42(1), 36–45.

Hodges, T.S., Wright, K.L., & McTigue, E. (2019). What do middle grades preservice teachers believe about writing and writing instruction? *RMLE Online: Research in Middle Level Education*, 42 (2) (not paginated).

Hodgson, J. (2013). Classroom activities. *English Teaching Forum*, 51(3), 46–52.

Hoff, K.E. & Ervin, R.A. (2013). Extending self-management strategies: The use of a classwide approach. *Psychology in the Schools*, 50(2), 151–164.

Holliman, A.J., Hurry, J., & Bodman, S. (2016). Children's reading profiles on exiting the Reading Recovery programme: Do they predict sustained progress? *Journal of Research in Reading*, 39(1), 1–18.

Hollo, A. & Wehby, J.H. (2017). Teacher talk in general and special education elementary classrooms. *Elementary School Journal*, 117(4), 616–641.

Horbach, J., Mayer, A., Scharke, W., Heim, S., & Günther, T. (2020). Development of behavior problems in children with and without specific learning disorders in reading and spelling from Kindergarten to Fifth Grade. *Scientific Studies of Reading*, 24(1), 57–71.

Horn, A.L., Gable, R.A., & Bobzien, J.L. (2020). Constant time delay to teach students with intellectual disability. *Preventing School Failure*, 64(1), 89–97.

Howard, V.F., Williams, B.F., & Lepper, C. (2014). *Very young children with special needs* (5th ed.), Boston: Pearson.

Hua, O., Shore, B.M. & Makarova, E. (2014). Inquiry-based instruction within a community of practice for gifted-ADHD college students. *Gifted Education International*, 30(1), 74–86.

Hugh, M.L., Conner, C., & Stewart, J. (2018). *Intensive Intervention Practice Guide: Using visual activity schedules to intensify academic interventions for young children with autism spectrum disorder*. Washington, DC: Office of Special Education Programs, US Department of Education.

Hughes, C.A., Morris, J.R., Therrien, W.J., & Benson, S.K. (2017). Explicit instruction: Historical and contemporary contexts. *Learning Disabilities Research & Practice*, 32(3), 140–148.

Hughes, S. (2014). *The Orton-Gillingham Language Approach: A research review*. Retrieved from: www.nessy.com/us/files/2014/06/Orton-Gillingham_Report-Final-Version.pdf.

Hutchison, A. & Woodward, L. (2014). A planning cycle for integrating digital technology into literacy instruction, *Reading Teacher*, 67(6), 455–464.

Hwang, J. (2019). Relationships among locus of control, learned helpless, and mathematical literacy in PISA 2012: Focus on Korea and Finland. *Large-scale Assessments in Education*, 7, Article 4 (not paginated).

Hwang, M.H., Choi, H.C., Lee, A., Culver, J.D., & Hutchison, B. (2016). The relationship between self-efficacy and academic achievement: A 5-year panel analysis. *Asia-Pacific Education Researcher*, 25(1), 89–98.

ICLI (International Communications Learning Institute). (2014). *Sound/Visual Phonics*. Retrieved from: www.SD-1817.ORG/.

IDA (International Dyslexia Association) (2017). Morphological awareness: One piece of the literacy pie. *Learning Difficulties Australia Bulletin*, 49(3), 23–25.

Idawati, D., Masitoh, S., & Bachri, B.S. (2020). Application of learning mobility orientation on social skill of blind children. *Journal of Education and Learning*, 9(1), 196–204.

IES (Institute of Education Sciences, US) (2009). *Success for All*. What Works Clearinghouse online document. Retrieved from: www.eric.ed.gov/ERICDocs/data/ericdocs2sql/content_storage_01/0000019b/80/44/d4/ec.pdf.

Imray, P. & Hinchcliffe, V. (2012). Not fit for purpose: A call for separate and distinct pedagogies as part of a national framework for those with severe and profound learning difficulties. *Support for Learning*, 27(4), 150–157.

Inclusive Technology. (2014). *Alternative and augmentative communication (AAC)*. Retrieved from: www.inclusive.co.uk/articles/alternative-and-augmentative-communication-aac-a280.

Institute of Education Sciences. (2013). *Beginning reading intervention report: Words Their Way*[TM]. What Works Clearinghouse. Retrieved from: http://whatworks.ed.gov.

Institute of Education Sciences. (2014). *Students with learning disabilities: Mastery Spelling*. What Works Clearinghouse[TM]. Retrieved from: https://files.eric.ed.gov/fulltext/ED544745.pdf.

Irving, J.A., Oppong, E., & Shore, B.M. (2016). Alignment of a high-ranked PISA mathematics curriculum and the "Parallel Curriculum" for gifted students: Is a high PISA mathematics ranking indicative of curricular suitability for gifted learners? *Gifted and Talented International*, 31(2),114–131.

Jacob, R. & Jacob, B. (2018). New evidence on the benefits of small group math instruction for young children. *Evidence Speaks Report* 2(55). Washington, DC: Center on Children and Families at Brookings.

Jacobsen, D.A., Eggen, P., & Kauchak, D. (2009). *Methods for teaching: Promoting student learning in K-12 classrooms* (8th ed.). Upper Saddle River, NJ: Pearson-Merrill.

James, J. & Steimle, A. (2014). Problem solvers: Jesse's train. *Teaching Children Mathematics*, 20(6), 346–349.

James, K. & Beringer, V. (2019). Brain research shows why handwriting should be taught in the computer age. *Learning Difficulties Australia Bulletin*, 51(1), 25–30.

Jenkins, A., Oakes, W., Booker, B., & Lane, K.L. (2013). Three-tiered models of prevention: Teacher efficacy and burnout. *Education and Treatment of Children*, 36(4), 95–127.

Jimenez, B.A., Lo, Y., & Saunders, A.F. (2014). The additive effects of scripted lessons plus guided notes on science quiz scores of students with intellectual disability and autism. *Journal of Special Education*, 47(4), 231–244.

Jo, W., Jang Hee, I., Harianto, R.A., So, J.H., Lee, H., Lee, H.J., & Moon, M.W. (2016). Introduction of 3D printing technology in the classroom for visually impaired students. *Journal of Visual Impairment & Blindness*, 110(2), 115–121.

John, N. (2017). *Examining the effectiveness of the Orton-Gillingham Reading Approach for poor readers in elementary*. University of Western Ontario: School of Communication Sciences and Disorders.

Kaczorowski, T.L., Hashey, A.I., & Di Cesare, D.M. (2019). An exploration of multimedia supports for diverse learners during core math instruction. *Journal of Special Education Technology*, 34(1), 41–54.

Kalogeropoulos, P., Russo, J.A., Sullivan, P., Klooger, M., & Gunningham, S. (2020). Re-enfranchising mathematically-alienated students: Teacher and tutor perceptions of the Getting Ready in Numeracy (G.R.I.N.) Program. *International Electronic Journal of Mathematics Education*, 15(1), Article em0545.

Kang, G.Y. (2018). Playing with digital tools with explicit scaffolding. *Reading Teacher*, 71(6), 735–741.

Kaplan, S.N (2019). Advocacy differentiating differentiation. *Gifted Child Today*, 42(1), 58–59.

Kaplan, S.N., Guzman, I., & Tomlinson, C.A. (2009). *Using the Parallel Curriculum Model in urban settings*. Thousand Oaks, CA: Corwin.

Karal, M.A. & Wolfe, P.S. (2018). Social Story effectiveness on social interaction for students with autism: A review of the literature. *Education and Training in Autism and Developmental Disabilities*, 53(1), 44–58.

Karbowski, C.F. (2020). See3D: 3D printing for people who are blind. *Journal of Science Education for Students with Disabilities*, 23(1). doi:10.14448/jsesd.12.0006.

Karich, A.C., Burns, M.K., & Maki, K.E. (2014). Updated meta-analysis of learner control with educational technology. *Review of Educational Research*, 84(3), 392–410.

Kast, M., Baschera, G., Gross, M., Jancke, L., & Meyer, M. (2011). Computer-based learning of spelling skills in children with and without dyslexia. *Annals of Dyslexia*, 61(2), 177–200.

Kempre, M.J., Verhoeven, L., & Bosman, A.M.T. (2012). Implicit and explicit instruction of spelling rules. *Learning and Individual Differences*, 22(6), 639–649.

Kervin, L. & Mantei, J. (2016). Digital writing practices: A close look at one Grade Three author. *Literacy*, 50(3), 133–140.

Kim, N.J., Belland, B.R., & Axelrod, D. (2019). Scaffolding for optimal challenge in K-12 problem-based learning. *Interdisciplinary Journal of Problem-based Learning*, 13(1), Article 3. (Online, not paginated.)

Kissane, B. (2017). Learning with calculators: Doing more with less. *Australian Mathematics Teacher*, 73(1), 3–11.

Kizilaslan, A. (2019). Linking theory to practice: Science for students with visual impairment. *Science Education International*, 30(1), 56–64.

Knackendoffel, A., Dettmer, P., & Thurston (2017). *Collaborating, consulting and working in teams for students with special needs* (8th ed.). Boston, MA: Pearson.

Knopp, K.A. (2019). The Children's Social Comprehension Scale (CSCS): Construct validity of a new social intelligence measure for elementary school children. *International Journal of Behavioral Development*, 43(1), 90–96.

Koegel, R.L. & Koegel, L.K. (2006). *Pivotal response treatments for Autism: Communication, social and academic development*. Baltimore, MD: Brookes.

Konrad, M. & Joseph, L.M. (2014). Cover-Copy-Compare: A method for enhancing evidence-based instruction. *Intervention in School and Clinic*, 49(4), 203–210.

Korpi, H., Peltokallio, L., & Piirainen, A. (2019). Problem-based learning in professional studies from the physiotherapy students' perspective. *Interdisciplinary Journal of Problem-based Learning*, 13(1) (not paginated). doi:10.7771/1541-5015.1732.

Koshy, V., Portman-Smith, C., & Casey, R. (2018). England policy in gifted education: Current problems and promising directions. *Gifted Child Today*, 41(2), 75–80.

Krawec, J.L. (2014). Problem representation and mathematical problem-solving of students of varying math ability. *Journal of Learning Disabilities*, 47(2), 103–115.

Kruit, P.M., Oostdam, R.J., van den Berg, E., & Schuitema, J.A. (2018). Effects of explicit instruction on the acquisition of students' science inquiry skills in grades 5 and 6 of primary education. *International Journal of Science Education*, 40(4), 421–441.

Kuczera, M., Field, S., & Windisch, H.C. (2016). *Building skills for all: A review of England*. Paris: OECD.

Kulakow, S. (2020). How autonomy support mediates the relationship between self-efficacy and approaches to learning. *Journal of Educational Research*, 113(1), 13–25.

Kumaravelu, G. (2018). Locus of control in school students and its relationship with academic achievement. *Journal on School Educational Technology*, 13(4), 63–66.

Kupzyk, S.S. & Daly, E.J. (2017). Teachers engaging parents as reading tutors. *Contemporary School Psychology*, 21(2), 140–151.

Kyriacou, C. & Zuin, A. (2018). Cyberbullying bystanders and moral engagement: A psychosocial analysis for pastoral care. *Pastoral Care in Education*, 36(2), 99–111.

Lacey, P. (2014). *Smart and scruffy targets*. Retrieved from: https://docs.google.com/viewer?a=v& pid=sites&srcid=Y2xpY2tzcGVjaWFsZWRuei5jb218c2Vuc29yeS1sZWFybm luZy1uenx1enxneDoyNDDdlYWE0NzhjOGFhMzY4.

Landers, E., Alter, P. & Walker, J.N. (2013). Teachers' perceptions of students' challenging behaviour and the impact of teacher demographics, *Education and Treatment of Children*, 36(4), 51–70.

Landstedt, E. & Persson, S. (2014). Bullying, cyber bullying and mental health in young people. *Scandinavian Journal of Public Health*, 42(2), 1–7.

Lane, K.L., Kalberg, J.R., & Menzies, H.M. (2013). *Developing school-wide programs to prevent and manage problem behaviors* (e-book). New York: Guilford Press.

Larson, T.A., Normand, M.P., Morley, A.J., & Miller, B.G. (2013). A functional analysis of moderate-to-vigorous physical activity in young children. *Journal of Applied Behavior Analysis*, 46(1), 199–207.

Lawrence, A.S., & Saileella, K. (2019). Self-regulation of higher secondary students in relation to achievement in mathematics. *ZENITH International Journal of Multidisciplinary Research*, 9(1), 258–265.

Lawson, M., Vosniadou, S., Van Deur, P., Wyra, M., & Jeffries, D. (2019). Teachers' and students' belief systems about the self-regulation of learning. *Educational Psychology Review*, 31(1), 223–251.

LDAA (Learning Disabilities Association of America). (2019). *Types of learning disabilities*. Online document retrieved from: https://ldaamerica.org/types-of-learning-disabilities/.

Leaf, J.B., Leaf, R., McEachin, J., Cihon, J.H., & Ferguson, J.L. (2018). Advantages and challenges of a home- and clinic-based model of behavioral intervention for individuals diagnosed with autism spectrum disorder. *Journal of Autism and Developmental Disorders*, 48(6), 2258–2266.

Learning Sciences Institute [Australia]. (2016). *Enhancing numeracy learning and teaching across the curriculum* Retrieved from: https://lsia.acu.edu.au/research/stem/.

Lee, S.M. & Oh, Y. (2017). The mediator role of perceived stress in the relationship between academic stress and depressive symptoms among E-Learning students with visual impairments. *Journal of Visual Impairment & Blindness*, 111(2), 123–134.

Lee, Y. (2019). Promoting students' motivation and use of SRL strategies in the web-based mathematics learning environment. *Journal of Educational Technology Systems*, 47(3), 391–410.

Leppien, J. & Purcell, J. (Eds). (2011). *Parallel curriculum units for science: Grades 6 to 12*. Thousand Oaks, CA: Corwin.

Levin, J. & Nolan, J.F. (2014). *Principles of classroom management* (7th ed.), Upper Saddle River, NJ: Pearson Educational.

Lewis, K. (2018). Lessons learned: Applying principles of Reading Recovery in the classroom. *Reading Teacher*, 71(6), 727–734.

Liberty, L.M. & Conderman, G. (2018). Using the self-regulated strategy development model to support middle-level writing. *Clearing House: A Journal of Educational Strategies, Issues and Ideas*, 91(3),118–123.

Lim, L., Arciuli, J., & Munro, N. (2018). Shared book reading behaviours of children with Down Syndrome before and after participation in the Multilit Reading Tutor Program: An exploratory study. *Australian Journal of Learning Difficulties*, 23(1), 31–51.

Lim, Z. & Lee, S.H. (2019). Effects of an interview article writing intervention using class-wide social network site on writing abilities and self-esteem of students with intellectual disabilities and peers' attitudes. *Journal of Special Education Technology*, 34(1), 27–40.

Lindelauf, J., Reupert, A., & Jacobs, K.E. (2018). Teachers' use of psycho-educational reports in mainstream classrooms. *Journal of Psychologists and Counsellors in Schools*, 28(1), 10–17.

Lindo, E.J., Weiser, B., Cheatham, J.P., & Allor, J.H. (2018). Benefits of structured after-school literacy tutoring by university students for struggling elementary readers. *Reading & Writing Quarterly*, 34(2), 117–131.

Lindstrom, J.H. (2019). Dyslexia in the schools: Assessment and identification. *Teaching Exceptional Children*, 51(3), 189–200.

Lipscomb, A.H., Anderson, M., & Gadke, D.L. (2018). Comparing the effects of Classdojo with and without tootling intervention in a postsecondary special education classroom setting. *Psychology in the Schools*, 55(10), 1287–1301.

Lithari, E. (2019). Fractured academic identities: Dyslexia, secondary education, self-esteem and school experiences. *International Journal of Inclusive Education*, 23(3), 280–296.

Liu, A. Y., Lacoe, J., Lipscomb, S., Haimson, J., Johnson, D.R., & Thurlow, M.L. (2018). *Preparing for life after high school: The characteristics and experiences of youth in special education. The National Longitudinal Transition Study 2012, Executive Summary*. Jessup, MD: National Center for Education Evaluation and Regional Assistance.

Logsdon, A. (2019). *Orthopedic impairments and special needs students*. Retrieved from: www.verywellfamily.com/what-is-orthopedic-impairment-2162506.

Loh, C.E. & Sun, B. (2019). 'I'd still prefer to read the hard copy': Adolescents' print and digital reading habits. *Journal of Adolescent & Adult Literacy*, 62(6), 663–672.

Lombardi, D. & Behrman, E.H. (2016). Balanced literacy and the underperforming English Learner in high school. *Reading Improvement*, 53(4),165–174.

Lovaas, O.I. & Smith, T. (2003). Early and intensive behavioral interventions in autism. In A.E. Kazdin & J.R. Weisz (Eds) *Evidence-based psychotherapies for children and adolescents* (pp. 325–340). New York: Guilford Press.

Luckner, J.L. & Movahedazarhouligh, S. (2019). Social-emotional interventions with children and youth who are deaf or hard of hearing: A research synthesis. *Journal of Deaf Studies and Deaf Education*, 24(1), 1–10.

Ludlow, B. (2014). Intensifying intervention: Kicking it up a notch. *Teaching Exceptional Children*, 46(4), 4.

Lum, J.D.K., Radley, K.C., Tingstrom, D.H., Dufrene, B.A., Olmi, D.J., & Wright, S.J. (2019). Tootling with a randomized independent group contingency to improve high school class-wide behavior. *Journal of Positive Behavior Interventions*, 21(2), 93–105.

Lussier, C.M.Swanson, H.L., & Orosco, M.J. (2014). The effects of mathematics strategy instruction for children with serious problem-solving difficulties. *Exceptional Children*, 80(2), 149–170.

Lyndon, H. (1989). 'I did it my way': An introduction to Old Way–New Way. *Australasian Journal of Special Education*, 13, 32–37.

Mac Cobb, S., Fitzgerald, B., & Lanigan-O'Keeffe, C. (2014). The Alert Program for self-management of behaviour in second level schools: Results of Phase 1 of a pilot study. *Emotional & Behavioural Difficulties*, 19(4), 410–425.

MacConville, R. & Rhys-Davies, L. (2007). Including pupils with visual impairment. In R. MacConville (Ed.) *Looking at inclusion: Listening to the voices of young people* (pp. 39–55). London: Paul Chapman.

MacSuga-Gage, A.S., Ennis, R.P., Hirsch, S.E., & Evanovich, L. (2018). Understanding and trumping behavioral concerns in the classroom. *Preventing School Failure*, 62(4), 239–249.

Magnusson, C., Roe, A., & Blikstad-Balas, M. (2019). To what extent and how are reading comprehension strategies part of language arts instruction? A study of lower secondary classrooms. *Reading Research Quarterly*, 54(2), 187–212.

Malik, S., Abd Manaf, U.K., Ahmad, N.A., & Ismail, M. (2018). Orientation and mobility training in special education curriculum for social adjustment problems of visually impaired children in Pakistan. *International Journal of Instruction*, 11(2), 185–202.

Mandelberg, J., Frankel, F., Cunningham, T., Gorospe, C., & Laugeson, E.A. (2014). Long-term outcomes from a parent-assisted social skills intervention for high-functioning children with autism spectrum disorders. *Autism*, 18(3), 255–263.

Manolev, J., Sullivan, A., & Slee, R. (2019). The datafication of discipline: ClassDojo, surveillance and a performative classroom culture. *Learning, Media and Technology*, 44(1), 36–51.

Mansour, M. & Wiener, J. (2019). *Social skills training for students with learning disabilities*. Retrieved from: www.ldatschool.ca/social-skills-training/.

Marchand-Martella, N.E., Martella, R.C., & Lambert, M.C. (2015). Targeted management tips to enhance the effectiveness of Tier 2, Guided Reading Instruction. *Intervention in School and Clinic*, 50(3), 169–172.

Mark, L., Värnik, A., & Sisask, M. (2019). Who suffers most from being involved in bullying—bully, victim, or bully-victim? *Journal of School Health*, 89(2), 136–144.

Martin, B.L., Sargent, K., Van Camp, A., & Wright, J. (2018). *Intensive intervention practice guide: Increasing opportunities to respond as an intensive intervention*. Washington, DC: US Department of Education, Office of Special Education Programs.

Martin, N.M. & Lambert, C. (2015). Differentiating digital writing instruction: The intersection of technology, writing instruction, and digital genre knowledge. *Journal of Adolescent & Adult Literacy*, 59(2), 217–227.

Martins, A.T., Faísca, L., Vieira, H., & Gonçalves, G. (2019). Emotional recognition and empathy both in deaf and blind adults. *Journal of Deaf Studies and Deaf Education*, 24(2), 119–127.

Masters, G. (2014) *Is school reform working?* A Research Development Occasional Paper. Melbourne: Australian Council for Educational Research.

Mathews, T.L., Vatland, C., Lugo, A.M., Koenig, E.A., & Gilroy, S.P. (2018). Training peer models to promote social skills: Considerations for practice. *Focus on Autism and Other Developmental Disabilities*, 33(3), 160–170.

Maycock, K.W. (2019). Chalk and talk versus flipped learning: A case study. *Journal of Computer Assisted Learning*, 35(1), 121–126.

Mays, D. (2020). Making plans for Michael: Providing for a student with moderate learning difficulties in a secondary academy. *Support for Learning*, 35(1), 83–100.

Mazurek, M.O. (2014). Loneliness, friendship and well-being in adults with autism spectrum disorders. *Autism*, 18(3), 223–232.

Mazurek, M.O., Curran, A., Burnette, C., & Sohl, K. (2019). ECHO Autism STAT: Accelerating early access to autism diagnosis. *Journal of Autism and Developmental Disorders*, 49(1), 127–137.

MCA (Middletown Center for Autism). (2019). *Differentiating the curriculum*. Retrieved from: http://best-practice.middletownautism.com/approaches-of-intervention/differentiating-the-curriculum/.

McCoach, D. B., Siegle, D., & Rubenstein, L.D. (2020). Pay attention to inattention: Exploring ADHD symptoms in a sample of underachieving gifted students. *Gifted Child Quarterly*, 64(2), 100–116.

McCollow, M.M., & Hoffman, H.H. (2019). Supporting social development in young children with disabilities: Building a practitioner's toolkit. *Early Childhood Education Journal*, 47(3), 309–320.

McConkey, R., Sadowsky, M., & Shellard, A. (2019). An international survey of obesity and underweight in youth and adults with intellectual disabilities. *Journal of Intellectual & Developmental Disability*, 44(3), 374–382.

McGeehan, B. (2018). Supporting students with epilepsy in the school setting. *Communique*, 47(3), 8.

McGrath, P. (2019). Education in Northern Ireland: Does it meet the needs of gifted students? *Gifted Education International*, 35(1), 37–55.

McKenna, J.W., & Bettini, E. (2018). Improving reading fluency skills for secondary students with emotional and behavioral disorders. *Beyond Behavior*, 27(2), 74–81.

McLaughlin, R., & Kamei-Hannan, C. (2018). Paper or digital text: Which reading medium is best for students with visual impairments? *Journal of Visual Impairment & Blindness*, 112(4), 337–350.

McLean, T.J., Ware, R.S., Heussler, H.S., Harris, S.M., &; Beswick, R. (2019). Barriers to engagement in early intervention services by children with permanent hearing loss. *Deafness & Education International*, 21(1), 25–39.

McMullan, J. & Keeney, S. (2014). A review of the literature on the social and environmental factors which influence children (aged 3–5 years) to be obese or overweight and the accuracy of parental perceptions. *Health Education Journal*, 73(2), 159–165.

Mendini, M. & Peter, P.C. (2019). Research note: The role of smart versus traditional classrooms on students' engagement. *Marketing Education Review*, 29(1), 17–23.

Meredith-Murphy, J., Hawkins, R.O., & Nabors, L. (2020). Combining social skills instruction and the Good Behavior Game to support students with emotional and behavioral disorders. *Contemporary School Psychology*, 24(2), 228–238.

Merrick, R. (2020). Pupil participation in planning provision for special educational needs: Teacher perspectives. *Support for Learning*, 35(1), 101–118.

Mesibov, G.B., Shea, V., & Schopler, E (2005). *The TEACCH Approach to Autism Spectrum Disorders*. New York: Kluwer Academic-Plenum.

Michael, R., Attias, J., & Raveh, E. (2019). Cochlear implantation and social-emotional functioning of children with hearing loss. *Journal of Deaf Studies and Deaf Education*, 24(1), 25–31.

Miller, S., Biggart, A., Sloan, S., & O'Hare, L. (2017). *Success for All: Evaluation report and executive summary*. London: Education Endowment Foundation.

Mohd-Syah, N.E., Hamzaid, N.A., Murphy, B.P., & Lim, E. (2016). Development of computer play pedagogy intervention for children with low conceptual understanding in basic mathematics operation using the dyscalculia feature approach. *Interactive Learning Environments*, 24(7), 1477–1496.

Mølster, T. & Nes, K. (2018). To what extent does information and communication technology support inclusion in education of students with learning difficulties? *Universal Journal of Educational Research*, 6(4), 598–612.

Montacute, R. (2018). *Potential for success: Fulfilling the promise of highly able students in secondary schools*. London: Sutton Trust.

Montgomery, D. (2008). Cohort analysis of writing in Year 7 following two, four and seven years of the National Literacy Strategy. *Support for Learning*, 23(1), 3–11.

Montgomery, D. (2012). The contribution of handwriting and spelling remediation to overcoming dyslexia. In T. Wydell (Ed.) *Dyslexia: A comprehensive and international approach* (pp. 109–146). New York: InTechOpen.

Moon, S.M., Kolloff, P., Robinson, A., Dixin, F., & Feldhussen, J.F. (2009). The Purdue Three-Stage Model. In J. Renzulli, E. Gubbins, K.S. McMillen, R.D. Eckert, & C. A. Little (Eds), *Systems and models for developing programs for the gifted & talented* (2nd ed., pp. 289–321). Waco, TX: Prufrock Press.

Morrill, M.S. (2018). Special education financing and ADHD medications: A bitter pill to swallow. *Journal of Policy Analysis and Management*, 37(2), 384–402.

Morrison, J.Q., Hawkins, R.O., & Collins, T.A. (2020). Evaluating the cost-effectiveness of the Dyslexia Pilot Project: A multitiered system of supports for early literacy. *Psychology in the Schools*, 57(4), 522–539.

Muijs, D. & Reynolds, D. (2017). *Effective teaching: Evidence and practice* (4th ed.). Thousand Oaks, CA: Sage.

Mund, M. & Neyer, F.J. (2019). Loneliness effects on personality. *International Journal of Behavioral Development*, 43(2), 136–146.

Murawski, W.W., & Scott, K.L. (Eds). (2019). *What really works with Universal Design for Learning*. Thousand Oaks, CA: Corwin.

Murray, A., Luo, T., & Franklin, T. (2019). Embracing a technologically enhanced environment: Teachers' experience educating students in an always-on and connected bring your own device (BYOD) classroom. *International Journal on E-Learning*, 18(1), 53–78.

Murray, A.L., Booth, T., Eisner, M., Auyeung, B., Murray, G., & Ribeaud, D. (2019). Sex differences in ADHD trajectories across childhood and adolescence. *Developmental Science*, 22(1), e12721.

Murray, B.A., McIlwain, M.J., Wang, C.H., Murray, G., & Finley, S. (2019). How do beginners learn to read irregular words as sight words? *Journal of Research in Reading*, 42(1), 123–136.

Mutlu, Y. & Akgün, L. (2017). The effects of computer assisted instruction materials on approximate number skills of students with dyscalculia. *Turkish Online Journal of Educational Technology*, 16(2), 119–136.

Mutlu, Y. & Akgün, L. (2019). Using computer for developing arithmetical skills of students with mathematics learning difficulties. *International Journal of Research in Education and Science*, 5(1), 237–251.

NAGC-CEC (National Association for Gifted Children-Council for Exceptional Children). (2013). *Teacher preparation standards in gifted and talented education*. Washington, DC: National Association for Gifted Children.

Nagro, S.A., Fraser, D.W., Hooks, S.D. (2019a). Lesson planning with engagement in mind: Proactive classroom management strategies for curriculum instruction. *Intervention in School and Clinic*, 54(3), 131–140.

Nagro, S.A., Hooks, S.D., & Fraser, D.W. (2019b). Over a decade of practice: Are educators correctly using tertiary interventions? *Preventing School Failure*, 63(1), 52–61.

National Autistic Society. (2016). *Choosing between mainstream and special school*. Retrieved from: www.autism.org.uk/about/in-education/choosing-school/mainstream-special.aspx.

National Autistic Society. (2018). *Causes of autism*. Retrieved from: www.autism.org.uk/about/what-is/asd.aspx.

NCES (National Centre for Education Statistics). (2018). *The condition of education*. Washington, DC: Institute of Education Sciences.

NCETM (National Center for Excellence in Teaching of Mathematics). (2014). *Learning maths outside the classroom in a special educational needs environment*. Retrieved from: www.ncetm.org.uk/resources/29014.

NCSiMERRA (National Centre of Science, Information and Communication Technology, and Mathematics Education for Rural and Regional Australia). (2009). *QuickSmart intervention research program data 2001–2008: Full report*. Armidale, NSW: University of New England.

Neale, A. (2019). A proactive targeted approach to preventing adolescent aggressive behaviours. *Pastoral Care in Education*, 37(1), 33–53.

Neilson, R. (2019). Spelling: Enabler or disabler? *Learning Difficulties Australia Bulletin*, 51(1), 22–24.

Nelson, G. & Powell, S.R. (2018). A systematic review of longitudinal studies of mathematics difficulty. *Journal of Learning Disabilities*, 51(6), 523–539.

Nelson, P.M., Parker, D.C., & Van Norman, E.R. (2018). Subskill mastery among elementary and middle school students at risk in mathematics. *Psychology in the Schools*, 55(6), 722–736.

Newbould, S. (2018). Classroom contract. *English Teaching Forum*, 56(4), 37–39.

Nguyen, T., Watts, T.W., Duncan, G J., Clements, D.H., Sarama, J.S., Wolfe, C., & Spitler, M.E. (2016). Which preschool mathematics competencies are most predictive of fifth grade achievement? *Early Childhood Research Quarterly*, 36(3), 550–560.

NHS (National Health Service: England). (2020). *Special educational needs and disability (SEND)*. Retrieved from: www.england.nhs.uk/learning-disabilities/care/children-young-people/send/.

Nicholson, T. & Dymock, S. (2018). *Writing for impact: Teaching students to write with a plan and spell well*. Wellington: NZCER Press.

Nields, A.N. (2014). *Preservice teachers' knowledge and perception of effective behavior management strategies*. ProQuest UMI Dissertations online.

Nielsen, A.M.V. (2017). Knowledge of conditional spelling patterns supports word spelling among Danish fifth graders. *Journal of Research in Reading*, 40(3), 313–332.

Nind, M. & Hewett, D. (2005). *Access to communication: Developing basic communication with people who have severe learning difficulties* (2nd ed.). London: Fulton.

Nipe, T.A., Dowdy, A., Quigley, J., Gill, A., & Weiss, M.J. (2018). Increasing the wearing of multiple prescription prosthetic devices. *Education and Treatment of Children*, 41(3), 331–344.

Noltemeyer, A., Palmer, K., James, A.G., & Petrasek, M. (2019). Disciplinary and achievement outcomes associated with School-Wide Positive Behavioral Interventions and Supports implementation level. *School Psychology Review*, 48(1), 81–87.

Nordahl, J., Beran, T., & Dittrick, C.J. (2013). Psychological impact of cyber-bullying: Implications for school counsellors. *Canadian Journal of Counselling and Psychotherapy*, 47(3), 383–402.

Northern Illinois University. (2014). *Situated learning*. Retrieved from: www.niu.edu/facdev/resources/guide/strategies/situated_learning.pdf.

NSW DEC (New South Wales Department of Education and Communities). (2015). *Differentiating content, process, product, learning environment*. Retrieved from: www.ssgt.nsw.edu.au/documents/3_content_pro_etal.pdf.

O'Connor, E. (2016). The use of "Circle of Friends" strategy to improve social interactions and social acceptance: A case study of a child with Asperger's syndrome and other associated needs. *Support for Learning*, 31(2), 138–147.

Oczkus, L.D. (2018). *Reciprocal teaching at work: Powerful strategies and lessons for improving reading comprehension* (3rd ed.). Alexandria, VA: ASCD.

OECD (Organization for Economic Cooperation and Development). (2006). *Starting Strong II: Early Childhood and Care*. Paris: OECD.

OECD (Organization for Economic Cooperation and Development). (2007). *Students with Disabilities, learning difficulties and disadvantages: Policies, statistics, and indicators*. Paris: OECD.

OECD (Organization for Economic Cooperation and Development). (2013). *OECD Skills Outlook 2013: First results from survey of adults*. Paris: OECD.

OECD (Organisation for Economic Cooperation and Development). (2016). *PISA 2015: Results in focus*. Retrieved from: www.oecd.org/pisa/pisa-2015-results-in-focus.pdf.

Ofsted (Office for Standards in Education). (2017). *Bold beginnings: The Reception curriculum in a sample of good and outstanding primary schools*. London: Ofsted.

Oh, S., Hailey, E., Azano, A., Callahan, C., & Moon, T. (2012). *What works in gifted education: Documenting the model-based curriculum for gifted students*. Evanston, IL: Society for Research on Educational Effectiveness.

Ohashi, L. (2018). *Self-directed learning and the teacher's role: Insights from two different teaching contexts*. Paper presented at the EUROCALL 26th Conference, Jyväskylä, Finland: Retrieved from: https://eric.ed.gov/?q=self-directed+learning&ff1=dtySince_2015&pg=4&id=ED590671.

Ohtani, K. & Hisaka, T. (2018). Beyond intelligence: A meta-analytic review of the relationship among metacognition, intelligence, and academic performance. *Metacognition and Learning*, 13(2), 179–212.

Okcu, B. & Sozbilir, M. (2019). Designing a bulb to teach electric circuits to visually impaired students. *Physics Teacher*, 57(2), 99–101.

Oppong, E., Shore, B.M., & Muis, K.R. (2019). Clarifying the connections among giftedness, metacognition, self-regulation, and self-regulated learning: Implications for theory and practice. *Gifted Child Quarterly*, 63(2), 102–119.

Orton, S.T. (1937). *Reading, writing and speech problems in children*. New York: Norton.

Ouelette, G., Senechal, M., & Haley, A. (2013). Guiding children's invented spelling: A gateway into literacy learning. *Journal of Experimental Education*, 81(2), 261–279.

Outhwaite, L.A., Faulder, M., Gulliford, A., & Pitchford, N.J. (2019). Raising early achievement in math with interactive apps: A randomized control trial. *Journal of Educational Psychology*, 111(2), 284–298.

Owiny, R.L., Spriggs, A.D., Sartini, E.C., & Mills, J.R. (2018). Evaluating response cards as evidence based. *Preventing School Failure*, 62(2), 59–72.

Ozturk, G. & Ohi, S. (2018). Understanding young children's attitudes towards reading in relation to their digital literacy activities at home. *Journal of Early Childhood Research*, 16(4), 393–406.

Pablico, J.R. (2016). *An exploratory study of differentiated instruction in the high school science classroom.* ProQuest LLC, PhD Dissertation, Southern University and Agricultural and Mechanical College. ERIC document number ED590951.

Pacello, J. (2019). Cultivating a process approach to writing: Student experiences in a developmental course. *Journal of the Scholarship of Teaching and Learning*, 19(2), 187–197.

Paige, D.D. (2018). Reading Recovery® won't fix poor core Tier-One reading instruction. *Reading Psychology*, 39(5), 492–497.

Papen, U., Watson, K., & Marriot, N. (2012). *The phonological influences on children's spelling.* Department of Linguistics and English Language, University of Lancaster. Retrieved from: www.lancs.ac.uk/fss/linguistics/staff/kevin/spelling.htm.

Pappano, L. (2014). Changing the face of math. *The Education Digest*, 79(6), 10–12.

Park, I. & Kim, Y.R. (2018). Effects of TEACCH structured teaching on independent work skills among individuals with severe disabilities. *Education and Training in Autism and Developmental Disabilities*, 53(4), 343–352.

Parsons, S.A. & Vaughn, M. (2013). A multiple case study of two teachers' instructional adaptations. *Alberta Journal of Educational Research*, 59(2), 299–318.

Pas, E.T., Ryoo, J.H., Musci, R., & Bradshaw, C.P. (2019). A state-wide quasi-experimental effectiveness study of the scale-up of school-wide positive behavioral interventions and supports. *Journal of School Psychology*, 73, 41–55.

Passolunghi, M.C., Cargnelutti, E., & Pellizzoni, S. (2019). The relation between cognitive and emotional factors and arithmetic problem-solving. *Educational Studies in Mathematics*, 100(3), 271–290.

Pawelski, C.E. (2007). Conductive education. In A.M. Bursztyn (Ed.) *The Praeger handbook of special education* (pp. 84–88). Westport, CT: Praeger.

Pearn, C. (2014). Reducing mathematics anxiety. *Teacher* magazine [online], 17 July. Retrieved from: http://teacher.acer.edu.au/article/reducing-mathematics-anxiety.

Pelkey, M.M. (2018). *A Kansas survey: Teaching writing to middle school students.* ProQuest LLC, Ed. D. Dissertation, University of Kansas. ERIC document number ED587312.

Peterson, J.M. & Hittie, M.M. (2010). *Inclusive Teaching: The Journey toward effective schools for all learners* (2nd ed.). Boston, MA: Pearson-Merrill.

Peterson, S. (2014). *Supporting struggling writers. What works? Research into Practice Monograph 49.* Government of Ontario Canada. Retrieved from: www.edu.gov.on.ca/eng/literacynumeracy/inspire/research/WW_StrugglingWriters.pdf.

Peterson, S. & Portier, C. (2014). Grade One peer and teacher feedback on student writing. *Education 3–13*, 42(3), 237–257.

Peterson, S.P., Rodriguez, N.M., & Pawich, T.L. (2019). Effects of modeling rote versus varied responses on response variability and skill acquisition during discrete-trial instruction. *Journal of Applied Behavior Analysis*, 52(2), 370–385.

Piaget, J. (1963). *Origins of intelligence in children.* New York: Norton.

Pieratt, J.R. (2011). *Teacher-student relationships in project-based learning: A case study of High-Tech Middle North County.* Online Proquest Dissertation and Theses.

Pierce, S. & Maher, A.J. (2020). Physical activity among children and young people with intellectual disabilities in special schools: Teacher and Learning Support Assistant perceptions. *British Journal of Learning Disabilities*, 48(1), 37–44.

Pitts, L., Gent, S., & Hoerger, M.L. (2019). Reducing pupils' barriers to learning in a special needs school: Integrating applied behaviour analysis into Key Stages 1–3. *British Journal of Special Education*, 46(1), 94–112.

Plucker, J., Glynn, J., Healey, G., & Dettmer, A. (2018). *Equal talents, unequal opportunities: A report card on state support for academically talented low-income students* (2nd ed.). Landsdowne, VA: Jack Kent Cooke Foundation.

Pokorski, E.A. (2019). Group contingencies to improve class-wide behavior of young children. *Teaching Exceptional Children*, 51(5), 340–349.

Powell, D. (2018). Governing the (un)healthy child-consumer in the age of the childhood obesity crisis. *Sport, Education and Society*, 23(4), 297–310.

Preston, A.I. (2016). *Effects of Singapore Model Method with explicit instruction on math problem solving skills of students at risk for or identified with learning disabilities*. ProQuest LLC: Ph.D. Dissertation, University of North Carolina at Charlotte. ERIC document number ED571121.

Prizant, B., Wetherby, A.M., Laurent, A.C., & Rydell, P.J. (2006). *The SCERTS® Model: A comprehensive educational approach for children with autism spectrum disorders*. Baltimore, MD: Brookes.

Puliatte, A. & Ehri, L.C. (2018). Do 2nd and 3rd Grade teachers' linguistic knowledge and instructional practices predict spelling gains in weaker spellers? *Reading and Writing: An Interdisciplinary Journal*, 31(2), 239–266.

Putman, R. (2017). Using research to make informed decisions about the spelling curriculum. *Texas Journal of Literacy Education*, 5(1), 24–32.

Quint, J. & Condliffe, B. (2018). *Project-based learning: A promising approach to improving student outcomes*. New York: Manpower Demonstration Research Corporation.

Rabideau, L.K., Stanton-Chapman, T.L., & Brown, T.S. (2018). Discrete Trial Training to teach alternative communication: A step-by-step guide. *Young Exceptional Children*, 21(1), 34–47.

Radovan, M. & Perdih, M. (2016). Developing guidelines for evaluating the adaptation of accessible web-based learning materials. *International Review of Research in Open and Distributed Learning*, 17(4), 166–181.

Ramberg, J. & Watkins, A. (2020). Exploring inclusive education across Europe: Some insights from the European Agency statistics on inclusive education. *FIRE: Forum for International Research in Education*, 6(1), 85–101.

Ramirez, G., Fries, L., Gunderson, E., Schaeffer, M.W., Maloney, E.A., Beilock, S.L., & Levine, S.C. (2019). Reading anxiety: An early affective impediment to children's success in reading. *Journal of Cognition and Development*, 20(1), 15–34.

Ramirez, G., Shaw, S.T., & Maloney, E.A. (2018). Math anxiety: Past research, promising interventions, and a new interpretation framework. *Educational Psychologist*, 53(3), 145–164.

Ramos, S. & de Andrade, A.M. (2016). ICT in Portuguese reference schools for the education of blind and partially sighted students. *Education and Information Technologies*, 21(3), 625–641.

Randall, N. (2016). *'It's differentiation Jim, but not as we know it!'*. Retrieved from Herts for Learning website at: www.hertsforlearning.co.uk/blog/its-differentiation-jim-not-we-know-it.

Ray, A. & Graham, S. (2019). Effective practices for teaching students who have difficulty with writing. *Learning Difficulties Australia Bulletin*, 51(1), 13–16.

Redford, K. (2019). Assistive technology: Promises fulfilled. *Educational Leadership*, 76(5), 70–74.

Regan, K., Evmenova, A.S., Sacco, D., Schwartzer, J., Chirinos, D.S., & Hughes, M.D. (2019). Teacher perceptions of integrating technology in writing. *Technology, Pedagogy and Education*, 28(1), 1–19.

Regan, K.S. & Martin, P.J. (2014). Cultivating self-regulation for students with mild disabilities. *Intervention in School and Clinic*, 49(3), 164–173.

Reid, E. & Horváthová, B. (2016). Teacher training programs for gifted education with focus on sustainability. *Journal of Teacher Education for Sustainability*, 18(2), 66–74.

Reimers, C. (2020). *Longitudinal analysis of behavior screening data in a school district implementing School-Wide Positive Behavior Interventions and Supports*. ProQuest LLC, Ed.S. Dissertation, University of Nebraska at Omaha. ERIC document number ED597652.

Renzulli, J. (2005). The three-ring conception of giftedness: A developmental model for promoting creative productivity. In R.J. Sternberg & J.E. Davidson (Eds), *Conceptions of giftedness* (2nd ed., pp. 246–279). New York: Cambridge University Press.

Renzulli, J. & Reis, S. (2014) *The Schoolwide Enrichment Model: A how-to guide for talent development* (3rd ed.). Waco, TX: Prufrock Press.

Renzulli, J., Reis, S., & Shaughnessy, M.F. (2014). A reflective conversation with Joe Renzulli and Sally Reis: About the Renzulli Learning System. *Gifted Education International*, 30(1), 24–32.

Reynolds, M., Wheldall, K., & Madelaine, A. (2007). Meeting initial needs in literacy (MINILIT): A ramp to MULTILIT for younger low-progress readers. *Australian Journal of Learning Disabilities*, 12(2), 67–72.

Reynolds, T., Zupanick, C.E. & Dombeck, M. (2014). *Onset and prevalence of intellectual disabilities*. Pecan Valley Centers Behavioral and Developmental Healthcare. Retrieved from: www.pvmhmr. org/poc/view_doc.php?type=doc&id=10329&cn=208.

Reynolds, T., Zupanick, C.E., & Dombeck, M. (2019). *Effective teaching methods for people with intellectual disabilities*. Retrieved from: www.mentalhelp.net/articles/effective-teaching-methods-for-people-with-intellectual-disabilities/.

Rhodes, M.G. (2019). Metacognition. *Teaching of Psychology*, 46(2), 168–175.

Ribeiro, F.S., Tonoli, M.C., Ribeiro, D.P., & Santos, F.H.D. (2017). Numeracy deficits scrutinized: Evidences of primary developmental dyscalculia. *Psychology & Neuroscience*, 10(2), 189–200.

Ritchotte, J.A., Matthews, M.S., & Flowers, C.P. (2014). The validity of the Achievement-Orientation Model for gifted middle school students: An exploratory study. *Gifted Child Quarterly*, 58(3), 183–198.

Roberts, D. (2012). *Spelling with Imagery (SWIM)*. Retrieved from: www.psych-online.co.uk/p3s.html.

Rochford, D. (2016). *Review of assessment for pupils working below the standard of national curriculum tests (The Rochford Review): Final report*. London: Standards and Testing Agency.

Rodriguez, S., Allen, K., Harron, J., & Qadri, S.A. (2019). Making and the 5E Learning Cycle. *Science Teacher*, 86(5), 48–55.

Rogers-Shaw, C., Carr-Chellman, D.J., & Choi, J. (2018). Universal Design for Learning: Guidelines for accessible online instruction. *Adult Learning*, 29(1), 20–31.

Ronimus, M., Eklund, K., Pesu, L., & Lyytinen, H. (2019). Supporting struggling readers with digital game-based learning. *Educational Technology Research and Development*, 67(3), 639–663.

Ronksley-Pavia, M., Grootenboer, P., & Pendergast, D. (2019a). Bullying and the unique experiences of twice exceptional learners: Student perspective narratives. *Gifted Child Today*, 42(1), 19–35.

Ronksley-Pavia, M., Grootenboer, P., & Pendergast, D. (2019b). Privileging the voices of twice-exceptional children: An exploration of lived experiences and stigma narratives. *Journal for the Education of the Gifted*, 42(1), 4–34.

Rose, J. (2009). *Identifying and teaching children and young people with dyslexia and literacy difficulties*. Nottingham: DCSF Publications. Retrieved from: http://publications.teachernet.gov.uk/default.aspx?PageFunction=productdetails&PageMode=publications&ProductId=DCSF-00659-2009&.

Rose, R. & Shevlin, M. (2020). Support provision for students with special educational needs in Irish primary schools. *Journal of Research in Special Educational Needs*, 20(1), 51–63.

Rosenblum, L.P., Cheng, L., & Beal, C.R. (2018). Teachers of students with visual impairments share experiences and advice for supporting students in understanding graphics. *Journal of Visual Impairment & Blindness*, 112(5), 475–487.

Rosenshine, B. & Meister, C. (1994). Reciprocal teaching: A review of research. *Review of Educational Research*, 64(4), 479–530.

Rouse, H., Goudie, A., Rettiganti, M., Leath, K., Riser, Q., & Thompson, J. (2019). Prevalence, patterns, and predictors: A statewide longitudinal study of childhood obesity. *Journal of School Health*, 89(4), 237–245.

Rubow, C.C., Vollmer, T.R., & Joslyn, P.R. (2018). Effects of the Good Behavior Game on student and teacher behavior in an alternative school. *Journal of Applied Behavior Analysis*, 51(2), 382–392.

Ruderman, M. (2016). *Children's vision and eye health: A snapshot of current national issues.* Chicago, IL: National Center for Children's Vision and Eye Health at Prevent Blindness.

Russell, J. & Cohn, R. (2012). *Snoezelen.* Stoughton, WI: Books on Demand.

Samur, Y. (2019). Kes Sesi: A mobile game designed to improve kindergarteners' recognition of letter sounds. *Journal of Computer Assisted Learning,* 35(2), 294–304.

Sanchez, M., Magnan, A., & Ecalle, J. (2012). Knowledge about word structure in beginning readers: What specific links are there with word reading and spelling? *European Journal of Psychology of Education,* 27(3), 299–317.

Sanchez, V.M. & O'Connor, R.E. (2015). Building Tier 3 intervention for long-term slow growers in Grades 3–4: A pilot study. *Learning Disabilities Research & Practice,* 30(4), 171–181.

Sandjojo, J., Zedlitz, A.E.E., Gebhardt, W.A., Hoekman, J., den Haan, J., & Evers, A.W.M (2019). Effects of a self-management training for people with intellectual disabilities. *Journal of Applied Research in Intellectual Disabilities,* 32(2), 390–400.

Satsangi, R., Hammer, R., & Hogan, C.D. (2019a). Video modeling and explicit instruction: A comparison of strategies for teaching mathematics to students with learning disabilities. *Learning Disabilities Research & Practice,* 34(1), 35–46.

Satsangi, R., Miller, B., & Savage, M.N. (2019b). Helping teachers make informed decisions when selecting assistive technology for secondary students with disabilities. *Preventing School Failure,* 63(2), 97–104.

Sauer, K., Patten, E., Roberts, K., & Schartz, M. (2018). Management of food allergies in schools. *Journal of Child Nutrition & Management,* 42(2). (Online, not paginated.)

Saulsbury, R., Kilpatrick, J.R., Wolbers, K.A., & Dostal, H. (2015). Getting students excited about learning: Incorporating digital tools to support the writing process. *Odyssey: New Directions in Deaf Education,* 16, 30–34.

Sayeski, K.L., Brown, M.R. (2011). Developing a classroom management plan using a tiered approach. *Teaching Exceptional Children,* 44(1), 8–17.

Sayi, A.K. (2018). Teachers' views about the teacher training program for gifted education. *Journal of Education and Learning,* 7(4), 262–273.

Scarparolo, G.E. & Hammond, L.S. (2018). The effect of a professional development model on early childhood educators' direct teaching of beginning reading. *Professional Development in Education,* 44(4), 492–506.

Schardt, A.A., Miller, F.G., & Bedesem, P.L. (2019). The effects of CellF-Monitoring on students' academic engagement: A technology-based self-monitoring intervention. *Journal of Positive Behavior Interventions,* 21(1), 42–49.

Scharer, P.L. & Zutell, J. (2003). The development of spelling. In N. Hall, J. Larson, & J. Marsh (Eds) *Handbook of early childhood literacy.* London: Sage.

Schulze, M.A. (2016). Self-management strategies to support students with ASD. *Teaching Exceptional Children,* 48(5), 225–231.

Schwab, S. (2019). Friendship stability among students with and without special educational needs. *Educational Studies,* 45(3), 390–401.

Scott, J.A., Goldberg, H., Connor, C.M., & Lederberg, A.R. (2019). Schooling effects on early literacy skills of young deaf and hard of hearing children. *American Annals of the Deaf,* 163(5), 596–618.

Seage, S.J. & Türegün, M. (2020). The effects of blended learning on STEM achievement of elementary school students. *International Journal of Research in Education and Science,* 6(1), 133–140.

Segedin, L., Fahrer, N., Ernst, J.V., Clark, A.C., Kelly, D.P., & DeLuca, V.W. (2019). Adapting instruction. *Technology and Engineering Teacher,* 78(4), 9–11.

Serhan, D. & Almeqdadi, F. (2020). Students' perceptions of using MyMathLab and WebAssign in mathematics classroom. *International Journal of Technology in Education and Science,* 4(1), 12–17.

Serry, T., Rose, M., & Liamputtong, P. (2014). Reading Recovery teachers discuss Reading Recovery: A qualitative investigation. *Australian Journal of Learning Difficulties,* 19(1), 61–73.

Sharp, E. & Shih-Dennis, M. (2017). Model Drawing Strategy for fraction word problem solving of fourth-grade students with learning disabilities. *Remedial and Special Education*, 38(3), 181–192.

Sherry, M.B. (2019). Emergence and development of a dialogic whole-class discussion genre. *Dialogic Pedagogy*, 7, 27–57.

Shimono, T.R. (2019). The effects of repeated oral reading and timed reading on L2 oral reading fluency. *Reading Matrix: An International Online Journal*, 19(1), 139–154.

Siegle, D. (2014). Technology: Differentiating instruction by flipping the classroom. *Gifted Child Today*, 37(1), 51–55.

Siegle, D., McCoach, D.B., & Roberts, A. (2017). Why I believe I achieve determines whether I achieve. *High Ability Studies*, 28(1), 59–72.

Slavin, R. & Madden, N.A. (2012). *Success for All: Summary of research on achievement outcomes.* Retrieved from: www.successforall.org/SuccessForAll/media/PDFs/Summary_of_Research_September_2012.pdf.

Slavin, R., Lake, C., & Groff, C. (2009a). Effective programs in middle and high school mathematics: a best-evidence synthesis. *Review of Educational Research*, 72(2), 839–911.

Slavin, R., Madden, N.A., Chambers, B., & Haxby, B. (2009b). *Two million children: Success for All* (2nd ed.). Thousand Oaks, CA: Corwin Press.

Slavin, R.E. & Madden, N.A. (2013). Success for All at 27: New developments in whole-school reform. *Journal of Education for Students Placed at Risk*, 18(3–4), 169–176.

Smith, A., Prendeville, P., & Kinsella, W. (2018). Using preferred interests to model social skills in a peer-mentored environment for students with special educational needs. *International Journal of Inclusive Education*, 22(8), 921–935.

Smith, B., Spooner, F., & Wood, C.L. (2013). Using embedded computer-assisted explicit instruction to teach science to students with autism spectrum disorder. *Research in Autism Spectrum Disorders*, 7(3), 433–443.

Smith, B.E. (2019). Collaborative multimodal composing: Tracing the unique partnerships of three pairs of adolescents composing across three digital projects. *Literacy*, 5(1), 14–21.

Smith, M.D., & Broomhead, K.E. (2019). Time, expertise and status: Barriers faced by mainstream primary school SENCos in the pursuit of providing effective provision for children with SEND. *Support for Learning*, 34(1), 54–70.

Smith, S.W., Poling, D.V., & Worth, M.R. (2018). Intensive intervention for students with emotional and behavioral disorders. *Learning Disabilities Research & Practice*, 33(3), 168–175.

Smithers, A. & Robinson, P. (2012). *Educating the highly able: The Sutton Trust Report.* London: The Sutton Trust.

Snow, C.E. (2018). Simple and not-so-simple views of reading. *Remedial and Special Education*, 39(5), 313–316.

Snowling, M.J., Lervåg, A., Nash, H.M., & Hulme, C. (2019). Longitudinal relationships between speech perception, phonological skills and reading in children at high-risk of dyslexia. *Developmental Science*, 22(1), e12723.

Southward, J.D. (2018). *Repeated reading as an intervention for high school students identified with a specific learning disability.* ProQuest LLC: PhD Dissertation from Texas Woman's University. ERIC document number ED590920.

Spanoudis, G.C., Papadopoulos, T.C., & Spyrou, S. (2019). Specific language impairment and reading disability: Categorical distinction or continuum? *Journal of Learning Disabilities*, 52(1), 3–14.

Spooner, F., Root, J.R., Saunders, A.F., & Browder, D.M. (2019). An updated evidence-based practice review on teaching mathematics to students with moderate and severe developmental disabilities. *Remedial and Special Education*, 40(3), 150–165.

Sprick, R. & Knight, J. (2018). Involving teachers in schoolwide behavior policy. *Educational Leadership*, 76(1), 48–53.

Stahmer, A.C. (2014). Effective strategies by any other name. *Autism*, 18(3), 211–212.

Stanton-Chapman, T.L., Walker, V.L., Voorhees, M.D., & Snell, M.E. (2016). The evaluation of a three-tier model of Positive Behavior Interventions and Supports for preschoolers in Head Start. *Remedial and Special Education*, 37(6), 333–344.

Steenbergen-Hu, S., Makel, M.C., & Olszewski-Kubilius, P. (2016). What one hundred years of research says about the effects of ability grouping and acceleration on K-12 students' academic achievement: Findings of two second-order meta-analyses. *Review of Educational Research*, 86(4), 849–899.

Steenbergen-Hu, S., Olszewski-Kubilius, P., & Calvert, E. (2020). The effectiveness of current interventions to reverse the underachievement of gifted students: Findings of a meta-analysis and systematic review. *Gifted Child Quarterly*, 64(2), 132–165.

Stevens, E.A., Park, S., & Vaughn, S. (2019). A review of summarizing and main idea interventions for struggling readers in Grades 3 through 12: 1978–2016. *Remedial and Special Education*, 40(3), 131–149.

Stockall, N. & Dennis, L.R. (2014). Using pivotal response training and technology to engage preschoolers with autism in conversations. *Intervention in School and Clinic*, 49(4), 195–202.

Stoeger, H., Hopp, M., & Ziegler, A. (2017). Online mentoring as an extracurricular measure to encourage talented girls in STEM: An empirical study of one-on-one versus group mentoring. *Gifted Child Quarterly*, 61(3), 239–249.

Storch, N. (2019). Collaborative writing. *Language Teaching*, 52(1), 40–59.

Strassman, B.K. & Schirmer, B. (2013). Teaching writing to deaf students: Does research offer evidence for practice? *Remedial and Special Education*, 34(3), 166–179.

Stripp, C. (2015). *How can we meet the needs of all pupils without differentiation of lesson content?* Retrieved from NCETM website at: www.ncetm.org.uk/resources/46830.

Stultz, S.L. (2017). Computer-assisted mathematics instruction for students with specific learning disability: A review of the literature. *Journal of Special Education Technology*, 32(4), 210–219.

Sullivan, A.L. & Sadeh, S.S (2014). Is there evidence to support the use of social skills interventions for students with emotional disabilities? *Journal of Applied School Psychology*, 30(2), 107–131.

Sutherland, K.S., Conroy, M.A., McLeod, B.D., Kunemund, R., & McKnight, K. (2019). Common practice elements for improving social, emotional, and behavioral outcomes of young elementary school students. *Journal of Emotional and Behavioral Disorders*, 27(2), 76–85.

Tam, V.C., Chan, J.W., Li, S.C., & Pow, J. (2018). Developing and managing school human capital for information and communication technology integration: A case study of a school-based e-learning project in Hong Kong. *International Journal of Leadership in Education*, 21(4), 447–461.

Tan, C. (2018). Whither teacher-directed learning? Freirean and Confucian Insights. *Educational Forum*, 82(4), 461–474.

Taylor, S. (2017). Contested knowledge: A critical review of the concept of differentiation in teaching and learning. *Warwick Journal of Education*, 1(1), 55–68.

Tee, A. & Reed, P. (2017). Controlled study of the impact on child behaviour problems of Intensive Interaction for children with ASD. *Journal of Research in Special Educational Needs*, 17(3), 179–186.

Templeton, S.R., Bear, D.R., Invernizzi, M.A., Johnston, F.R., Flanigan, K., Townsend, D.R., Helman, L., & Hayes, L. (2015). *Vocabulary their way: Word study with middle and secondary students* (2nd ed.). Boston, MA: Pearson.

Terband, H. Coppens-Hofman, M., Reffeltrath, M., & Maassen, B. (2018). Effectiveness of speech therapy in adults with intellectual disabilities. *Journal of Applied Research in Intellectual Disabilities*, 31(2), 236–248.

Thompson, A.M. (2014). A randomized trial of the self-management training and regulation strategy for disruptive students. *Research on Social Work Practice*, 24(4), 414–427.

Thompson, D. (2013). Obese children more likely to have asthma. *Health Day News Online*. Retrieved from: http://consumer.healthday.com/respitory-and-allergy-information-2/asthma-news-47/asthma-and-obesity-679009.html.

Thompson, J.L., Wood, C.L., Preston, A., Stevenson, B. (2019). Teaching unison responding during small-group Direct Instruction to students with autism spectrum disorder who exhibit interfering behaviors. *Education and Treatment of Children*, 42(1), 1–23.

Thomson, S., De Bortoli, L., & Underwood, C. (2017). *PISA 2015: Reporting Australia's results*. Retrieved from: https://research.acer.edu.au/ozpisa/22/.

Thornton, J. (2013). The 4E Wiki Writing Model: Redefining collaboration for technological relevance. *Curriculum and Teaching Dialogue*, 15(2), 49–62.

Tincani, M. & Twyman, J.S. (2016). *Enhancing engagement through active student response*. Philadelphia, PA: Center on Innovations in Learning, Temple University.

Tomlinson, C. & Imbeau, M.B. (2014). *A differentiated approach to the Common Core: How do I help a broad range of learners succeed with challenging curriculum?* Alexandria, VA: Association for Supervision and Curriculum Development.

Tomlinson, C.A., Kaplan, S.N., Purcell, J.H., Leppien, J.H., Burns, D.E., Renzulli, J.S., Imbeau, M.B., & Strickland, C.A. (2008). *The Parallel Curriculum* (2nd ed.), Thousand Oaks, CA: Corwin Press.

Tong, Y., Kinshuk, D., & Wei, X. (2020). Teaching design and practice of a project-based blended learning model. *International Journal of Mobile and Blended Learning*, 12(1), 33–50.

Toro, B. (2019). Memory and standing balance after multisensory stimulation in a Snoezelen Room in people with moderate learning disabilities. *British Journal of Learning Disabilities*, 47(4), 270–278.

Torrington, J. (2013). Using guided inquiry in a Year 3 classroom. *Access*, 27(4), 22–24.

Tracey, L., Chambers, B., Slavin, R.E., Hanley, P., & Cheung, A. (2014). Success for All in England: Results from the third year of a national evaluation. *SAGE OPEN*, 2014 4. doi:10.1177/2158244014547031.

Tracy-Bronson, C.P., Causton, J.N., & MacLeod, K.M. (2019). Everybody has the right to be here: Perspectives of related service therapists. *International Journal of Whole Schooling*, 15(1), 132–174.

Troia, G. (2014). *Evidence-based practices for writing instruction* (Document No. IC-5). University of Florida. Retrieved from: http://ceedar.education.ufl.edu/tools/innovation-configuration/.

Trump, C.E., Pennington, R.C., Travers, J.C., Ringdahl, J.E., Whiteside, E.E., & Ayres, K.M. (2018). Applied Behavior Analysis in special education: Misconceptions and guidelines for use. *Teaching Exceptional Children*, 50(6), 381–393.

Tunmer, W.E., Chapman, J.W., Greaney, K.T., Prochnow, J.E., & Arrow, A.W. (2013). Reading Recovery and the failure of the New Zealand national literacy strategy. *LDA Bulletin*, 45(3), 13–17.

Turnbull, A., Turnbull, R., Wehmeyer, M.L., & Shogren, K.A. (2019). *Exceptional lives: Practice, progress and dignity in today's schools* (9th ed.), Upper Saddle River, NJ: Pearson.

Turner, K. (2019). One-to-one learning and self-determination theory. *International Journal of Instruction*, 12(2), 1–16.

Turner, W.D. & Solis, O.J. (2017). The misnomers of differentiating instruction in large classes. *The Journal of Effective Teaching*, 17(3), 64–76.

University of Washington. (2012). *Working together: Computers and people with learning disabilities*. Online document retrieved from: www.washington.edu/doit/Brochures/Technology/atpwld.html.

Ünlü, E., Vuran, S., & Diken, I.H. (2018). Effectiveness of discrete trial training program for parents of children with autism spectrum disorder. *International Journal of Progressive Education*, 14(3), 12–31.

Urtubey, L.J. (2020). Supporting Latinx families in special education decisions. *Educational Leadership*, 77(4), 40–45.

US Department of Education. (2004). *Individuals with Disabilities Education Improvement Act, Public Law 108–446:108th Congress*. Retrieved from: http://idea.ed.gov/download/statute.html.

US Department of Education. (2014). *Digest of education statistics.* Washington, DC: Institute of Educational Sciences.

van de Pol, J., Mercer, N., & Volman, M. (2019). Scaffolding student understanding in small-group work: Students' uptake of teacher support in subsequent small-group interaction. *Journal of the Learning Sciences*, 28(2), 206–239.

Van Geel, M., Keuning, T., Frèrejean, J., Dolmans, D., van Merriënboer, J., & Visscher, A.J. (2019). Capturing the complexity of differentiated instruction. *School Effectiveness and School Improvement*, 30(1), 51–67.

VanTassel-Baska, J. (2015). Common Core State Standards for students with gifts and talents. *Teaching Exceptional Children*, 47(4), 191–198.

Vatterott, C. (2018). *Rethinking homework: Best practices that support diverse needs* (2nd ed.). Alexandria, VA: Association for Supervision and Curriculum Development.

Vincent, K. (2020). Closing the gap: Supporting literacy through a computer-assisted-reading-intervention. *Support for Learning*, 35(1), 68–82.

Virues-Ortega, J., Julio, F.M., & Pastor-Barriuso, R. (2013). The TEACCH program for children and adults with autism: A meta-analysis of intervention studies. *Clinical Psychology Review*, 33(8), 940–953.

Vise, A. (2019). *Teaching students with intellectual disabilities: Tips and strategies.* Retrieved from: www.brighthubeducation.com/special-ed-inclusion-strategies/9893-teaching-students-with-intellectual-disabilities/.

Vogl, K. & Preckel, F. (2014). Full-time ability grouping of gifted students: Impacts on social self-concept and school-related attitudes. *Gifted Child Quarterly*, 58(1), 51–68.

Vollmer, L.E., Gettinger, M., & Begeny, J.C. (2019). Training preservice general education teachers in Response to Intervention: A survey of teacher educators throughout the United States. *Journal of Applied School Psychology*, 35(2), 122–145.

Vukovic, R. (2019). Intervention programs: Emphasising progress. *Teacher* magazine [online], 14 May (not paginated).

Walcott, C.M., Marett, K., & Hessel, A.B. (2014). Effectiveness of a computer-assisted intervention for young children with attention and reading problems. *Journal of Applied School Psychology*, 30(2), 83–106.

Waller, A. (2019). Telling tales: Unlocking the potential of AAC technologies. *International Journal of Language & Communication Disorders*, 54(2), 159–169.

Walsh, R.L. & Jolly, J.L. (2018). Gifted education in the Australian context. *Gifted Child Today*, 41(2), 81–88.

Waltz, S.B. (2019). Tutor training for service learning: Impact on self-efficacy beliefs. *Mentoring & Tutoring: Partnership in Learning*, 27(1), 26–43.

Wang, C., Berry, B., & Swearer, S.M. (2013). The critical role of school climate in effective bullying prevention. *Theory into Practice*, 52(4), 296–302.

Wang, C.H., Shannon, D.M., & Ross, M.E. (2013). Students' characteristics, self-regulated learning, technology self-efficacy, and course outcomes in online learning. *Distance Education*, 34(3), 302–323.

Wang, L. & Li, J. (2019). Development of an innovative dual-coded multimedia application to improve reading comprehension of students with imagery deficit. *Journal of Educational Computing Research*, 57(1), 170–200.

Wang, W.L. & Kuo, C.Y. (2019). Relationships among teachers' positive discipline, students' well-being and teachers' effective teaching: A study of special education teachers and adolescent students with learning disabilities in Taiwan. *International Journal of Disability, Development and Education*, 66(1), 82–98.

Wass, M., Ching, T.Y.C., Cupples, L., Wang, H.C.Lyxell, B., Martin, L., Button, L., Gunnourie, M., Boisvert, I., McMahon, C., & Castles, A. (2019). Orthographic learning in children who are deaf or hard of hearing. *Language, Speech, and Hearing Services in Schools*, 50(1), 99–112.

Watkins, L., O'Reilly, M., Kuhn, M., & Ledbetter-Cho, K. (2019). An interest-based intervention package to increase peer social interaction in young children with autism spectrum disorder. *Journal of Applied Behavior Analysis*, 52(1), 132–149.

Watts, G.W., Bryant, D.P., & Carroll, M.L. (2019). Students with emotional-behavioral disorders as cross-age tutors: A synthesis of the literature. *Behavioral Disorders*, 44(3), 131–147.

Weale, S. (2020). Schools converting toilet blocks into isolation booths. *Guardian* [online], 18 January. Retrieved from: https://uk.news.yahoo.com/schools-converting-toilet-blocks-isolation-170100289.html.

Webb, E. (2019). *Teach for attention! A tool belt of strategies for engaging students with attention challenges.* Golden Valley, MN: Free Spirit Publishing.

Webster, J. (2018). *Behavior contracts to support good behavior.* Retrieved from: www.thoughtco.com/behavior-contracts-support-good-behavior-3110683.

Weeks, C., Hill, V., & Owen, C. (2017). Changing thoughts, changing practice: Examining the delivery of a group CBT-based intervention in a school setting. *Educational Psychology in Practice*, 33(1), 1–15.

Wehmeyer, M.L., Shogren, K.A., & Thompson, J.R. (2018). Self-determination and adult transitions and supports. *New Directions for Adult and Continuing Education*, 160, 53–62.

Weierink, L., Vermeulen, R.J., & Boyd, R.N. (2013). Brain structure and executive functions in children with cerebral palsy: A systematic review. *Research in Developmental Disabilities: A Multidisciplinary Journal*, 34(5), 1678–1688.

Westwood, P. (2011). The problem with problems: Potential difficulties in using problem-based learning as the core method for teaching mathematics in the primary years. *Australian Journal of Learning Difficulties*, 16(1), 5–18.

Westwood, P. (2014). *Teaching spelling: Exploring commonsense strategies and best practices.* Abingdon, Oxon: Routledge.

Westwood, P. (2016). *Teaching and learning difficulties* (2nd ed.). Melbourne: Australian Council for Educational Research.

Westwood, P. (2017). *Learning disorders: A response-to-intervention perspective.* London: Routledge.

Westwood, P. (2018a). *Inclusive and adaptive teaching: Meeting the challenge of diversity in the classroom* (2nd ed.). Abingdon, Oxon: Routledge.

Westwood, P. (2018b). Learning to spell: Enduring theories, recent research and current issues. *Australian Journal of Learning Difficulties*, 23(2), 137–152.

Westwood, P. (2019). Are we teaching our students to write? *Learning Difficulties Australia Bulletin*, 51(1), 10–12.

Wheldall, K., Wheldall, R., Madelaine, A., Reynolds, M., & Arakelian, S. (2017). Further evidence for the efficacy of an evidence-based, small group, literacy intervention program for young struggling readers. *Australian Journal of Learning Difficulties*, 22(1), 3–13.

Wienen, A.W., Reijnders, I., van Aggelen, M.H., Bos, E.H., Batstra, L., & de Jonge, P. (2019). The relative impact of school-wide positive behavior support on teachers' perceptions of student behavior across schools, teachers, and students. *Psychology in the Schools*, 56(2), 232–241.

Williams, C. (2018). Learning to write with interactive writing instruction. *Reading Teacher*, 71(5), 523–532.

Willson, A.M. & Falcon, L.A. (2018). Seeking equilibrium: In what ways are teachers implementing a balanced literacy approach amidst the push for accountability? *Texas Journal of Literacy Education*, 6(2), 73–93.

Wilson, H.E. & Adelson, J.L. (2018). Perfectionism: Helping gifted children learn healthy strategies and create realistic expectations. *Parenting for High Potential*, 7(3), 8–11.

Wiskow, K.M., Matter, A.L., & Donaldson, J.M. (2019). The Good Behavior Game in preschool classrooms: An evaluation of feedback. *Journal of Applied Behavior Analysis*, 52(1), 105–115.

Wissink, I.B., van Vugt, E.S., Smits, I.A.M., Moonen, X., & Stams, G. (2018). Reports of sexual abuse of children in state care: A comparison between children with and without intellectual disability. *Journal of Intellectual & Developmental Disability*, 43(2), 152–163.

Witzel, B. & Mize, M. (2018). Meeting the needs of students with dyslexia and dyscalculia. *SRATE Journal*, 27(1), 31–39.

Wolfe, Z.M. (2019). "You explore, I guide, we learn!": Developing an inquiry-based teaching curriculum. *Childhood Education*, 95(4), 30–35.

Wolter, J.A. & Dilworth, V. (2014). The effects of a multi-linguistic morphological awareness approach for improving language and literacy. *Journal of Learning Disabilities*, 47(1), 76–85.

Wolter, J.A. & Green, L. (2013). Morphological awareness intervention in school-age children with language and literacy deficits: A case study. *Topics in Language Disorders*, 33(1), 27–41.

Wong, M.E. & Law, J.S.P. (2016). Practices of assistive technology implementation and facilitation: Experiences of teachers of students with visual impairments in Singapore. *Journal of Visual Impairment & Blindness*, 110(3), 195–200.

Woods, D.M., Ketterlin Geller, L., & Basaraba, D. (2018). Number sense on the number line. *Intervention in School and Clinic*, 53(4), 229–236.

Worley J., Fodstad J., & Neal, D. (2014). Controversial treatments for autism spectrum disorders. In J. Tarbox, D. Dixon, P. Sturmey, & J. Matson (Eds) *Handbook of early intervention for autism spectrum disorders* (pp. 487–509). New York: Springer.

Wright, R. (2003). Mathematics Recovery: A program of intervention in early number learning, *Australian Journal of Learning Disabilities*, 8(4), 6–11.

Wright, S., Fugett, A., & Caputa, F. (2013). Using E-readers and Internet resources to support comprehension. *Educational Technology & Society*, 16(1), 367–379.

Wyse, D. (2018). Choice, voice and process – Teaching writing in the 21st Century: Revisiting the influence of Donald Graves and the process approach to writing. *English in Australia*, 53(3), 82–91.

Yan, J. & Li, D. (2019). Deaf and hard of hearing students' understanding of causal and adversative connectives in sentence reading. *American Annals of the Deaf*, 163(5), 554–575.

Yang, D.C. & Lin, Y.C. (2015). Using calculator-assisted instruction to enhance low-achievers in learning number sense: A case study of two fifth graders in Taiwan. *Journal of Education and Learning*, 4(2), 64–72.

Yeh, C.C. (2017). Shared time, shared problems? Exploring the dynamics of paired writing conferences. *Pedagogies: An International Journal*, 12(3), 256–274.

Yu, L. & Zhu, X. (2018). Effectiveness of a SCERTS model-based intervention for children with autism spectrum disorder in Hong Kong: A pilot study. *Journal of Autism and Developmental Disorders*, 48(11), 3794–3807.

Yuen, M.T., Chan, S., Chan, C., Fung, D.C.L., Cheung, W.M., Kwan, T., & Leung, F.K.S. (2018). Differentiation in Key Learning Areas for gifted students in regular classes: A project for primary school teachers in Hong Kong. *Gifted Education International*, 34(1), 36–46.

Zhang, W. & Zhu, C. (2020). Blended learning as a good practice in ESL courses compared to F2F learning and online learning. *International Journal of Mobile and Blended Learning*, 12(1), 64–81.

Zimmerman, B.S., Rasinski, T.V., Was, C.A., Rawson, K.A., Dunlosky, J., Kruse, S., & Nikbakht, E. (2019). Enhancing outcomes for struggling readers: Empirical analysis of the fluency development lesson. *Reading Psychology*, 40(1), 70–94.

Index